D1134608

STOCK

130923

ADI
Shelves   3/7/00

361.61094   SUR

Survival of the European Welfare State

Survival of the European Welfare State takes a novel perspective on the state of European welfare states. The challenges to the welfare state are indisputable, ranging from changing demographic, social and family structures to high levels of unemployment, rising entitlements and the growth of social expenditure. 'Crisis', 'breakdown' and 'dismantlement' have emerged as the catchphrases of both academic and media analyses of European welfare states since the late 1970s. *Survival of the European Welfare State* challenges the premises behind such reductive attitudes, focusing instead on the survival of the welfare state in Europe and its possible future development. Its international panel of experts offer thorough national and transnational studies of social policy and welfare reform activities in West European countries during the 1990s, and come to the conclusion that European voters and governments are unlikely to allow fundamental elements of the welfare state's architecture to fall apart.

Survival of the European Welfare State provides an alternative, more optimistic interpretation of the position of European welfare states on the threshold of a new century. It aims at increasing both theoretical understanding and empirical knowledge of recent welfare reforms in areas including Spain, Britain, Germany, Denmark and the European Union. It is a valuable resource for all students, researchers and practitioners interested in the welfare state.

Stein Kuhnle is Professor of Comparative Politics at the University of Bergen, Norway. He has written extensively and published in many languages on comparative welfare state development in Scandinavia and Europe. His previous publications include *Small States Compared: Politics of Norway and Slovenia* (with B. Bucar) and *Government and Voluntary Organisations: A Relational Perspective* (with P. Selle).

Routledge/ECPR Studies in European Political Science

Formerly edited by Hans Keman, *Vrije University, The Netherlands*; now edited by Jan W. van Deth, *University of Mannheim, Germany on behalf of the European Consortium for Political Research*

The Routledge/ECPR Studies in European Political Science series is published in association with the European Consortium for Political Research – the leading organisation concerned with the growth and development of political science in Europe. The series presents high-quality edited volumes on topics at the leading edge of current interest in political science and related fields, with contributions from European scholars and others who have presented work at ECPR workshops or research groups.

Survival of the European Welfare State

Edited by Stein Kuhnle

London and New York

First published 2000
by Routledge
11 New Fetter Lane, London EC4P 4EE

Simultaneously published in the USA and Canada
by Routledge
29 West 35th Street, New York, NY 10001

Routledge is an imprint of the Taylor & Francis Group

© 2000 edited by Stein Kuhnle

Typeset in Baskerville
by MHL Typesetting Ltd, Coventry
Printed and bound in Great Britain by
Biddles Ltd, Guildford and King's Lynn

All rights reserved. No part of this book may be reprinted or
reproduced or utilised in any form or by any electronic,
mechanical, or other means, now known or hereafter
invented, including photocopying and recording, or in any
information storage or retrieval system, without permission
in writing from the publishers.

British Library Cataloguing in Publication Data
A catalogue record for this book is available
from the British Library

Library of Congress Cataloging in Publication Data
Survival of the European welfare state/edited by Stein Kuhnle.
     p.   cm. – (Routledge/ECPR studies in European political
  science, 14)
    Includes bibliographical references and index.
    1. Europe–Social policy.   2. Public welfare–Europe.
3. Welfare state.   I. Kuhnle, Stein.
II. Series.

HN373.5.S87   2000

361.6'1'094–dc21   99-054191

ISBN 0-415-21291-X

Contents

Figures

Tables

Contributors

Matti Alestalo (b. 1944), Professor of Sociology at University of Tampere, Finland. E-mail: ssmaal@haapa.uta.fi.

Giuliano Bonoli (b. 1968), Research Fellow in the Department of Social Work and Social Policy, University of Fribourg, Switzerland. E-mail: giuliano.bonoli@unifr.ch.

Francis G. Castles (b. 1943), Professor and Head of Political Science Program at Australian National University, Canberra, Australia. E-mail: francis.castles@anu.edu.au.

Pål Eitrheim (b. 1971), Consultant in Statoil in Department for Risk and Issues, Stavanger, Norway. E-mail: peit@statoil.com.

Gerda Falkner (b. 1964), Associate Professor at the Institute for Government at University of Vienna, Austria. E-mail (current): falkner@mpi-fg-koeln.mpg.de.

Maurizio Ferrera (b. 1955), Professor of Public Policy at University of Pavia, Italy. E-mail: ferrera@unipv.it.

Jørgen Goul Andersen (b. 1953), Professor of Political Sociology at Aalborg University, Denmark. E-mail: goul@socsci.auc.dk.

Anton Hemerijck (b. 1958), Associate Professor in Public Administration at Leiden University, The Netherlands. E-mail: hemerijck@fsw.leidenuniv.nl.

Stein Kuhnle (b. 1947), Professor of Comparative Politics, University of Bergen, Norway. E-mail: stein.kuhnle@isp.uib.no.

Philip Manow (b. 1963), Senior Research Fellow at the Max-Planck Institute in Cologne, Germany. E-mail: manow@mpi-fg-koeln.mpg.de.

François-Xavier Merrien (b. 1951), Professor at Faculty of Political and Social Sciences, University of Lausanne, Switzerland. E-mail: fmerrien@issp.unil.ch.

Luis Moreno (b. 1950), Senior Research Fellow at Spanish National Research Council, Madrid, Spain. E-mail: lmorfer@iesam.csic.es.

Richard Parry (b. 1953), Senior Lecturer in Social Policy at University of Edinburgh, Scotland, United Kingdom. E-mail: richard.parry@ed.ac.uk.

Bo Rothstein (b. 1954), August Röhss Professor in Political Science at University of Gothenburg, Sweden. E-mail: bo.rothstein@pol.gu.se.

Kees van Kersbergen (b. 1958), Professor of National Political Systems, University of Nijmegen, The Netherlands. E-mail: c.vankersbergen@bw.kun.nl.

Series editor's preface

The spread of welfare state provisions will certainly be remembered as one of the most positive accomplishments of the outgoing century. In an increasing number of countries the poor, the sick, the disabled, the very young, the very old and the unemployed are offered support in a wide variety of ways. Starting with the Bismarck legislation in Germany more than a century ago, every European state has initiated provisions and regulations in an attempt to secure minimum living conditions for its citizens. Originally meant for the sick and disabled, coverage in many countries was rapidly expanded to other categories. By the end of the 1970s, European welfare states essentially provided an income guarantee for each citizen if circumstances make it impossible for them to earn an income. Without welfare state provisions poverty, inequality and human misery would entail even more social exclusion than can be observed already. And although the cross-national differences in these provisions are evident, the common goal of reducing individual and social risks experienced in industrial capitalism by providing public arrangements is easily discernible.

Despite the historically unprecedented success of the welfare state to guarantee minimal living conditions to virtually each and every citizen, the heydays of the development of welfare state arrangements in the first decades after the Second World War were not followed by a widespread feeling of gratefulness and satisfaction. On the contrary. Like the plot of some antique tragedy, the honourable intentions and provisions of the welfare state became the object of severe criticism at the very moment that the accomplishments of its arrangements were unquestionable. Marxists, conservatives, and neo-liberals all agreed that welfare state provisions contradict the logic of capitalism, hinder the appropriate functioning of market regulations, make people dependent instead of autonomous, and above all imply the financial bankruptcy of the nation state due to its uncontrollable costs. Especially concerning this last aspect, rather mechanical predictions of down-going spirals of financial and budgetary distress were omnipresent. Besides, these economic problems would surely mean the end of democratic decision-making processes ('The line we dare not cross'). To the embarrassment of many proponents, welfare state provisions gradually became depicted as part of the causes, and no longer as a part of the solutions, of the problems of modern societies. A wave of very fashionable interpretations and warnings about a nearing catastrophe reached the columns of virtually every journal and newspaper in the late 1970s and 1980s.

Afterwards it is cheap and easy to make fun about the obviously unrealistic predictions of the many 'crises' of the welfare state presented about two decades ago. But if we drop the ideological bias so clearly visible in many analyses, it cannot be denied that the development of welfare state provisions indeed presents a number of very serious social, economic and political complications, and that, in the long run, these provisions and their intended benevolent consequences cannot be taken for granted. So the widely shared but somewhat uncritical support for welfare state provisions in the initial phases, was extended with genuine concern about the opportunities to maintain the basic idea behind these arrangements, in a period of economic decline and severe financial and budgetary restrictions. What was urgently needed, then, was a grave reform of the welfare state in order to maintain its principles.

The contributions to this volume all deal with the difficult and always painstaking attempts to reform European welfare states. As becomes clear from even a very brief glimpse at these efforts, the national differences are noteworthy and one wonders whether we are really dealing with treatments of similar difficulties. A closer look at reforms in welfare states which usually are considered to belong to the same 'model', 'type' or 'family' reveals an astonishing array of diversity and differences. Even for the Scandinavian countries (see Chapters 3, 4 and 5) the impression of differences overshadows the idea of similar reforms designed to deal with similar problems in more or less similar countries. This notion is reinforced by the direct comparisons of the Dutch and German experiences (Chapter 7) and the reforms implemented in France and Switzerland (Chapter 8). Even the development of new welfare states in Southern Europe shows remarkable cross-national differences (Chapter 9 and 10). These nation-specific policies to reform the welfare state, however, should not come as a surprise. As Stein Kuhnle reminds us in his introduction 'social insurance was a political invention', and so very different welfare state provisions developed in different countries. These provisions, in turn, were consolidated in different economic, cultural, ideological, social and political institutional settings. Although many diagnoses of the 'crises' of the welfare state are remarkably similar, the condition of the patients, the acute symptoms, and the history of the illnesses are too different to expect results from some general or simple therapies. Reform policies also belong to the category 'political inventions', even if they mainly consist of 'creeping disentitlement'.

In addition to the inherent problems of welfare states basically rooted in conflicts between the logic of advanced capitalism and the need for redistributive policies, the ongoing process of European integration presents a new and more uniform challenge. It is hard to imagine a further outgrowth of European integration without implications for national welfare state arrangements. The tremendous cross-national differences between these arrangements will not simply urge for different reform policies in different countries. Exactly these differences constitute a crucial obstacle for the integration process and the question arises in which ways European treaties (see Chapter 11) and institutional frameworks (see Chapter 12) have an impact on the problems and prospects of attempts to harmonise national welfare state arrangements.

As the contributions to this volume show, contemporary welfare state analyses surpassed the phase of fashionable apocalyptic prophesies without many complications or damage. The apparent national differences in welfare state provisions and reform policies are well-documented, but it remains difficult to predict which reform programmes will be successful under which conditions. A more fruitful approach is to differentiate systematically between the questions (i) whether it is possible to maintain the welfare state, (ii) whether it is desirable to do that, and (iii) whether it is likely that these arrangements survive (as Jørgen Goul Andersen suggests in his analysis of the Danish experiences). Although the challenges remain formidable, the experiences with European welfare states and their reforms suggest a cautious, but positive answer to each of these questions.

Jan W. van Deth, *Series Editor*
Mannheim

Preface

The title of this book is identical to the title of a roundtable convened by the editor during the Research Sessions of the *European Consortium for Political Research* in Bergen in September 1997. The choice of 'survival' in the title was and is very conscious. It may be said to represent a hypothesis: the survival of a fundamental and relatively comprehensive state and public responsibility for the welfare of citizens in European nation-states is both *possible* and *likely*. According to a number of mass surveys, the survival of the welfare state is also considered *desirable* by a vast majority of European citizens, which in turn may conveniently help our hypothesis come true. But the title of the book also serves another purpose. It is intended to convey a novel perspective on the status and prospect of the idea and institutions of advanced European welfare states. The title implicitly takes issue with the many voices of inevitable 'crisis', 'breakdown', 'dismantlement' and 'end' of welfare states that have made themselves loud and clear in the international community through books, journals, magazines and newspapers during the last quarter of the twentieth century. There is no disputing the view that challenges abound: changing demographic, social and family structures; seemingly persistent high levels of unemployment in large parts of Europe; rising entitlements and growth of social expenditure; increased mobility of capital and financial transactions across national boundaries in an economically more integrated global world. But challenges to welfare state development are historically nothing new. Is there any reason to believe that European welfare states are in a more critical condition at the turn of the second millennium than they were 50 years ago? If European democracies provided the proper institutional settings for public policy solutions to social problems, needs and demands during the 1950s and 1960s, why should we not consider it likely that consolidated European democracies a generation later are able to deal with diverse challenges to the welfare state? We may be allowed to test the proposition that continuous reforms in the field of social and welfare policy are predictable and likely elements of highly developed capitalist democracies. And the proposition that reforms may not jeopardise the survival of European welfare states. Even if state and public welfare is provided with a 'little less of the same' or in slightly new ways, the term 'survival' seems justified.

Contributions to this book are mainly based on papers especially prepared for the roundtable in Bergen in September 1997. Chapters 8 and 12 are revised versions of papers first presented at a panel on 'Rethinking the Welfare State' that the editor convened during the World Congress of the *International Political Science Association* in Seoul, Republic of Korea, in August 1997. Chapter 7 was later commissioned to achieve a more balanced coverage of empirical developments in all the four major types of (West) European welfare states during the 1990s. The contributions in this book embody a range of views and interpretations of recent and current developments of national welfare states in Europe, but analyses of 'crises', 'challenges', successful reforms and unsuccessful reform efforts all relate to the 'survival-thesis'. The aim of the book is to provide a more informed empirical basis for interpretations of welfare state development in a historical and comparative perspective, and thus also a better basis for theorising about the European welfare state(s).

The book would not have been possible without support of various kinds. First, I thank the *European Consortium for Political Research* for supporting the idea of a roundtable on 'Survival of the European Welfare State' during its research sessions in Bergen. Second, I thank the Norwegian Research Council and the Faculty of Social Sciences at the University of Bergen for financial support making the roundtable possible. Third, I thank all authors for their original contributions to this book, and for discussions of social policies and welfare states at many and varied venues during the last decade. Fourth, I wish to extend special thanks to the European Forum at the European University Institute for inviting me as a Jean Monnet Fellow during the 1998–99 Forum Research Project on 'Recasting the European Welfare State'. My six months' stay in Florence gave me the opportunity to meet and discuss topical issues relevant to this book with a number of internationally leading welfare state researchers, and gave me the time needed to finalise this book project. Finally, I thank my Department of Comparative Politics at the University of Bergen for providing me with a continuously inspiring context for research. And as part of this context, I thank especially Terese Zeil for assisting me with diligence, calm and humour in the editorial and technical preparation of the manuscript.

Stein Kuhnle
Bergen

Part I

European welfare states in perspective

1 Introduction

Growth, adjustments and survival of European welfare states

Stein Kuhnle and Matti Alestalo

Growth

The Bismarckian legislation in the 1880s can be considered as the point of departure for the initiation of the modern welfare state. Comparative studies of the development of social insurance legislation show, however, that the last decades of the nineteenth century and the first decade of the twentieth century witnessed for the most part the introduction and extension only of occupational injuries insurance schemes in Europe. Limited old-age insurance and sickness insurance were introduced in some countries. During the inter-war years social insurance was extended in terms of new risks covered (unemployment), in terms of population coverage, and in terms of countries that introduced all four major schemes of social security. In the aftermath of the Second World War many countries made extensive social reforms. As a result, almost all West European countries had rather comprehensive social insurance programmes for occupational injuries, old age, sickness and unemployment by the year 1950. The following three decades can be characterised as the major growth period of the European welfare state. Differences between European countries began to diminish and major schemes were close to covering the total adult population in many countries (Flora and Alber 1981: 37–80). However, by the early 1980s important variations between European countries persisted, and aggregate data on social expenditure and government employment bear out underlying institutional differences (see Tables 1.1 and 1.2).

Over the last 20 years academic and media attention to the 'state of the welfare state' has been dominated by much negatively framed analysis and discussion. In most countries cuts in social benefits and various kinds of adjustments in social programmes have been made. But, as the relative figures in Table 1.1 imply, there was still growth in social expenditure in the 1980s and 1990s (cf. Chapters 3 and 9 for data for selected countries on very significant growth of social expenditures in absolute terms). Figures on social expenditure as a proportion of gross domestic product (GDP) indicate a converging trend across the various types of European welfare states, and growth in Continental European countries seems to have reached its limits. Scandinavian countries and the United Kingdom reached the high Continental level in the 1990s. Southern European countries show remarkable

Table 1.1 Social expenditure as a percentage of gross domestic product in different types of European welfare states, 1980–95: unweighted averages[a]

	1980	1990	1995
Continental Europe	28.1	29.6	30.1
Scandinavia	25.6	28.1	32.1
Southern Europe	15.0	18.0	22.2
United Kingdom	21.5	24.3	27.7

Sources: Sosiaali- ja terveyministeriö (1998) *Sosiaaliturva Suomessa 1996* (p. 32; figures based on Eurostat and Nordic Social Statistical Committee); Nordiska Statistiska Sekretariatet (1984) *Social trygghet i de nordiska länderna 1981* (p. 93); Nordic Social Statistical Committee (1998) *Social Protection in the Nordic Countries 1996* (p. 144).

Notes
a   Classification of countries:
Continental Europe: Austria, Belgium, France, Germany, The Netherlands; Scandinavia: Denmark, Finland, Norway, Sweden; Southern Europe: Greece, Italy, Portugal, Spain.

Table 1.2 Government employment as a percentage of total employment in different types of European welfare states, 1974–95: unweighted averages[a]

	1974	1985	1995
Continental Europe	14.7	18.7	18.8[b]
Scandinavia	20.0	26.9	29.4
Southern Europe	10.5	14.2	15.5[c]
United Kingdom	19.6	21.5	14.4

Source: OECD (1997) *Historical Statistics 1960–1995* (p. 44).

Notes
a   For classification of countries, see Table 1.1. The OECD definition of government employment stemming from the System of National Accounts includes 'producers of government services', i.e. those who are employed by central and local bodies in administration, defence, health, education and social services. The definition excludes most public enterprises (see Alestalo *et al.* 1991: 37–45).
b   Figure for Belgium is for 1994.
c   Figure for Portugal is for 1993.

growth since 1980 and are 'catching up' with the most 'advanced' European welfare states. Figures for government employment give a similar picture in the case of Scandinavia and Continental Europe. The share of public employment has not increased in Continental countries during the last two decades, while the share has increased markedly in Scandinavia where on average close to one-third of total employment is in the public sector. The effects of Thatcherism appear evident in the case of the UK where the share of public employment by 1995 had fallen to a level below that of the Southern European countries.

Similar challenges

The discussion of causes, effects and consequences of the welfare state encapsulates a methodological problem. The post-war expansion of the welfare state makes it highly difficult to 'explain' its variations and developments by conventional factors (population dynamics, major changes in social structures and changes in family structures). The problem is that the development of the welfare state itself has had an increasing impact on these processes. For example, the scope and quality of health services have had effects on population dynamics and, similarly, increased female employment is connected with child and old age care services, not to mention the effect of the increased public services on the continuous growth of the middle classes. Thus, discussions of similar challenges of European welfare states should be conducted only with great caution (Alestalo and Flora 1994: 65–66).

We shall concentrate our discussion of similar challenges on population dynamics and the increasing participation of women in the labour force. Tables 1.3 and 1.4 clearly point out the major demographic trend. Europeans are getting older and older. The rapid decline in fertility rates and the increasing number and proportion of old people presents a crucial challenge for European societies. The declining birth rate is most dramatic in Southern Europe, but is apparent also in Continental Europe, especially in Germany (Castles 1998: 265).

The gender revolution has increased female labour force participation throughout Europe, and European societies have begun to resemble each other

Table 1.3 Total fertility rate (average number of children per woman aged 15–44) in different types of European welfare states, 1960–93: unweighted averages[a]

	1960	1974	1993
Continental Europe	2.70	1.73	1.52
Scandinavia	2.57	1.88	1.86
Southern Europe	2.64	2.52	1.31
United Kingdom	2.69	1.81	1.76

Source: Castles (1998: 265).

Note
a   For classification of countries, see Table 1.1.

Table 1.4 Population aged 65 and more as a proportion of the total population in different types of European welfare states, 1961–97: unweighted averages[a]

	1961	1970	1980	1990	1997
Continental Europe	11.3	12.8	13.4	14.4	15.2
Scandinavia	10.3	12.1	14.4	15.8	15.7
Southern Europe	8.4	9.9	12.1	14.0	15.6[b]
United Kingdom	11.7	12.8	15.1	15.7	15.2

Sources: OECD (1974) *Labour Force Statistics 1961–1972* (pp. 128–369); OECD (1998) *Labour Force Statistics 1977–1997* (pp. 177–467).

Notes
a   For classification of countries, see Table 1.1.
b   Figure for Greece is from 1996.

Table 1.5 Female labour force as a percentage of total female population aged 15–64 in different types of European welfare states, 1960–95: unweighted averages[a]

	1960	1974	1995
Continental Europe	42.1	44.9	59.2[b]
Scandinavia	48.9	60.9	72.5
Southern Europe	31.6	37.6	49.0
United Kingdom	46.1	54.3	66.0

Source: OECD (1997) *Historical Statistics 1960–1995* (p. 41).

Notes
a   For classification of countries, see Table 1.1.
b   Figure for Austria is from 1994.

more and more. There are, however, inter-country variations. The Scandinavian and British figures for female labour force participation rates have been relatively high since the 1970s, but female participation rates have increased markedly also in Continental and Southern European countries since the mid-1970s (see Table 1.5). All over Europe women have been the traditional providers of unpaid family care for the young and old. On this background, the intertwinement of welfare state challenges is straightforwardly spelled out by Pekka Kosonen: 'If women participate in paid work, for instance, child care and services for the elderly must be organized by the public sector (or some other organization)' (Kosonen 1994: 100).

Why expect less state welfare?

Despite some indicators of increasing convergence between European welfare states there still exists striking institutional differences. In all societies, a number of distinct providers offer welfare: the family, civil society, the market and the state (see Figure 1.1, based on Alestalo and Flora 1994: 67). The market may provide welfare in two ways, either in the form of responding to demand for individual or collective insurance or services or in the form of firms offering welfare to their own employees. For reasons of graphical parsimony, 'the state' in Figure 1.1 embraces both central and local government. By 'civil society' we refer to the complex of social organisations and associations 'that are not strictly production-related nor governmental or familial in character' (Rueschemeyer *et al.* 1992: 6). The total output of welfare is the result of various combinations of inputs from these sectors or institutions, and countries can be classified as different *types of welfare states* by characteristics of the 'welfare mix' (see Figure 1.2). Our classification comes close to the ones made by Liebfried (1993), Ferrera (1997) and Kosonen (1994), and the geographical clustering of countries as presented in Tables 1.1–1.5 corresponds rather nicely to a meaningful differentiation of types of welfare states by their historical institutional characteristics.

The providers of welfare and the interrelationships between them have had varying importance over time and across 'the four social Europes'. For example,

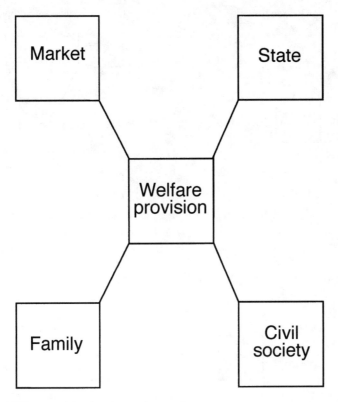

Figure 1.1 Welfare provision in advanced countries.

the state has had an overall importance in Scandinavia; families and voluntary organisations (e.g. Catholic Church) relatively more importance in Southern Europe. Much research has gone into why different 'regimes' (Esping-Andersen 1990), 'types' or 'models' (Leibfried 1993) of welfare states have developed in Europe. Research has focused on factors such as characteristics of pre-industrial social structures, political institutions, degree of homogeneity of population, culture, problem perceptions and preferences that induce different political-institutional solutions, and the observation that new ideas, new solutions hit political systems and societies at different points in 'developmental time'. At this present day, with much economic determinism dominating political debate and policy studies in general and welfare state studies in particular (e.g. the claim that globalisation of capital mobility and financial transactions leads to shrinking welfare states) we do well to remember that social insurance was a political invention. It was a politically motivated invention leading to the establishment and cross-national spread of institutions which in the beginning were weakly correlated with scope of industrialisation, level of economic development, 'problem pressure' and degree of democracy. Thus, social insurance – and a variety of different principles of coverage, financing and organisation – was introduced

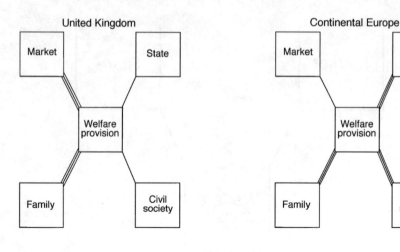

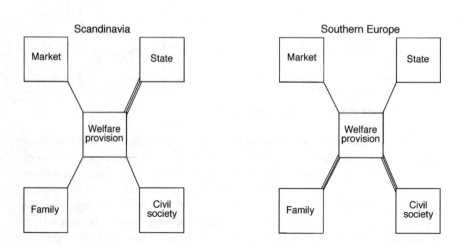

Figure 1.2 Types of welfare states in Europe.

and consolidated in different economic, social and political institutional settings, and different relationships between different welfare providers, and different weight to different providers, were established. Pre-social insurance structures and institutions (e.g. the supranational Catholic Church, the family in Southern Europe; an early merged state and church bureaucracy, local government in Scandinavia; guilds and mutual benefit societies in Continental Europe) have a long-lasting impact, as do the early social insurance institutions established.

Institutional inertia is one factor why different welfare state types persist in Europe, and one factor why welfare states persist and are likely to do so. Politics and institutions matter.

By speaking of 'types' of welfare states instead of 'regimes' and 'models' we want to point out the tentative character of this kind of classification and to take into consideration the piecemeal history of the making of European welfare states. Welfare states have seldom been established as a result of big plans or big fights, but mostly as results of complex processes and successive steps of social and political engineering in European history.

Since the early 1980s interest has been growing in the welfare role played by the market, family and voluntary organisations among political and bureaucratic elites, mass media, social science researchers and, to some extent, voters. Paradoxically, this new attention, frequently based on sharp criticism of the allegedly bureaucratic, inefficient and costly welfare state, emanated from political leaders of the 'less advanced' Western welfare states: Thatcher in Britain and Reagan in the USA. But this paradox serves to emphasise the importance of political rather than economic factors for policy change. Likewise, welfare cutbacks have subsequently not been more pronounced in the expensive and comprehensive Scandinavian countries than in leaner welfare states. A more general indicator of an increased attention devoted to non-state welfare providers came in an OECD publication: 'New relationships between action by the state and private action must be thought; new agents for welfare and well-being developed; the responsibilities of individuals for themselves and others reinforced. It is in this sense that the emergence of the Welfare Society is both inevitable and desirable' (OECD 1981: 12). This political statement was based upon perceptions of demographic and economic challenges and implied a clear ambition to shift the burden of welfare responsibilities among the various welfare providers.

Modifications of welfare programmes have occurred all over Europe since then, but without affecting much the overall cost of the welfare state (given demographic composition, entitlements, and increasing welfare needs). The UK, where social expenditure has increased both relative to GDP and in absolute terms, is a case in point. The new awareness of other possible welfare providers than the state may have been induced by economic or financial imperatives and constraints. Modifications of schemes could be looked upon simply as pragmatic adjustments to 'economic realities' as defined by those in a position to define. But the new awareness can also be interpreted as an indicator of a major ideological shift: that the state's strong role in welfare provision is not considered a good thing, that maximum state-organised welfare is not necessarily an expression of the most progressive welfare policy, that voluntary organisations offer other qualities in welfare provision, and that market competition can stimulate both better and more efficient health and other welfare service delivery.

On the rhetorical-ideological level the welfare state has also been claimed to undermine individual initiative, threaten economic prosperity, create 'dependency culture' (as if the market, the family and voluntary organisations do not create dependencies). These arguments and beliefs to justify less state welfare may be fictional or real. We still lack a model that explains how and why the boundaries between market, state, voluntary agencies and the family in the provision of social welfare change over time and across countries (Paci 1987). It is also an empirical, under-researched question to what extent boundaries in fact have changed. One hypothesis could be that, controlled for demographic composition, as people and countries become richer, more resources will be spent on welfare because meeting welfare needs have high priority for individuals and their collective representatives as well as for governments in democratic societies. Thus, although there have been cuts and adjustments of benefits in many social security schemes in European countries, the overall governmental expenditure effort has increased in absolute terms. We lack systematic comparative data, but what may have happened since the 1980s at a general level is that welfare provided by other resource allocation mechanisms have increased at the same time. Thus we may observe not so much a shift in the welfare mix formula as a simultaneous growth of all kinds of welfare provision. Welfare provision is not a zero-sum game between providers. For example, one hypothesis for what has happened in terms of welfare provision in at least some of the Scandinavian countries during the 1980s and 1990s would be: more state and more market, and perhaps even more voluntary and family care. The case of Scandinavia also implies that extensive public services may be conducive to the present coexistence of high female labour force participation and relatively high fertility rates, both of which in turn may help consolidate the economy and prospects for the survival of the welfare state. Which again goes to show that the supply of extensive public services is not simply a cost factor in the arithmetic of the welfare state.

Ideology and rhetoric aside: why is it likely that the relative role (if not necessarily the absolute role) of the state will decline in the decades ahead? Our argument would go like this: More wealth in society and higher incomes for a large part, for a substantial majority, of the population in a country give greater meaning to the concept 'freedom of choice'. Or to adapt the concepts and theory developed by Albert Hirschman (1970): greater individual economic resources make *exit* from an organisation possible. Greater individual resources thus indirectly make it more likely that possible alternative providers will arise (if laws permit) as a reaction to subjectively felt poor quality, or declining quality of services. Or as a response to unmet demand, in – in this case – the public state welfare system (e.g. waiting lists for health operations; infrequent home help services; low income replacement in public pension schemes). As long as the state provides a near monopoly of social insurance, health and welfare services, the use of political *voice* to demand better or more services is realistically the only option open for dissatisfied voters. When the majority of the population was relatively less well off, one would expect – at least for historical reasons in a Scandinavian context – that demands for equal and universal access to welfare resulted in political pressure for more state welfare. Income and wealth mean freedom of choice. One hypothesis could be that people are rather pragmatic as to choosing between public and private providers of welfare as long as services are considered good, satisfactory and efficient. If one values equality of quality of services, or equal access to the best possible services, the problem is of course that a dual public–private welfare system most likely will become socially differentiated. Private providers are likely to pay better wages for professional employees as their services are catered to the economically well-off, who are both able and willing to pay for high quality. The concomitant risk is that such client groups will lose interest in paying taxes for a public system for which they will have a decreasing need, thus causing further differentiation of private and public service provision and deterioration of the public system. Still, the possibility of 'exit' does not necessarily lead to massive exit. The threat of exit can be efficient, and the use of voice can be more productive once the threat of exit is real. And there is also the possibility that public and private welfare provisions are not substitutes: people can have both, or even more kinds of welfare provision at the same time.

There is also a third possibility (and fourth, if we consider the family) beyond the dichotomy public vs. private or market welfare provision, namely provision by voluntary organisations and institutions. These have been, and can be, more or less dependent upon or integrated with either the market or government (Kuhnle and Selle 1992; Gidron *et al.* 1992). Burt Weisbrod (1977) argues that changes over time and across countries in the substitution ratios among the three sectors can be explained in terms of political demand and changes in per capita income levels. Until a political majority is able to demand public provision of a collective good, the minority will have to remain satisfied with voluntary organisations. A sufficiently coherent political demand emerges as society becomes more democratised, and as society generates sufficient national income it moves to supplant traditional family or charitable provisions with public welfare. Once per capita income reaches a relatively high level, and we should add: with a relatively equal income distribution producing a large 'middle class', consumers develop diversified needs and seek market substitutes for the public provision of goods. This perspective may supplement the *exit-voice* perspective. A graphic illustration of the hypothesised relationship between income levels (and distributions) in society and size of the welfare state would be an inverted U-curve. Low income levels result in poorly developed welfare states. As income increases, demand for (and supply of) welfare state provision increases. But when income increases beyond certain levels and is relatively evenly distributed, market and other substitutes to public welfare are likely to develop because consumers (voters, patients, clients, gainfully employed) develop or can act upon their more diversified needs. Thus, there is less need for a big welfare state. Perhaps paradoxically, the combination of a rich society and a well-developed welfare state may cause market and 'third sector' (civil society) welfare provision to develop as complements, supplements or even substitutes to public welfare. Accordingly, we may expect that in (European) societies with high levels of income, a large middle class, a large and growing class of well-off, highly educated pensioners, and in a situation where welfare needs enjoy high priority, more space for market and 'third sector' solutions will be opened. European economic integration offers more space and may accelerate growth of market supply of welfare. Once this space is being filled, the relative importance of the state will decline. The longer term scenario will be that experience with more mixed welfare provision will induce new generations to lower their expectations somewhat towards the welfare state, thus indirectly making it possible for (somewhat downsized) welfare states to survive (see also Chapter 2). With the EU and EEA the market for welfare, health and social insurance services is no longer limited to the territory of the nation state. Supply and demand will grow across national boundaries. The likely development of a greater proportion of transnational firms as well as transnational households may also undermine the present strong position of national welfare states. Also, a likely more ethnically and culturally heterogenous composition of 'national' populations may make it more difficult to preserve or create the political consensus for unified state welfare solutions (Barry 1983; Østerud 1999).

A new 'social Europe'?

Besides the *similar* domestic challenges, European welfare states face a *common* external challenge (Flora 1993): international, first of all European, economic integration. The future of European national welfare states is influenced by European integration and wider international developments even if it can be argued that 'welfare states are national states' (Swaan 1990). European welfare states are fundamentally national in character, and within the European Union social policy is primarily a national responsibility (see Chapter 11). The strength of national welfare states may in itself be an argument against active European level policy-making in this field: it may be argued that there is no immediate apparent need for the European level to be engaged. The bond between social policy development and political legitimacy at the national level appears obvious. On the other hand, European economic integration will in various ways affect national welfare state development. European integration may be perceived either as a threat to comprehensive national welfare states or as a process which will in the long run strengthen a 'Social Europe' in which national welfare states will continue to play a crucial role. A social dimension is clearly evident in EU policies on structural funds, in provisions for the coordination of social rights for people moving between member states (including EEA members) and in directives imposing minimum standards, for example health and security at work places, working hours and for maternity leave and benefits. There exists, however, no direct taxation or social contributions to EU. Although this may change, welfare policies and institutions in all likelihood will and must remain largely national for the foreseeable future. National welfare states will, however, continuously be affected by the process of European integration in two ways (Leibfried and Pierson 1995): both the exclusive legislative authority (i.e. sovereignty) and the actual capacity to decide on what policies or laws must be followed within the national territory (i.e. autonomy) are affected in the realm of social policy. National social policy is steadily becoming more 'European', although there is no unidirectional nor any unidimensional development. Harmonisation of national schemes is unlikely due to complex institutional differences and legal entrenchment. A possible pressure for actual harmonisation can arise from a consideration of the effects of the principles of free movement of labour and the sustenance of social rights within the entire EU (EEA) territory. An underlying interest for harmonisation might be to avoid unfair competition from so-called 'social dumping'. But it is doubtful whether any country would be interested in imposing less generous welfare schemes on other countries. So far the welfare state has expanded in the lesser developed welfare states in Europe (see Chapters 9 and 10), and cuts in the most comprehensive welfare states have clearly been motivated by domestic financial and demographic challenges rather than by a perception of increased intra-European or global competition, although the EU (in particular the Maastricht criteria for EMU membership) and the ill-defined monster of 'globalisation' can be used by governments as convenient 'blame avoidance' references. Another motivation for harmonisation is the possibility of people moving to the country with the most generous welfare systems. This has hardly happened, and labour mobility across national boundaries has been limited during the three decades that free mobility has been permitted in the EU territory, most likely because of factors such as differences in language, culture and employment conditions. Most of the labour migration that has taken place has come from outside into the EU, and this will probably remain a great welfare challenge. A new challenge will have to be met if or when efforts to extend the EU eastwards to incorporate the poorer former communist countries succeed.

The Maastricht criteria for membership in the EMU led member states to make public expenditure cutbacks and reforms to social security and welfare arrangements. The EMU represents a tightening of the macroeconomic background to 'Social Europe' (Teague 1998). With or without EMU the problems of sustaining advanced national welfare states are substantial. As long as taxing and 'active social policy integration' are largely outside the European agenda, the nation-states will maintain prime responsibility and accountability for welfare. A critical question is whether national tax systems can be sustained or not in a Europe (and world) with open borders. This is a question of incentives and mobility of tax objects, and of course, a question of political will and decision-making at the European or intergovernmental level. A general minimum level of value added tax at 15 per cent has been agreed upon within the EU, and so far there is little evidence that European integration will fuel 'social dumping'. The social wage is only one factor in decisions on investments. On the other hand, there is little doubt that the enhanced exit option for business strengthens their hand in bargaining with governments and trade unions. Unless EMU is followed by some kind of a political union, with central taxation and (more) redistribution, a common monetary policy and a common currency may sharpen the economic imbalance between member countries. If the legitimacy of redistribution is questioned within many national states today (e.g. Italy, Belgium, the UK, Spain, Germany), one may surely estimate that establishing legitimacy for redistribution at the supranational European level is a tremendous challenge. A feeling of common identity is sometimes perceived as a necessary prerequisite for legitimate redistributive policies (e.g. Offe 1984), and we may safely assume that national identity on average ranks higher than European identity. Whatever way we look at EMU, it creates big dilemmas for the further development of

European integration. There exists an asymmetry between economic integration and political integration in the EU, creating a 'coordination deficit' and 'democratic deficit' (Scharpf 1996, 1997). There exists a mismatch between the free movement of capital and the lack of proper supranational governance structures. Member states have been very reluctant to develop institutions designed to create European-wide forms of economic and social governance. On the other hand, national legal, political and financial scope for positive social policy action remains despite European integration, and political actions by the EU are also imaginable in order to avoid the erosion of 'Social Europe'. Lipietz (1997) suggests that one way out of the dilemma is to create 'an alternative Social Europe', a regime with four key functions:

1   The reduction of social dumping by the enactment of Union-wide common labour market ground rules and more tightly coordinated national employment policies.
2   The control of fiscal dumping which entices the member states to attract mobile international capital by offering minimal taxation.
3   The reduction of high unemployment through launching a Europe-wide recovery plan.
4   The reorganisation of the European labour market so that social equity, ecological demands and economic performance are made compatible.

But for such a plan to be implemented, the EU would need new fiscal and social policy competences, which can only be done through the building of some kind of democratic political federation. This is, as hinted at, not an idea that brings the European masses of voters into the streets, country and mountain roads for unbridled celebration and cheers for the time being. The inclusion of Central and East European states into the EU over a 5–10 year period makes it less likely that institutions and governance structures for an alternative (supranational) 'Social Europe' will be agreed upon. But there might be other, less radical options. Scharpf (1996), for example, has suggested that to avoid competition between different national social rules, the member states should commit themselves to EU-level regulations that establish multi-level social standards. The idea is that the level of social protection should be linked to a member state's level of economic development, thus minimising the harmful side-effects of crude harmonisation. Member states should also adopt a European directive that binds them not to push total welfare expenditure below a mutually agreed share of GDP. Thus, member states would not have to commit themselves to any, highly problematic, institutional harmonisation. The European welfare state would survive, probably also the four different types of it.

Structure of the book

The book is divided into three parts. Without denying crucial challenges of various kinds and urgencies, all chapters relate to the (likely) prospect of survival of the European welfare state. A 'little less of the same' is interpreted as 'survival', as is welfare provided in somewhat varied forms and 'mixtures' as long as the state retains a fundamental responsibility for the welfare of its citizens. The use of the term 'survival' frames the analysis and debate on the welfare state differently than the use of the term 'crisis'. The way analyses and debates are framed may in turn affect the politics of the welfare state (see also Chapter 13).

Chapters 1 and 2 make up *Part I* and represent efforts to put the development and present status of West European welfare states in perspective. In the introductory chapter we have pointed to trends of growth and adjustments of welfare states, provided some comparative data on four different types of European welfare states, and discussed domestic and external challenges to national welfare states which make changes in welfare states likely without seriously threatening their existence. In Chapter 2, Kees van Kersbergen critically reviews current theoretical and empirical welfare state literature and proposes a set of hypotheses for the declining resistance of welfare states to change. Little empirical evidence confirms radical changes in welfare states induced by the dramatic crises that many theories forcefully have prophesied. The welfare state has turned out to be more resilient than many expected. The resilience hypothesis may, however, be put to a tougher test, and the conclusion is that in order for the welfare state to survive it must, paradoxically, be transformed.

Part II consists of eight chapters that in various ways deal with problems, challenges, more or less successful reforms and reform efforts during the 1990s in the four major 'social Europes' distinguished between in this introductory chapter. Some of the chapters are comparative, some national case studies. Pål Eitrheim and Stein Kuhnle present in Chapter 3 a comparative review and interpretation of what has happened to major social security programmes in four Scandinavian countries. Primarily Sweden and Finland have made significant cuts in benefits, but basic universal institutions remain intact. Matti Alestalo stresses in Chapter 4 the past as a determinant of the present in a case study of the reactions to the sudden economic downturn and mass unemployment in the beginning of the 1990s in Finland. Denmark is presented as an interesting test case of the sustainability of the 'Scandinavian model' by Jørgen Goul Andersen in Chapter 5, in which he shows that critical problems have been solved without significant institutional change and without sacrificing basic normative principles. The United Kingdom is covered in Chapter 6 by Richard Parry, who shows that Tony Blair's government seems committed to a 'strong Treasury' with firm control of public expenditure in order to prevent tax rises and in order to target spending more precisely on Labour's priorities. The chapter indicates that there is no suggestion that the British government is prepared to move to the average European level of transfers from taxes and contributions into welfare expenditure, thus making the survival of the welfare state in Britain a continuing issue. Analyses of developments in Continental Europe are covered by two comparative chapters. Chapter 7 by Anton Hemerijck, Philip Manow and Kees van Kersbergen compares the Netherlands and Germany – two countries which show striking similarities of the institutional features of the production system and of the welfare regime. They find different political responses to the 'welfare without work' crisis. Both 'survive', but differently and with different social, economic and political outcomes and divergent prospects. The Dutch case illustrates that the 'welfare without work' equilibrium is not inevitable. The second chapter on Continental European welfare states contrasts reform efforts in centralised France and federal Switzerland. François-Xavier Merrien and Giuliano Bonoli show in Chapter 8 how different institutionalisation of relationship patterns between the state and civil society, combined with different political cultures, make for different results to reform efforts motivated by similar challenges. Perhaps paradoxically, a weak state like Switzerland has more successfully implemented reforms than a strong state like France. Southern Europe is also covered by two chapters, both based in a comparative Southern European setting, but one concentrates on the case of Spain (Chapter 9) and the other deals with Portugal, Spain, Greece and Italy, with some concentration on Italy (Chapter 10). Luis Moreno places Spain within the Southern European frame of reference and describes how universalisation of social entitlements has made Spain converge to Northern European types of welfare states. Moreno argues that a concerted effort within the EU may be required if goals for the preservation of institutions for social solidarity are to be accomplished in Spain and Europe. Maurizio Ferrera outlines in Chapter 10 the main problems and reform challenges of social protection in Southern Europe. The Iberian countries seem to be in a relatively better shape than Greece, which struggles with the most critical problems, and Italy where he finds that some promising and significant steps have been taken in recent years to eradicate distributive and allocative distortions.

Part III of the book includes three chapters that from different angles discuss the prospect of a consolidation of European welfare states and one final short chapter which summarises the 'survival' perspective. The possible common challenge of European integration (and international global competition) for national welfare states is discussed more or less explicitly in several chapters throughout the book, but Gerda Falkner offers in Chapter 11 a direct interpretation of the implications of the Maastricht and Amsterdam treaties for the European Union and European social policies. She sketches the basic division of social policy competences between the EU and member states, and concludes that the likelihood of survival of the European welfare state would be higher if the EU played a more active, supportive role. In Chapter 12, Francis G. Castles asks whether European welfare states in trouble might have anything to learn from looking to non-European institutional designs of welfare states in the world. No quick fixes are found to be readily available, and he concludes that European welfare states struggling with high unemployment and weak economic growth might be better served by looking at relatively successful welfare state reform efforts in selected European countries, like Denmark, the Netherlands and Norway. Bo Rothstein addresses in Chapter 13 – with particular reference to Sweden – the future of the national universal welfare state model in light of the challenges it is perceived to face. Instead of the traditional focus on societal forces (economy, ideology, political power, class structure, etc.) the argument is that the future of the universal welfare state depends upon the political and economic logic of the institutions of the universal welfare state. Based on the 'theory of contingent consent' the argument is that the electoral and economic support for the welfare state depends on how well the social policies it produces in the future will be able to match three requirements posed by the theory. These are substantive justice, procedural justice and control of 'free-riding'. Rothstein, addressing most economists' alleged (mis)understanding of what the welfare state is about, concludes with a positive evaluation of the economic viability of the universal welfare state given that a general demand for social insurance and welfare services is *there*, and given, among other things, that universal systems are more cost-efficient than private insurance systems.

The final Chapter 14 by Stein Kuhnle is a brief summary view of the possible lessons to be drawn from European welfare state development in the 1990s.

References

Alestalo, M., Bislev, S. and Furåker, B. (1991) 'Welfare State Employment in Scandinavia', in J. E. Kolberg (ed.) *The Welfare State as Employer*, Armonk: M. E. Sharpe.

Alestalo, M. and Flora, P. (1994) 'Scandinavia: Welfare States in the Periphery – Peripheral Welfare States?', in M. Alestalo, E. Allardt, A. Rychard and W. Wesolowski (eds) *The Transformation of Europe. Social Conditions and Consequences*, Warsaw: IFIS Publishers.

Barry, B. (1983) 'Self-Government Revisited', in D. Miller and L. Siedentop (eds) *The Nature of Political Theory*, Oxford: Clarendon Press.

Castles, F. G. (1998) *Comparative Public Policy*, Cheltenham: Edward Elgar.

Esping-Andersen, G. (1990) *The Three Worlds of Welfare Capitalism*, Cambridge: The Polity Press.

Ferrera, M. (1997) 'Four Social Europes between Universalism and Selectivity', in Y. Meny and M. Rhodes (eds) *A New Social Contract*, London: Macmillan.

Flora, P. (1993) 'The National Welfare States and European Integration', in L. Moreno (ed.) *Social Exchange and Welfare Development*, Madrid: Consejo Superior de Investigaciones Científicas.

Flora, P. and Alber, J. (1981) 'Modernization, Democratization and the Development of Welfare States in Western Europe', in P. Flora and A. J. Heidenheimer (eds) *The Development of Welfare States in Europe and America*, New Brunswick: Transaction Books.

Gidron, B., Kramer, R. M. and Salamon, L. M. (eds) (1992) *Government and the Third Sector. Emerging Relationships in Welfare States*, San Francisco: Jossey-Bass Publishers.

Hirschman, A. O. (1970) *Exit, Voice, and Loyalty*, Cambridge, MA: Harvard University Press.

Kosonen, P. (1994) 'European Transformation: The Social Dimension', in M. Alestalo, E. Allardt, A. Rychard and W. Wesolowski (eds) *The Transformation of Europe*, Warsaw: IFIS Publishers.

Kuhnle, S. and Selle, P. (eds) (1992) *Government and Voluntary Organizations. A Relational Perspective*, Aldershot: Avebury.

Leibfried, S. (1993) 'Towards a European Welfare State? On Integrating Poverty Regimes in the European Community', in C. Jones (ed.) *New Perspectives on the Welfare State in Europe*, London: Routledge.

Leibfried, S. and Pierson, P. (1995) 'Semisovereign Welfare States: Social Policy in a

Multitiered Europe', in S. Leibfried and P. Pierson (eds) *European Social Policy: Between Fragmentation and Integration,* Washington DC: Brookings Institution.

Lipietz, A. (1997) 'The Post-Fordist World: Labour Relations, International Hierarchy and Global Ecology', *Review of International Political Economy,* 4, 1: 1–41.

Nordic Social Statistical Committee (1998) *Social Protection in the Nordic Countries 1996,* Copenhagen.

Nordiska Statistiska Sekretariatet (1984) *Social trygghet i de nordiska länderna 1981,* Nordisk statistisk skriftserie 43, Helsingfors.

OECD (1974) *Labour Force Statistics 1961–1972,* Paris: OECD.

—— (1981) *The Welfare State in Crisis,* Paris: OECD.

—— (1997) *Historical Statistics 1960–1995,* Paris: OECD.

—— (1998) *Labour Force Statistics 1977–1997,* Paris: OECD.

Offe, C. (1984) *Contradictions of the Welfare State,* London: Hutchinson.

Østerud, Ø. (1999) *Globaliseringen og nasjonalstaten,* Oslo: AdNotam Gyldendal.

Paci, M. (1987) 'Long Waves in the Development of Welfare Systems', in C. Maier (ed.) *Changing Boundaries of the Political,* Cambridge: Cambridge University Press.

Rueschemeyer, D., Huber, E. and Stephens, J. D. (1992) *Capitalist Development and Democracy,* Cambridge: The Polity Press.

Scharpf, F. (1996) 'Europas olösliga ekvation?', *Moderna Tider* (October): 16–25.

—— (1997) 'Economic Integration, Democracy and Welfare States', *Journal of European Public Policy,* 4, 1: 18–36.

Sosiaali- ja terveyministeriö (1998) *Sosiaaliturva Suomessa 1996,* SVT Sosiaaliturva 1998: 1, Helsinki.

Swaan, A. de (1990) 'Perspectives for Transnational Social Policy', paper presented at World Congress of Sociology, 9–13 July, Madrid.

Teague, P. (1998) 'Monetary Union and Social Europe', *Journal of European Social Policy,* 8, 2: 117–38.

Weisbrod, B. (1977) *The Voluntary Non-Profit Sector: An Economic Analysis,* Lexington, MA: Heath.

2 The declining resistance of welfare states to change?[1]

Kees van Kersbergen

Introduction

'Crisis' was one of the buzzwords of many a welfare state study in the 1970s and early 1980s. Looking at these studies some 10 to 20 years later, it is striking to note how deep the vocabulary of emergency had entered social scientific theories already in this period (see Schmidt 1983; Mishra 1984; Panich 1986; Moran 1988; Alber 1988). Allegedly there was a fiscal crisis (O'Connor 1973), a crisis of governability caused by overload (Crozier *et al.* 1975; King 1975; Birch 1984), a crisis of legitimacy (Habermas 1976; Wolfe 1979; see Offe 1984), a crisis of liberal democracy (Brittan 1975; Crozier *et al.* 1975; Bowles and Gintis 1982), and a crisis of culture (Bell 1979) and 'utopian energies' (Habermas 1985).

At the heart of all these crises stood the welfare state, celebrated as an extraordinary political organisation, but increasingly viewed as an accomplishment which had reached its utter limits (Flora 1985, 1986–87), a view shared by the OECD (1981, 1985). Marxist analyses in particular theorised that the redistributive logic of the welfare state contradicted the generic logic of capitalism, governed as this system is by the functional needs of profitability and accumulation, and that this contradiction posed a threat to legitimacy and would necessarily lead to the transformation of the welfare state (e.g. O'Connor 1973; Ginsburg 1979; Gough 1979; Offe 1984; but see Skocpol 1980). The prospects for the welfare state were argued to be gloomy and its core structures were likely to be transformed radically as they were dysfunctional to the accumulation needs of capital.

Many such sweeping statements and general predictions about the welfare state, its contradictions and its precarious future were made, but often without any specification of the temporal horizon within which these were to occur. Moreover, the empirical evidence for the proclaimed collapse was usually meagre or entirely absent. These were arguably mostly analyses of administrative failures, studies of social needs and risks still to be covered, critiques of (unintended) distributional effects of social policies (e.g. Piven and Cloward 1971; Wilson 1977; Hadley and Hatch 1981; Harris and Seldon 1987), or highly abstract exercises in Marxology.

In the 1980s, the conservative and neo-liberal attack on the welfare state inspired a second wave of crisis theories. The assaults on the British and American welfare states were readily heralded as proof of a new era in which the cherished institutionalisation of equality and justice – as most analysts had come to see the welfare state – had come to an end and was rapidly giving way to the institutionalisation of inequality for the sake of economic growth and efficiency. The paradox was that the harshest attack on the welfare state took place in those nations that had the most residual type of welfare system and that a comparable assault did not occur – at least not until the late 1980s – in the highly developed welfare states in Scandinavia and on the European continent (see Jones Finer 1996).

More recently, predictions of crisis and dismantling derive from theories that focus on the increasing interdependence, internationalisation or globalisation of national economies (for critical overviews see Thompson *et al.* 1994/1995; Hirst and Thompson 1995, 1996; Boyer and Drache 1996; Gummett 1996; Rhodes 1996b; Taylor-Gooby 1997; Thompson 1997). The crisis-inclined theories now argue that these macro-processes are compelling national welfare states to dismantle their social systems radically for reasons of international competitiveness, that different national systems are rapidly converging around a lowest common social denominator that is a far cry from the welfare state of the golden age, and that the role of the state will be diminished in order to make room for 'welfare pluralism' (Mishra 1996) with a more extensive role for private and voluntary initiative. A similar account is given of the effects of European integration. Severe risks of 'social tourism','social dumping'or 'regime shopping'arise as the European nation-states gradually abandon their economic borders. National welfare states, again for the sake of competitiveness, necessarily adjust their social systems drastically in a struggle for survival in a common market that, paradoxically, was itself invented to facilitate and regulate economic competition and to preserve welfare (Adnett 1995; Aspinwall 1996; Begg and Nectoux 1995; Ferrera 1994; Kosonen 1994, 1995; Leibfried and Pierson 1995; Rhodes 1996a; Streeck 1996b).

Empirical and historical research necessarily lags behind sweeping theories. But whenever empirical evidence is presented, there seems to be little confirmation of radical changes induced by the dramatic crises that the theories so forcefully prophesied. No doubt, the empirical studies record extensively the immense pressures on, as well as the massive challenges to, the welfare state. Moreover, they provide evidence for incremental adjustment in the major programmes, decreasing growth of social expenditures and retrenchment. But they also demonstrate the substantial gap between the crisis theories and the conservative or neo-liberal political rhetoric of retrenchment on the one hand and the actual resistance against change of most of the welfare state's core programmes on the other hand.

Welfare state research in the early 1990s further documented empirically that welfare states have been remarkably resistant to change notwithstanding the mounting challenges they face. Not surprisingly, a major explanatory problem for these dominant welfare state theories was the persistence rather than 'crisis' or 'breakdown' of the major institutions of the welfare state. Both macro- and meso-institutional theories started to identify the crucial institutional mechanisms (e.g. path dependency and lock-in) that explain welfare state persistence. Moreover, a major prediction of this body of literature is that these mechanisms also will preclude the institutional transformation of welfare states in the next decade or so (Pierson 1994, 1996; Esping-Andersen 1996a; George and Taylor-Gooby 1996; Kitschelt *et al*. 1999). This review is inspired by the critical observation that – in contradiction to this prediction – some recent empirical studies find considerable and increasing variation in institutional and policy adjustments among welfare states that were once broadly similar in design. Moreover, the source of this variation dates back to the mid-1980s (Clasen and Gould 1995; Kelsey 1995; Sainsbury 1996; Hemerijck and van Kersbergen 1997; Visser and Hemerijck 1997; European Commission 1998; Boix 1998; Huber and Stephens 1998; Rhodes 1997; Camissa 1998; Cavanna 1998; Swank 1998). This observation raises two issues: (a) whether persistence has indeed been a prominent characteristic of contemporary welfare state development; and (b) whether and to what extent mainstream welfare state theories are capable of identifying and explaining the institutional and social policy changes that do occur.

This chapter is organised as follows. The second section is a review of the major findings of current empirical research on the welfare state. The studies extensively document both the pressures towards change and the institutional persistence of most welfare state regimes. The third section discusses two major explanations for this observed persistence. The fourth considers some questions and possible challenges to the neo-institutionalist explanation of resistance, provides a discussion of what constitutes fundamental change or transformation, and then elaborates arguments that may support the hypothesis that a more fundamental transformation of the welfare state is more likely than the consensus around the resistance thesis indicates. The final section is the conclusion.

Challenges, pressures and resistance

Present-day European welfare states are under pressure to adjust their institutional arrangements to changing political, social and economic circumstances. The fundamental reason for this is that the conditions under which the post-war welfare state has emerged, as well as the assumptions upon which social policies were formulated and implemented, are no longer valid. The literature (e.g. European Commission 1993; Regini 1995; Esping-Andersen 1996a; George 1996; Rhodes 1997; Slomp 1996; Kitschelt *et al*. 1999) highlights the following changes.

First, the relatively stable balance between generations is being challenged by an ageing population, whereby ageing is a combined effect of an increased life expectancy and a decreasing fertility rate. An ageing population will be putting an ever greater claim on national resources, particularly on health, social care and pensions, without substantially contributing to these resources.

Second, the traditional family, towards which so many social policies were targeted, is no longer dominant. The double income, double career household is a more frequent phenomenon. The number of divorced, single-person and single-parent households spirals and single parents tend to claim a larger share of social benefits or – if they manage to combine a job and child rearing – need to carry the considerable financial burden of child care themselves, which they may not be able to sustain without assistance.

Third, slackening economic growth and the post-industrialisation of labour markets (i.e. deindustrialisation, the growth of the service economy and new technologies and flexibilisation (Esping-Andersen 1993)) have decreased job security and the continuity of employment generally and have caused a rise in irregular and atypical employment. The kind of stable employment patterns and trajectories that appear to have belonged to a growing, industrial economy are being challenged. Consequently, the financial logic of social security arrangements are jeopardised.

Fourth, changing relations between men and women with respect to the division of labour within and outside the family (paid work and unpaid care), as well as the increasing differentiation of the life cycle and of careers, have challenged the gender assumptions of many welfare state arrangements.

Fifth, politically recognised systems of interest intermediation and centralised collective bargaining, which historically have accorded a firm social and economic basis to the welfare state, have been eroded to a considerable extent, sometimes as a result of deliberate policy decisions, but generally speaking as a result of the weakening position of organised labour.

Sixth, new risks and needs have arisen to which neither those who defend the welfare state nor those who opt for rollback have viable answers.

Finally, relatively fixed relations between national states are in a state of flux as a result of the end of the Cold War, continuing and accelerating economic globalisation and the intensification of European economic and political integration, particularly the Economic and Monetary Union (EMU). The attempt of national governments to meet the criteria of EMU is intensifying the public political debate on welfare restructuring. The predicted outcome of this debate is apparently a dwindling autonomy of national states in the realm of social policy-making.

However, in spite of these mounting challenges, until the beginning of the 1990s empirical research finds predominantly that the European welfare states have been resistant to change to a remarkable extent. The conclusion of most of these studies[2] is that in Europe the welfare state is not being abandoned, but adjusted incrementally and reconstructed partially. So far, no political constellation has emerged in a welfare state that will be able to induce the discontinuation of existing patterns of social policy, or the radical abolishment of core programmes. In other words, changes have taken place, but these were predominantly incremental, and did not alter the basic institutional design of welfare states.

The major findings from current research are the following:

1   There is ample empirical documentation of the immense pressures on and formidable challenges to the existing welfare states.
2   There is abundant evidence for incremental adjustments in the major programmes, for the decreasing growth of social expenditures, and for moderate retrenchments.

3   There is persisting institutional variation and continuing divergence among the developed welfare states.
4   Policies of adjustment are largely governed by the institutional logics of the welfare states' distinctive regime properties.
5   Partly because of this, there are few signs of radical or fundamental transformation; moreover, such a transformation is unlikely.

Explaining institutional resistance

The dominant literature of the early 1990s aimed to explain the resistance of European welfare states to change (see Becker 1998). The major question of this body of literature has been why welfare states have been so impervious to fundamental change in spite of the social, economic and political transformation they have experienced, and in spite of the mounting pressures they are facing.

There are two major theoretical explanations that emerge from these studies. The first approach focuses on the idea that national publics are 'attached' to their national systems of welfare. The second approach centres on meso- and macro-institutional and political mechanisms of resistance and offers the most elaborate generalisations theoretically speaking.

As to the first type of explanation, detailed case studies and comparative accounts document the considerable and persisting support of national publics for their welfare states (Sihvo and Uusitalo 1995; Hantrais 1996; Niero 1996; Ferrera 1997; Gould 1996; Stephens 1996; van Kersbergen 2000). Moreover, time and again public opinion research finds considerable public support for the welfare state and little, if any, decline in patterns of public attachment to the national systems. The welfare state is well entrenched in national political cultures (Roller 1992; Ploug and Kvist 1996; Goul Andersen 1997; Svallfors 1995). Cross-national studies allow for similar conclusions, as there is little evidence to support a declining popularity hypothesis. This holds true for the equality dimension (Roller 1995) and the security dimension of the welfare state (Pettersen 1995) and does not only apply to the Scandinavian welfare states (Svallfors 1993; on Britain, see Taylor-Gooby 1988; Jowell 1990).

The second approach to the explanation of resistance to change centres on meso- and macro-institutional and political mechanisms. The explanation of resistance to change is found in historical-institutionalist arguments of path dependency, lock-in and electoral hazard. One can distinguish between two levels of analysis in contemporary studies: the ones that focus on meso-level, i.e. programmatic obstacles to reform; and the ones that study the macro-level, i.e. resilient regime-characteristics.

Pierson's (1994; 1996) work focuses on the meso-level and offers the building blocks of a comparative theory of retrenchment politics, all resting on his core argument that 'frontal assaults on the welfare state carry tremendous electoral risks' (Pierson 1996: 178). There are four conditions under which radical retrenchments and fundamental reform are likely:

1   When electoral risks are estimated as limited.
2   When financial crises create an acute sense of emergency.
3   When the properties of political institutions facilitate the capacity to hide the visibility of retrenchment and to avoid blame.
4   When politicians manage to alter the institutional logic so as to generate a more favourable context for reform.

Nevertheless, governments that are seeking radical reform find it difficult to develop the means that minimise the political hazards. 'Everywhere, retrenchment is a difficult undertaking. The welfare state remains the most resilient aspect of the postwar political economy' (Pierson 1996: 179).

Pierson's theory is derived from the conviction that the politics of retrenchment is fundamentally different from the politics of welfare state expansion. The difference pertains to the fact that whereas welfare expansion involves popular policies, retrenchment does the opposite and tends to affront voters and vested interests that have come about through the growth of the welfare state. The politics of retrenchment, for instance cutting on benefits, does not lend itself so easily to credit-claiming as, for instance, the introduction of new benefits does. Shifting the goals from expansion to retrenchment is electorally risky, because it imposes 'tangible losses on concentrated groups of voters in return for diffuse and uncertain gains' (Pierson 1996: 145) and the attempt to avoid the blame is paramount. Moreover, voters react more strongly to negative than positive incentives. 'Retrenchment advocates thus confront a clash between their policy preferences and their electoral ambitions' (Pierson 1996: 146).

The development of the welfare state has produced a new political context by having created a host of interests, solid networks of interests groups, and patterns of mass popularity around social programmes. The result is that 'the emergence of powerful groups surrounding social programs may make the welfare state less dependent on the political parties, social movements, and labor organizations that expanded social programs in the first place' (Pierson 1996: 147). In addition, there may arise powerful feedback mechanisms that may make change difficult.

Other empirical studies document the mechanisms that tend to impede radical transformation. Stephens (1996) provides two arguments that help explain the resistance of the Swedish welfare state to rollback. First, the supposedly negative effects of increasing economic integration into the world market can be questioned. Globalisation has no necessary and direct effect on the transformation of social policies. 'The assumption that market integration will necessarily exert a strong downward pressure on social provisions is based on the assumption that the competitive advantage of low wages will be more important than the advantage of capital intensity and highly qualified labour' (Stephens 1996: 57), which is far from clear. Second, the Scandinavian welfare states were particularly well-prepared institutionally to deal with the challenge of globalisation and integration as 'they were built so as to maximize the competitiveness of the domestic manufacturing export sector' (Stephens 1996: 57). The prospects for the Nordic welfare states are linked to these characteristics. Therefore, some programmes are more likely to be adjusted than others, i.e. 'those programmes which positively support international competitiveness and/or market conforming are most likely to survive the axe, and those which do not are likely to be restructured to do so' (Stephens 1996: 59; see Huber and Stephens 1998).

The macro-analysis is paramount in Esping-Andersen's work (1996a). He emphasises the resilience of macro-level regime characteristics and policy legacies of the different welfare state regimes. This analysis looks at the by now famous three worlds of welfare capitalism (Esping-Andersen 1990; see Lessenich and Ostner 1998) in terms of their capacity to respond to the major challenges discussed above. The post-industrial trajectories of these welfare state regimes are path-dependent to the extent that they correspond to the specific regime features. The 'liberal' regime is characterised by a persistent downward pressure on low-skill wage levels, which is likely to create profound poverty traps and greater inequality. The 'social democratic' regime cannot maintain full employment, continues to be characterised by very high levels of taxation, and experiences great difficulty in upholding active labour market policies. The continental, conservative regime is trapped in a vicious cycle of 'welfare without work', where a growing group of labour market outsiders depends on a shrinking group of insiders. For all regimes holds that . . . 'the contemporary politics of the welfare state is a politics of the status quo' (Esping-Andersen 1996c: 266–67).

The general thesis that may be distilled from the literature is that while the context of welfare state policies has changed, this has not led to the dismantling of existing welfare state regimes or single programmes, because enduring sources of support persist, even in the face of failing policies, programmes and institutions. Welfare state regimes have been stabilised and change in core social policies is predominantly incremental. The institutionalist theories of resistance, although concentrating on different levels, contain four basic arguments (Pierson 1996; Esping-Andersen 1996b). First, there is the protection of a welfare state regime that stems from it being the status quo. Second, the welfare state's political defence may depend no longer predominantly on organised labour, but may have found other powerful defenders instead, who owe their job, income, status, services, etc. to the welfare state. Third, the political (especially electoral) costs of radical retrenchment are prohibitively high, as most social policies are still very popular among the electorate. Finally, in addition to the political impediments, there are 'technical' obstacles to change which are related to institutional inertia. To give but one example, there is the problem of finding alternative funding systems for pay-as-you-go pension systems.

Criticism and hypotheses

Two concerns need to be mentioned. First, the cross-national comparative analyses that document the resistance of developed welfare states to change empirically rely predominantly on data covering the period until 1990. However, it is conceivable that pressures on the core programmes of social protection have been building up since then. There should be a growing awareness among researchers that it is

important to test the existing theories against recent data. Second, the institutionalist arguments tend to be biased so heavily towards conceptualising and
theorising the institutional mechanisms of persistence and resistance (path
dependency, lock-in, electoral hazard, etc.) that evidence of institutional change
and fundamental transformation is difficult to recognise (but see Alston *et al.* 1996).
In spite of the powerful mechanisms against radical change, it may be that in the
light of contemporary developments the resistance argument is stretched too far.

From these concerns the following questions can be formulated. How to
conceptualise 'change', 'radical change', 'fundamental transformation' or 'drastic
reform'? How to identify (radical) change and what is the empirical evidence for
this in the 1990s? To what extent is the politics of retrenchment still governed by
the logic of (institutional) resistance? How to explain the changes that do occur
and how to account for cross-national and cross-sectional (within country)
variation in (institutional) transformations? To what extent are the forces of
accelerating globalisation and European integration capable of effectively
overriding resistance?

It is difficult to define precisely, conceptualise accurately, and operationalise
and then identify correctly a radical change or fundamental transformation, if
only for the prosaic reason that contemporary developments are the object of
analysis. Nevertheless, there are four arguments that challenge the mainstream
welfare state theories that predict continuing persistence. From these arguments
four sets of hypotheses can be derived that will (or should) guide further research.

Politics for markets

One can speak of a fundamental transformation if the core social programmes
and institutions – taken as a system constituting the distinctive features of a
national welfare state regime – no longer guarantee the protection of citizens
against the hardships of the market. 'The core question', according to Streeck
(1996b: 300) 'of political economy at a time when economic relations systematically outgrow the boundaries of nation-states . . . is whether by undermining
the economic governing capacity of the nation-state, internationalization
undermines the capacity of society to civilize its economy.' According to Streeck,
this is exactly what is happening. Neither the nation-states nor the European
Union has the power to govern the internationalised economy. Moreover, the
constitution of the Union is such that it is highly unlikely that this power will be
claimed in the near future. In fact, 'European integration has become locked in a
negative, market-making, deregulatory mode, and in an institutional trajectory
that almost certainly rules out progress . . . from national to supranational
distributive intervention, and thus perfectly fits the interests behind the
"Thatcherist" *alliance of neo-liberalism and nationalism* that has come to dominate
European integration' (Streeck 1996b: 302, original emphasis; a 'nightmare
scenario' for Europe is envisioned by Amin 1997, chapter 6).

National welfare states are affected negatively by European economic
integration, and a supranational, European level of social policy is not replacing

the declining protective capacity of national welfare states. The Union is restricted in terms of authoritative capacities in the social policy realm. In fact, national welfare states are 'marketising' to the extent that governments are forced to comply with the demands of increasingly mobile production factors. 'In the process national social policy regimes and the national social compacts that sustain them are bound to be fundamentally transformed' (Streeck 1996a: 88).

The hypothesis can be formulated that the 'politics against markets' becomes a 'politics for markets', where national political activity is more preoccupied with the internationalisation of the national economy – bringing macroeconomic policies in line with the functional demands of international markets and deregulating the economy to attract investors – than with protecting the national population against the internationalising market.

Overriding resistance

The level of pressure – from various directions and a variety of sources – on the welfare states has been building up to such an extent that more radical adjustments are being chosen that may override the mechanisms of resistance. The economic, social and political context of the national politics of retrenchment is rapidly changing. National social policy is now strongly embedded in the European Union's attempt to facilitate the Union and the member states to remain or become competitive economies. The criteria for entry into the EMU have forced national governments to follow more radical adjustment policies than those that seemed electorally safe from the politician's short-term perspective. In the context of national social policy changes, the European Union has long functioned as a whipping-boy for the politics of blame avoidance (Weaver 1986; Anderson 1995), but may now increasingly become the major point of reference for the 'there-is-no-alternative-for-the-national-interest' arguments that underpin the proposals of more radical shifts in national policy. National governments have tried to meet the criteria of Maastricht.[3] The hypothesis is that it is likely that reform proposals are particularly aiming at overriding the defence mechanisms against change by politically making use of the EMU criteria as weapons in the national political struggles (see Pacolet 1996).

Institutional transformation

One can identify a radical reform when single core programmes are abolished or redefined in such a way that the former institutional logic is entirely replaced by a new one, as in the case of privatisation of public schemes, in the case of deregulation and marketisation by 'bringing the market into the state', or in the case of modifying substantially the rules of a programme (eligibility criteria, contribution standards, level of means testing, replacement rates, number of waiting days, funding, etc.).

However, there are some caveats here. First, privatisation can mean many things and does not necessarily lead to a radical reduction of protection or to the abolishment of established and accustomed rights. It may simply amount to radically more efficient ways of performing the originally intended function of social schemes by shifting responsibilities and making visible formerly hidden costs. As a result, a fundamental change in the institutional rules may hardly have any effect in terms of outcomes. The privatisation of the Dutch sickness scheme, which legally forces employers to seek private insurance for their employees, may be an example (see Hemerijck and van Kersbergen 1997). Sickness insurance is still mandatory, but its execution is privatised. Second, as Castles (1989, 1996; see Castles and Mitchell 1993) has rightly pointed out, there are alternative ways to provide social protection. In terms of outcomes the often championed strategy of universalism is not necessarily superior to more particularist approaches. Castles (1996: 112) is right when he stresses that . . .

> in the area where a needs-based system should deliver – i.e. where need is greatest – it does, at least, deliver outcomes at least as satisfactory as those of most other types of welfare states. That is a feature of such systems which may be of very considerable appeal to nations seeking to establish viable systems of social protection for the first time or to streamline existing systems under the pressure of fiscal exigency.

Nevertheless, if the development from 'marginalism' to institutionalism and universalism in major social programmes has indeed historically fostered radically greater equality in some contexts, then it may very well be that the reverse evolution will increase inequality greatly (Jäntti *et al.* 1996). In general, there may be radical institutional changes that have hardly any dramatic consequences, whether distributional or in terms of coverage and level of protection. Nevertheless, the hypothesis is that radical social policy reforms are most likely to result from institutional changes *within* the existing schemes.

Creeping disentitlement

Contemporary welfare state development is characterised by 'creeping disentitlement'. Under this general hypothesis a cluster of five hypotheses can be formulated.

(1) Radical transformation does not necessarily result from radical measures. Weakening or relaxing indexation in major social schemes is an illustration of a policy of incremental change that over time has significant effects. Lowering replacement rates once, say, by 5 per cent, may not be radical, but performing this operation several times over many years, of course, is. Increasing retirement age, lowering pensions, introducing (moderate) means tests, and increasing the number of earning years for assessment are by themselves perhaps not drastic measures, but their combined effect may be harmful, particularly for those who depend on a public pension only. Thus, European citizens may have suffered already a much larger loss of protection under sustained retrenchment policies than has been empirically documented so far, a deterioration of social security

that can be contributed to the accumulation of a host of small-scale measures. The hypothesis is that small, incremental changes – commonly taken as signs of the resilience of welfare states – can at a certain point in time result in a more fundamental transformation when, as a consequence of the accumulation of small measures, a social programme ceases to offer the level of protection for which it was originally designed (see Pierson 1996: 157).

(2) The incremental strategy of reform in one area of social policy undermines the (financial) viability in other areas, because the ex-beneficiaries of one programme become the clientele of another scheme. The hypothesis is that, ultimately, this leads to a greater reliance on (means tested or otherwise restricted) social assistance (see Gough and Eardly 1996).

(3) According to Wilding (1992), the real impact and lasting legacy of Thatcherism in Britain is to be found at the level of changing attitudes and approaches rather than in any radical policy transformation. Even if the structural characteristics of the welfare state have not been transformed fundamentally, the politics of welfare has, that is to say 'the political and ideological debate about the value of welfare – and thus about the nature of citizenship, the meaning of individual responsibility and the obligations of the state to the disadvantaged members of the community – has changed' (Waddan 1997: 168). The hypothesis is that over the longer term small adjustments gradually weaken vested interests, change ideas and approaches, alter public attitudes, transform the normative and political discourse on the welfare state, and cause instability and a greater susceptibility to fundamental change.

(4) A new generation has been brought up in a context of declining expectations and with the political language of retrenchment. It is this generation which is now becoming economically, socially and politically active (the cohort born around 1973–75). This cohort, although raised in the welfare state, has been taught not to expect too much from it. This group is not part of the stable social and political coalition that once supported the growth of the welfare state and there is no guarantee that this generation will develop the same patterns of solidarity as those upon which the welfare state was constructed. The hypothesis is that this generation will be much less attached politically to the welfare state than the preceding generations that built it and profited from it. Research on public attitudes towards the welfare state that would look not only at sectoral and occupational variation, but would also include an analysis of age group differences, might test the plausibility of the cohort effect (see Pettersen 1995: 230).

(5) Retrenchment is electorally a risky policy because of its tangible losses and uncertain gains. It is therefore often the case that the politicians advocating retrenchment tend to play off one group against another (Pierson 1996: 147) and hit those groups hardest that are poorly organised and electorally harmless. Analyses that concentrate on specific groups, e.g. single mothers, ethnic groups, long-term unemployed, flexi-workers, irregular and atypical workers, may uncover more dramatic changes than those studies that concentrate on particular programmes. The hypothesis is that gradual retrenchment policies through

salami-tactics produce dramatic results in terms of a decreasing level of social protection and rising poverty among specific groups.

Conclusion

The conclusion is that many theories have predicted the end of the welfare state, but the welfare state turned out to be more resilient than expected. The welfare state continued to function, even under deteriorating economic conditions. The real characteristic of welfare state development in the 1980s and 1990s was resistance against change. Institutionalist accounts of welfare state development are generally convincing to the extent that they explicitly focus on institutional persistence. However, this chapter has looked at a number of arguments and hypotheses that may imply a qualification of the resilience argument. There may be far more radical or fundamental changes than we expected or have so far observed (see Clayton and Pontusson 1998). Still, not every radical reform of the welfare state necessarily leads to the collapse of the welfare state.

The chance for survival of the welfare state is gloomy if the political debate over restructuring continues to assume the inherent mechanisms of resistance of the status quo. In his imaginative reflection on the current state of the welfare state and its future, Esping-Andersen (1996c: 256) offers what he sees as the only viable scenario for the welfare state to transform. The focus is on equality and protection, the two fundamental properties of the welfare state. Inequality is increasingly difficult to avoid and this demands a radical innovation in thinking and a stronger emphasis on a viable combination of education and active social policies. 'The most logical solution', says Esping-Andersen (1996c: 264),

> is that we rethink the idea of redistribution and rights: accepting inequalities for some, here and now, but guaranteeing at the same time that those who fare less well 'here and now' will not always do so; that underprivilege will not be a permanent fixture of anyone's life course. This kind of dynamic, life-chances commitment to equality is arguably a positive-sum solution in that it stresses a social policy more explicitly designed to optimize the self-reliant capacities of the citizenry. Again, the core of such a model's social citizenship guarantees would combine education and proactive income maintenance.

This, however, assumes a fundamental alteration in the traditional manner in which we tend to think of the welfare state as well as a radical transformation of its institutions and core policies. If it is the case that because 'a major overhaul of the existing welfare state edifice must occur if it is meant to produce a positive-sum kind of welfare for postindustrial society' (Esping-Andersen 1996c: 267), then the political mission is both immense and paradoxical. The political and institutional defence mechanisms of the 'old order' have to be broken down, while at the same time new and innovative coalitions have to be forged that can initiate a 'new order'. The immensity concerns the fact that this has to be accomplished in such a way that the existing level of social protection is guaranteed while at the same time the systems are reorganised. The paradox is that in order for the welfare state to survive, it must be transformed.

Notes

1   For helpful comments I would like to thank Sven Bislev, John D. Stephens, Jonas Pontusson, Duane Swank, Christoffer Green-Pedersen, and Stein Kuhnle.
2   On Continental Europe, see Esping-Andersen (1996b). On Germany, see Lawson (1996); Pierson (1996); Alber (1998). On Italy, see Ferrera (1997); Niero (1996); Saraceno and Negri (1994). On France, see Hantrais (1996). On Scandinavia, see Kangas (1995); Gould (1996); Kosonen (1996); Pierson (1996); Stephens (1996); Huber and Stephens (1998). On the United Kingdom, see Taylor-Gooby (1996); Pierson (1996). On the Antipodes, see Castles (1996). On convergence of national systems and other comparative perspectives, see Ferrera (1994); Kangas (1994); Kosonen (1995); Ervik and Kuhnle (1996); Garrett and Mitchell (1996); Esping-Andersen (1996c); Rhodes (1996a, 1997); Gough *et al.* (1997); Stephens *et al.* (1999).
3   This logic seems to have inspired the French President Chirac to call for early elections so as to prevent the coincidence of the EMU decision and national elections, that is to say trying to prevent the danger that the elections would turn into an EU referendum. The idea was that in this way the extra retrenchment policies necessary for EMU could be announced after the elections without endangering France's entry into monetary union, while still guaranteeing a Gaullist electoral victory. However, the Gaullists lost the elections and a socialist government took over.

References

Adnett, N. (1995) 'Social Dumping and European Economic Integration', *Journal of European Social Policy*, 5, 1: 1–12.

Alber, J. (1988) 'Is there a Crisis of the Welfare State? Cross-national Evidence from Europe, North America, and Japan', *European Sociological Review*, 4, 3: 181–207.

—— (1998) 'Der deutsche Sozialstaat im Licht international vergleichender Daten', *Leviathan*, 26, 2: 199–227.

Alston, L. J., Eggertsson, T. and North, D. C. (eds) (1996) *Empirical Studies in Institutional Change*, Cambridge: Cambridge University Press.

Amin, S. (1997) *Capitalism in the Age of Globalization. The Management of Contemporary Society*, London and New Jersey: Zed Books.

Anderson, C. (1995) *Blaming the Government. Citizens and the Economy in Five European Democracies*, Armonk, NY: M.E. Sharpe.

Aspinwall, M. (1996) 'The Unholy Social Trinity: Modelling Social Dumping under Conditions of Capital Mobility and Free Trade', *West European Politics*, 19, 1: 125–50.

Becker, U. (1998) 'Der Wohlfahrtsstaat am Kreuzweg', *Politische Vierteljahresschrift*, 39, 3: 610–24.

Begg, J. and Nectoux, F. (1995) 'Social Protection and Economic Union', *Journal of European Social Policy*, 5, 4: 285–302.

Bell, D. (1979) *The Cultural Contradictions of Capitalism*, London: Heinemann.

Birch, A. (1984) 'Overload, Ungovernability and Delegitimation', *British Journal of Political Science*, 14, 2: 135–60.

Boix, C. (1998) *Political Parties, Growth and Equality. Conservative and Social Democratic Strategies in the World Economy*, Cambridge: Cambridge University Press.

Bowles, S. and Gintis, H. (1982) 'The Crisis of Liberal Democratic Capitalism: the Case of the US', *Politics and Society*, 11, 1: 51–93.

Boyer, R. and Drache, D. (eds) (1996) *States Against Markets. The Limits of Globalization*, London and New York: Routledge.

Brittan, S. (1975) 'The Economic Contradictions of Democracy', *British Journal of Political Science*, 5, 2: 129–59.

Camissa, A. M. (1998) *From Rhetoric to Reform? Welfare Policy in American Politics*, Boulder, CO: Westview.

Castles, F. G. (1989) 'Social Protection by other Means: Australia's Strategy of Coping with External Vulnerability', in F. G. Castles (ed.) *The Comparative History of Public Policy*, Cambridge: Polity Press.

—— (1996) 'Needs Based Strategies of Social Protection in Australia and New Zealand', in G. Esping-Andersen (ed.) *Welfare States in Transition. National Adaptations in Global Economies*, London: Sage.

Castles, F. G. and Mitchell, D. (1993) 'Worlds of Welfare and Families of Nations', in F. G. Castles (ed.) *Families of Nations*, Aldershot: Dartmouth.

Cavanna, H. (ed.) (1998) *Challenges to the Welfare State: Internal and External Dynamics for Change*, Cheltenham: Edward Elgar.

Clasen, J. and Gould, A. (1995) 'Stability and Change in Welfare States: Germany and Sweden in the 1990s', *Policy and Politics*, 23, 3: 189–201.

Clayton, R. and Pontusson, J. (1998) 'Welfare-state Retrenchment Revisited: Entitlement Cuts, Public Sector Restructuring, and Inegalitarian Trends in Advanced Capitalist Societies', *World Politics*, 51, 1: 67–98.

Crozier, M., Huntington, S. P. and Watanuki, J. (eds) (1975) *The Crisis of Democracy*, New York: New York University Press.

Ervik, R. and Kuhnle, S. (1996) 'The Nordic Welfare Model and the European Union', in B. Greve (ed.) *Comparative Welfare Systems: the Scandinavian Model in a Period of Change*, New York: St. Martin's Press.

Esping-Andersen, G. (1990) *The Three Worlds of Welfare Capitalism*, Cambridge: Polity Press.

—— (ed.) (1993) *Changing Classes. Stratification and Mobility in Post-Industrial Societies*, London: Sage.

—— (ed.) (1996a) *Welfare States in Transition. National Adaptations in Global Economies*, London: Sage.

—— (1996b) 'After the Golden Age? Welfare State Dilemmas in a Global Economy', in G. Esping-Andersen (ed.) *Welfare States in Transition. National Adaptations in Global Economies*, London: Sage.

—— (1996c) 'Positive-sum Solutions in a World of Trade-offs?', in G. Esping-Andersen (ed.) *Welfare States in Transition. National Adaptations in Global Economies*, London: Sage.

European Commission (1993) *Social Protection in Europe*, Brussels: European Communities.

—— (1998) 'The Welfare State in Europe. Challenges and Reforms', *European Economy 1997*, 4, Brussels: European Communities.

Ferrera, M. (1994) 'European Social Policy: Towards Convergence?', *Politico*, 59, 3: 525–37.

—— (1997) 'The Uncertain Future of the Italian Welfare State', *West European Politics*, 21, 1: 231–41.

Flora, P. (1985) 'History and Current Problems of the Welfare State', in S. N. Eisenstadt and O. Ahimer (eds) *The Welfare State and its Aftermath*, London: Croom Helm.

Flora, P. (ed.) (1986–87) *Growth to Limits*, vols 1, 2, 4, Berlin: De Gruyter.

Garrett, G. and Mitchell, D. (1996) 'Globalization and the Welfare State: Income Transfers in the Industrial Democracies', Paper presented at the Annual Meetings of the American Political Science Association, San Francisco, 28 August–1 September 1996.

George, V. (1996) 'The Future of the Welfare State', in V. George and P. Taylor-Gooby (eds) *European Welfare Policy. Squaring the Welfare Circle*, Basingstoke: Macmillan.

George, V. and Taylor-Gooby, P. (eds) (1996) *European Welfare Policy. Squaring the Welfare Circle*, Basingstoke: Macmillan.

Ginsburg, N. (1979) *Class, Capital and Social Policy*, London: Macmillan.

Gough, I. (1979) *The Political Economy of the Welfare State*, London: Macmillan.

Gough, I. and Eardley, T. (1996) 'Diverse Systems, Common Destinations? A Comparative Study of Social Assistance in OECD Countries', Paper presented at the Annual Meeting of Research Committee 19 of the International Sociological Association, Australian National University, Canberra, Australia, 19–23 August.

Gough, I., Bradshaw, J., Ditch, J., Eardley, T. and Whiteford, P. (1997) 'Social Assistance in OECD Countries', *Journal of European Social Policy*, 7, 1: 17–44.

Goul Andersen, J. (1997) 'The Scandinavian Welfare Model in Crisis? Achievements and Problems of the Danish Welfare State in an Age of Unemployment and Low Growth', *Scandinavian Political Studies*, 20, 1: 1–31.

Gould, A. (1996) 'Sweden: the Last Bastion of Social Democracy', in V. George and P. Taylor-Gooby (eds) *European Welfare Policy. Squaring the Welfare Circle*, Basingstoke: Macmillan.

Greve, B. (ed.) (1996) *Comparative Welfare Systems. The Scandinavian Model in a Period of Change*, Basingstoke: Macmillan.

Gummett, P. (ed.) (1996) *Globalization and Public Policy*, Cheltenham: Edward Elgar.

Habermas, J. (1976) *Legitimation Crisis*, London: Heinemann.

—— (1985) 'Die Krise des Wohlfahrtsstaates und die Erschöpfung utopischer Energien', in J. Habermas, *Die neue Unübersichtlichkeit*, Frankfurt a. M.: Suhrkamp.

Hadley, R. and Hatch, S. (1981) *Social Welfare and the Failure of the State: Centralised Social Services and Participatory Alternatives*, London: Allen & Unwin.

Hantrais, L. (1996) 'France: Squaring the Welfare Triangle', in V. George and P. Taylor-Gooby (eds) *European Welfare Policy. Squaring the Welfare Circle*, Basingstoke: Macmillan.

Harris, R. and Seldon, A. (1987) *Welfare without the State: a Quarter-Century of Suppressed Public Choice*, London: Institute of Economic Affairs.

Hemerijck, A. and van Kersbergen, K. (1997) 'A Miraculous Model? Explaining the New Politics of the Welfare State in the Netherlands', *Acta Politica*, 32, 3: 258–301.

Hirst, P. and Thompson, G. (1995) 'Globalization and the Future of the Nation-state', *Economy and Society*, 24, 3: 408–42.

—— (1996) *Globalization in Question. The International Economy and the Possibilities of Governance*, Cambridge: Polity Press.

Huber, E. and Stephens, J. D. (1998) 'Internationalization and the Social Democratic Model: Crisis and Future Prospects', *Comparative Political Studies*, 31, 3: 353–97.

Jäntii, M., Kangas, O. and Ritakallio, V.-M. (1996) 'From Marginalism to Institutionalism: Distributional Consequences of the Transformation of the Finnish Pension Regime', *Review of Income and Wealth*, 42, 2: 473–91.

Jones Finer, C. (1996) 'European Social Policy: Subject or Subject-matter?', *Government and Opposition*, 31, 4: 497–507.

Jowell, R. (1990) *British Social Attitudes*, Aldershot: Gower.

Kangas, O. (1994) 'The Merging of Welfare State Models? Past and Present Trends in Finnish and Swedish Social Policy', *Journal of European Social Policy*, 4, 2: 79–94.

—— (1995) 'Attitudes on Means-tested Social Benefits in Finland', *Acta Sociologica*, 38, 4: 299–310.

Kelsey, J. (1995) *The New Zealand Experiment. A World Model for Structural Adjustment?*, Auckland: Auckland University Press.

King, A. (1975) 'Overload: Problems of Governing in the 1970s', *Political Studies*, 23, 2/3: 284–96.

Kitschelt, H., Lange, P., Marks, G. and Stephens, J. D. (eds) (1999) *Continuity and Change in Contemporary Capitalism*, Cambridge: Cambridge University Press.

Kosonen, P. (1994) *European Integration. A Welfare State Perspective*, Helsinki: University of Helsinki.

—— (1995) 'European Welfare State Models: Converging Trends', in T. P. Boye (ed.) 'Work and Welfare in Europe, Part II: Reshaping the European Welfare States', *International Journal of Sociology*, 25, 1: 81–110.

—— (1996) 'Nordic Welfare States in the 1990s: Internal and External Pressures', paper for the ISA Annual Meeting of Research Committee 19, 19–22 August, Australian National University, Canberra.

Lawson, R. (1996) 'Germany: Maintaining the Middle Way', in V. George and P. Taylor-Gooby (eds) *European Welfare Policy. Squaring the Welfare Circle*, Basingstoke: Macmillan.

Leibfried, S. and Pierson, P. (eds) (1995) *European Social Policy. Between Fragmentation and Integration*, Washington, DC: The Brookings Institute.

Lessenich, S. and Ostner, I. (1998) *Welten des Wohlfahrtskapitalismus. Der Sozialstaat in vergleichender Perspektive*, Frankfurt/New York: Campus.

Mishra, R. (1984) *The Welfare State in Crisis*, Brighton: Wheatsheaf.

—— (1996) 'The Welfare of Nations', in R. Boyer and D. Drache (eds) *States Against Markets. The Limits of Globalization*, London and New York: Routledge.

Moran, M. (1988) 'Crises of the Welfare State', *British Journal of Political Science*, 18, 4: 397–414.

Niero, M. (1996) 'Italy: Right Turn for the Welfare State?', in V. George and P. Taylor-Gooby (eds) *European Welfare Policy. Squaring the Welfare Circle*, Basingstoke: Macmillan.

O'Connor, J. (1973) *The Fiscal Crisis of the State*, New York: St. Martin's Press.

OECD (1981) *The Welfare State in Crisis*, Paris: OECD.

—— (1985) *Social Expenditure 1960–1990. Problems of Growth and Control*, Paris: OECD.

Offe, C. (1984) *Contradictions of the Welfare State*, London: Hutchinson.

Pacolet, J. (ed.) (1996) *Social Protection and the European Economic and Monetary Union*, Aldershot: Avebury.

Panich, L. (1986) *Working Class Politics in Crisis*, London: Verso.

Pettersen, P. A. (1995) 'The Welfare State: the Security Dimension', in O. Borre and E. Scarbrough (eds) *The Scope of Government*, Oxford: Oxford University Press.

Pierson, P. (1994) *Dismantling the Welfare State? Reagan, Thatcher, and the Politics of Retrenchment*, Cambridge, Cambridge University Press.

—— (1996) 'The New Politics of the Welfare State', *World Politics*, 48, 2: 143–79.

Piven, F. F. and Cloward, R. (1971) *Regulating the Poor: The Functions of Public Welfare*, New York: Pantheon Books.

Ploug, N. and Kvist, J. (1996) *Social Security in Europe: Development or Dismantlement?*, The Hague: Kluwer Law International.

Regini, M. (1995) *Uncertain Boundaries. The Social and Political Construction of European Economies*, Cambridge: Cambridge University Press.

Rhodes, M. (1996a) 'A New Social Contract? Globalisation and West European Welfare States', EUI Working Papers 96/43, the Robert Schuman Centre, Florence.

—— (1996b) 'Globalization and West European Welfare States: a Critical Review of Recent

Debates', *Journal of European Social Policy*, 6, 4: 305–27.

—— (1997) 'The Welfare State: Internal Challenges, External Constraints', in M. Rhodes, P. Heywood and V. Wright (eds) *Developments in West European Politics*, Basingstoke: Macmillan.

Roller, E. (1992) *Einstellungen der Bürger zum Wohlfahrtsstaat der Bundesrepublik Deutschland*, Opladen: Westdeutscher Verlag.

—— (1995) 'The Welfare State: the Equality Dimension', in O. Borre and E. Scarbrough (eds) *The Scope of Government*, Oxford: Oxford University Press.

Sainsbury, D. (1996) *Gender, Equality and Welfare States*, Cambridge: Cambridge University Press.

Saraceno, C. and Negri, N. (1994) 'The Changing Italian Welfare State', *Journal of European Social Policy*, 4, 1: 19–34.

Schmidt, M. G. (1983) 'The Welfare State and the Economy in Periods of Economic Crisis: a Comparative Study of 23 OECD Nations', *European Journal of Political Research*, 17, 6: 641–59.

Sihvo, T. and Uusitalo, H. (1995) 'Economic Crises and Support for the Welfare State in Finland 1975–1993', *Acta Sociologica*, 38, 3: 251–62.

Skocpol, T. (1980) 'Political Response to Capitalist Crisis: Neo-marxist Theories of the State and the Case of the New Deal', *Politics and Society*, 10: 155–201.

Slomp, H. (1996) *Between Bargaining and Politics: an Introduction to European Labor Relations*, Westport, CT: Praeger.

Stephens, J. D. (1996) 'The Scandinavian Welfare States: Achievements, Crisis, and Prospects', in G. Esping-Andersen (ed.) *Welfare States in Transition. National Adaptations in Global Economies*, London: Sage.

Stephens, J. D., Huber, E. and Ray, L. (1999) 'The Welfare State in Hard Times', in H. Kitschelt, P. Lange, G. Marks and J. D. Stephens (eds) *Continuity and Change in Contemporary Capitalism*, Cambridge: Cambridge University Press.

Streeck, W. (1996a) 'Neo-voluntarism: a New European Social Policy Regime?', in G. Marks *et al. Governance in the European Union*, London: Sage.

—— (1996b) 'Public Power Beyond the Nation-state: the Case of the European Union', in R. Boyer and D. Drache (eds) *States Against Markets. The Limits of Globalization*, London and New York: Routledge.

Svallfors, S. (1993) 'Dimensions of Inequality: a Comparison of Attitudes in Sweden and Britain', *European Sociological Review*, 9, 3: 267–87.

—— (1995) 'The End of Class Politics? Structural Cleavages and Attitudes to Swedish Welfare Policies', *Acta Sociologica*, 38, 1: 53–74.

Swank, D. (1998) 'Funding the Welfare State: Globalization and the Taxation of Business in Advanced Market Economies', *Political Studies*, 46, 4: 671–92.

Taylor-Gooby, P. (1988) 'The Future of the British Welfare State: Public Attitudes, Citizenship and Social Policy under the Conservative Governments of the 1980s', *European Sociological Review*, 4, 1: 1–19.

—— (1996) 'The United Kingdom: Radical Departures and Political Consensus', in V. George and P. Taylor-Goody (eds) *European Welfare Policy: Squaring the Welfare Circle*, Basingstoke: Macmillan.

—— (1997) 'In Defense of Second-best Theory: State, Class and Capital in Social Policy', *Journal of Social Policy*, 26, 2: 171–98.

Thompson, H. (1997) 'The Nation-state and Internationl Capital Flows in Historical Perspective', *Government and Opposition*, 32, 1: 84–113.

Thompson, P., Flecker, J. and Wallace, T. (1994/1995) 'Back to Convergence? Globalization and Societal Effects on Work Organization', in T. P. Boye (ed.) 'Work and Welfāre in a Changing Europe, Part I: Transformation of the European Societies', *International Journal of Sociology*, 24, 4: 83–108.

van Kersbergen, K. (2000) 'Political Allegiance and European Integration', *European Journal of Political Research*, 37: 1.

Visser, J. and Hemerijck, A. (1997) *'A Dutch Miracle'. Job Growth, Welfare Reform and Corporatism in the Netherlands*, Amsterdam: Amsterdam University Press.

Waddan, A. (1997) *The Politics of Social Welfare. The Collapse of the Centre and the Rise of the Right*, Cheltenham: Edward Elgar.

Weaver, R. Kent (1996) 'The Politics of Blame Avoidance', *Journal of Public Policy*, 6, 4: 371–98.

Wilding, P. (1992) 'The British Welfare State: Thatcherism's Enduring Legacy', *Policy and Politics*, 20, 3: 210–21.

Wilson, E. (1977) *Women and the Welfare State*, London: Tavistock.

Wolfe, A. (1979) *The Limits of Legitimacy*, London: Macmillan.

Part II

National welfare state reforms in the 1990s: comparative and case studies

3 Nordic welfare states in the 1990s

Institutional stability, signs of divergence[1]

Pål Eitrheim and Stein Kuhnle

Introduction: the Nordic type of welfare state

Since the 1960s all of the Nordic countries – Denmark, Finland, Iceland, Norway and Sweden – have made up a distinct type of welfare state sharing the following characteristics (Esping-Andersen 1990; Kuhnle 1990):

- Comprehensive in terms of welfare needs covered and services offered.
- Universal population coverage.
- High degree of redistribution.
- General taxation as major source of financing.
- Large share of public sector employment in general and in the broadly defined welfare sector in particular (social security, health, social services, education).
- High degree of services-in-kind.

A combination of specific historical circumstances may have been conducive to the development of the Scandinavian or Nordic variant of European welfare state models: small size; relatively egalitarian pre-industrial agricultural societies; 'peasants were carriers of freedom and equality' (Sørensen and Stråth 1997: 8); homogeneous populations in terms of language, religion, culture; early fusion between church and state bureaucracies after the Reformation – giving legitimacy to the strong position of the state and also giving local government ('communes') an early important role in matters of education and welfare.

As all other European welfare states, the Nordic ones have, but to a varying degree, experienced great challenges in the 1990s. In the following paragraphs we shall look at trends in social security reform activity in all of the Nordic countries with the exception of Iceland, put changes in perspective and discuss why things have changed (or not) in the light of the economic and political contexts of social policy development. For a more comprehensive interpretation of developments in Finland and Denmark in particular, see Chapters 4 and 5 in this volume.

State of the welfare states in the 1990s

Table 3.1 offers a snapshot of some indicators of overall change during the period 1990–95. All countries, except Sweden, spent substantially more resources per capita in real terms on social purposes in 1995 than in 1990, and a declining share of expenditures was spent on services (rather than cash transfers) in Finland and Sweden, while the opposite trend was evident in Denmark, and especially in Norway. Social expenditure as a percentage of gross domestic product is an ambiguous indicator, which is clearly evident from Table 3.1: the percentage is higher in 1995 than in 1990 in Sweden thanks to several years of declining GDP in the 1990s, and in spite of slightly lower social expenditure in absolute terms at fixed prices in 1995.

In Denmark, Finland and Norway, social expenditure per inhabitant increased as much as 16–21 per cent in real terms during the five-year period, hardly signs of major welfare state retrenchment. The decline in Sweden was negligible. Increased expenditure may indicate rising problems and needs, more people with welfare entitlements, and/or indicate changes towards more generous or comprehensive welfare states. Table 3.1 does indicate that in Finland and Sweden the scope of services-in-kind has been cut, while this does not seem apparent in Denmark, and definitely not in Norway. Through Tables 3.2 to 3.5 we shall provide comparative illustrations of major characteristics of social security schemes in 1990 and 1997 in order to reflect on the state of the welfare state in the Nordic countries. We do not review changes in the health and service sector, but should

Table 3.1 Social expenditure as a percentage of GDP, social expenditure per inhabitant, 1995 prices, in national currencies (Kr/Fm), and relative share of expenditures on services, in the Nordic countries, 1990 and 1995

| | *Social expenditure* | | *Share of expenditures on services (%)* |
	As % of GDP	*Per inhabitant*	
Denmark			
1990	29.7	51,104	34
1995	33.7	62,288	35
Finland			
1990	25.7	28,988	37
1995	32.8	35,322	30
Norway			
1990	26.4	50,503	35
1995	27.4	58,181	42
Sweden			
1990	34.8	67,481	41
1995	35.8	66,692	39

Sources: NOSOSCO (1992, 1997).

Table 3.2 Parental leave benefits and child allowance schemes in the Nordic countries, 1990 and 1997

	Denmark		Finland		Norway		Sweden	
	1990	1997	1990	1997	1990	1997	1990	1997
Duration (weeks)[1]	28	28	44	44	28/35	42/52	64	64
Weeks available to father	10	12[2]	26	26	22/29	33/42	32	32
Compensation (per cent)	90–100 (up to income ceiling)	100 (up to income ceiling)	80/50/30	70/40/25	100/80 (up to income ceiling)	100/80 (up to income ceiling)	90 (up to income ceiling)	75[3] (up to income ceiling)
Child allowance	Universal — flat rate under age 18	Universal — flat rate under age 18	Universal — flat rate under age 17	Universal — flat rate under age 17	Universal — flat rate under age 16	Universal — flat rate under age 16	Universal — flat rate under age 16	Universal — flat rate under age 16

Sources: NOSOSCO (1992); Ploug and Kvist (1994); Social Security Programs Throughout the World (1997); national web-sites of social security authorities.

Notes
1   Includes both immediately prior to and after birth.
2   As of 1 April 1998 two additional weeks are reserved for the father.
3   For the first 12 months; a flat rate benefit of 60 SEK per day for the additional three months.

mention that there has been no change in the general principle of universal, and basically free, coverage of health and hospital services throughout the 1990s in all four countries, although fees for medical consultations, same-day treatments, and medicines to some extent have been introduced.

All countries have held on to their universal child allowance schemes, and had, in a European comparison, relatively generous schemes for maternity benefits for the gainfully employed in 1990. The duration of parental leave is left unchanged in Finland and Sweden, but has been extended substantially in Norway, and both in Norway and Denmark the number of weeks available to the father has been increased, during the first seven years of the decade. Only Denmark and Norway have not reduced the replacement rate, while the two neighbouring states have decided to cut compensation by 10–15 percentage points. A major extension of the parental leave period was introduced only in Norway, gradually from 28/35 weeks in 1990 to 42/52 weeks at 100/80 per cent wage compensation. In 1993, it was instituted that four weeks of the total leave period should be reserved for the father, and in 1994 a so-called 'time account system' was introduced, which allows for the combination of reduced work hours and receipt of benefits. Special arrangements exist for single parents.

Kindergarten coverage in 1990 was relatively high, especially in Denmark and Sweden (64 per cent and 48 per cent coverage for children 0–6 years; in Norway

33 per cent), in 1995: 65 per cent in Denmark, 59 in Sweden, 44 in Norway and 39 per cent in Finland (NOSOSCO 1997).

Table 3.3 contrasts basic features in the sickness benefit system in 1990 with characteristics of the system in 1997. It indicates no changes in general scope of the sickness insurance during 1990–97: On both occasions the schemes were open to all gainfully employed persons, including self-employed. We note a tightening of the qualifying conditions in Finland and Sweden, while no such change has been implemented in Denmark or Norway. Only in Norway has the replacement rate remained stable, while it is significantly reduced in the three other Nordic countries. In all countries the benefit was paid for at least 50 weeks, but by 1997 both Sweden and Norway had introduced an upper maximum of 52 weeks. Norway and Denmark have maintained a system free of waiting days and with a two-week employer's period. Finland still has no employer's period, but has increased the number of waiting days to nine, while Sweden has introduced one waiting day and an employer's period of four weeks, compared to none in 1990. The sickness cash benefit scheme is the most frequently and extensively reformed area of the Swedish social security system in the 1990s. Reforms were induced by rising sickness absenteeism and costs in the 1980s, and by a dramatic rise in the number of persons receiving permanent and temporary disability pensions (33 per cent increase 1981–94). In Finland a general reduction of the benefit level dependent upon income brackets was introduced in 1992. Apart from a structural change of financing, through the reduction of state funds to municipalities from 75 per cent to 50 per cent in 1992, no major changes have been made in the Danish sickness benefit system in the 1990s. Minor alterations have been implemented as part of the general reform work in other benefit systems (e.g. job training, education, parental leave).

Basic features of the unemployment insurance schemes are presented in Table 3.4. As in 1990, only Norway has an unemployment insurance scheme covering all gainfully employed and self-employed. The other three countries have kept a voluntary insurance system with a relatively high coverage, and also non-insured are entitled to cash benefits as unemployment assistance. With regards to waiting days, only Denmark has managed to avoid them, whereas the Swedish system – originally without waiting days – now has five. In Finland the number of waiting days has increased from five to seven, while Norway had three both in 1990 and in 1997. All four Nordic countries have stricter qualifying conditions in 1997 compared to 1990, especially evident in Denmark and Norway. The normal replacement rate has only been significantly altered in Sweden, where it has decreased by 10 percentage points (and even more for a period in 1996–97). Finally, the maximum benefit duration has also been subject to reforms, most evident in Denmark, where the total period is limited from nine to five years during the period of analysis. All countries offered support for education of unemployed and had active labour market programmes in 1990. These schemes have been significantly improved during the 1990s. In Finland a partially means-tested benefit known as labour market support was introduced in 1994 to secure the basic livelihood of long-term unemployed and young people with no job

Table 3.3 Sickness insurance in the Nordic countries, 1990 and 1997

	Denmark		Finland		Norway		Sweden	
	1990	1997	1990	1997	1990	1997	1990	1997
Membership	Gainfully employed incl. self-employed	Gainfully employed incl. self-employed	Gainfully employed incl. self-employed	Gainfully employed incl. self-employed	Gainfully employed incl. self-employed	Gainfully employed incl. self-employed	Gainfully employed incl. self-employed	Gainfully employed incl. self-employed
Qualifying conditions	120 hrs. of work within 3 months employment	120 hrs. of work within 13 weeks employment	3 months employment	Employed last 3 months and annual income ≥ 5,070 FIM	a) 2 weeks employed; *and* b) annual income ≥ 18,250 NOK	a) 2 weeks employed; *and* b) annual income ≥ 21,250 NOK	Annual income ≥ 6,000 SEK	a) Income ≥ 24% of basic amount; *and* b) 4 weeks of employment *or* 2 weeks of work
Normal compensation (per cent)	100 up to specified max.	90 up to specified max.	80/50/30 dep. on income	70/40/25 dep. on income	100 up to 6 times basic amount	100 up to 6 times basic amount	90 up to 7.5 times basic amount	75 up to 7.5 times basic amount[1]
Max. benefit duration (weeks)	52 within 18 months	52 within 18 months	50	50	52 (but no real upper limit)	52	No upper limit	52
Employer's period (weeks)	2	2	none	none	2	2[2]	none	4[3]
Waiting days	0	0	7	9	0	0	0	1

Sources: NOSOSCO (1992); Social Security Programs Throughout the World (1997); national web-sites of social security authorities.

Notes
1 Increased to 80 per cent as of 1 January 1998.
2 Increased to 17 days as of 1 April 1998.
3 Reduced to two weeks as of 1 April 1998.

Table 3.4 Unemployment insurance in the Nordic countries, 1990 and 1997

	Denmark		Finland		Norway		Sweden	
	1990	1997	1990	1997	1990	1997	1990	1997
Membership	Voluntary	Voluntary	Voluntary	Voluntary	Compulsory	Compulsory	Voluntary	Voluntary
Waiting days	0	0	5	7	3	3	0	5
Qualifying conditions	a) 12 months membership; *and* b) 26 weeks of work within last 3 years	a) 12 months membership; *and* b) 52 weeks of unsubsidised work within 3 years	a) 6 months membership; *and* b) 26 weeks of work (18 hours per week) within last 2 years	a) 10 months membership; *and* b) 18 hrs. of work per week during last 2 years	Income equal to min. 75% of basic amount during last 3 years or last 3 months	a) Annual income min. 125% of basic amount; *or* b) average income during last 3 years equal to basic amount	a) 12 months membership; *and* b) 75 days of work during 4 months within latest 12 months	a) 12 months membership; *and* b) Worked minimum: – 70 hrs. per month for 6 months; *or* – 450 hrs. for 180 consecutive work days
Normal compensation (per cent)	90 (up to specified max.)	90 (up to specified max.)	Income-related Average ?	Income-related Average 58	Average 62 (up to specified max.)	Average 62 (up to specified max.)	90 (up to specified max)	80 (up to specified max)
Max. benefit duration	780 days within 3 years up to 9 years	5 years: • 2 years of *benefit* • 3 years of *activation*	500 days within 4 years (900 for 55+ years)	500 days within 4 years (900 for 57+ years)	480 days for 80 weeks	156/78 weeks depending on income previous or latest 3 years	300 days (450 for 55+ years)	300 days (450 for 57+ years)

Sources: NOSOSCO (1992, 1997); Social Security Programs Throughout the World (1997), national web-sites of social security authorities.

experience, but the scheme was restricted in 1996. Conditions for the unemployed have generally and gradually been improved during the 1990s in Norway (with the exception of the stricter income qualifying condition). For example, unemployed who wanted to set up their own business were granted an extra six months of benefits as of 1992. Simultaneously, the waiting period for re-qualification was abolished in cases where the labour market authorities were unable to offer any kind of work or job training. Hence, the *de facto* maximum benefit period was extended to 186 weeks.

Table 3.5 shows that all four countries had universal pension systems covering all residents in 1990, and with the exception of Denmark they had earnings-related supplementary pension schemes for employees and self-employed (in Denmark only all employees were entitled to a modest non-earnings-related supplement).[2] In principle pension benefits were taxable, but with many exceptions for groups with small or basic pensions.

With the exception of Sweden, 40 years of membership is now required for obtaining a full pension in all of the four Nordic countries, but with the implementation of the new pension reform in 2001, 40 years of membership will also be required in Sweden. The basic structure of the pension system is unaltered in Norway. The same holds true in Denmark, although the introduction of a partial income test of the 'pensions supplement' part of the basic pension in 1994 can be seen as a potentially significant structural adjustment. Nevertheless, a more profound and far-reaching structural change of the pension schemes has taken place in Finland and has been initiated in Sweden. Finland introduced a new system in 1996–97. Sweden will in 2001 move from a 'defined benefit' to a 'defined contribution' system. The employer and every insured will pay a contribution of 9.25 per cent each of the earnings of the insured, of which 2.5 per cent can be invested according to the preferences of the individual contributors. Common to both systems in the future is a closer link between contributions and payments, and a restriction of the previously universal basic amount to people with no, or low, employment-derived pension. The reform is the result of a broad cross-party majority initiative in the Swedish parliament in 1994. An agreement was reached in 1996, and a law passed in June 1998.

In Finland the old age-pension system has seen several changes in the 1990s: index linking and cuts in the employment-derived pension part; introduction of an employee contribution of 3 per cent for occupational pensions; lowering of age limit for part-time pensions and the increase of retirement age for some groups in the public sector from 63 to 65 years. The pension reform of 1996–97 implies a greater importance of work history, and the minimum national pension, hitherto a universal benefit, was restricted to pensioners with employment-derived pensions below a certain limit, thus introducing a system similar to what was later decided upon in the Swedish reform. In Norway, the old-age pension system has been maintained, but in order to save future pension expenditure, the rules for calculating the earnings-dependent supplementary pension were modified in 1992.

Table 3.5 Old-age pensions in the Nordic countries, 1990 and 1997

	Denmark		Finland		Norway		Sweden	
	1990	1997	1990	1997	1990	1997	1990	1997[1]
Pensionable age	67	67	65	65	67	67	65	65
Scope of basic pension	Universal: all residents	Universal: all residents, but partial income-testing	Universal: all residents	Universal: all residents, but partial income-testing	Universal: all residents	Universal: all residents	Universal: all residents	Universal: all residents
System characteristics	a) Universal basic amount + pensions supplement depending on income b) Labour market supplement depending on work history for employees	a) Partially income-tested basic amount b) Supplement based on work history for employees	a) Universal basic amount depending on marital status and local residence + income-depending supplement b) Supplementary pension depending on membership duration and income for employees and self-employed	a) Basic amount restricted to pensioners with low/no employment derived pension b) Supplementary pension depending on income and work history for employees and self-employed	a) Universal basic amount depending on marital status + special supplement for those not receiving b) b) Supplementary pension depending on income and work history for employees and self-employed	a) Universal basic amount depending on marital status + special supplement for those not receiving b) b) Supplementary pension depending on income and work history for employees and self-employed	a) Universal basic amount b) Supplementary pension depending on income and work history for employees and self-employed	a) Universal basic amount b) Supplementary pension depending on income and work history for employees and self-employed

Max. pension after (years)	40	40	40	40	40	40	30	30
Financing of a + b	Premium-free. Taxes: 'pay-as-you-go'	Premium-free. Taxes: 'pay-as-you-go'	Social contributions and taxes	Social contributions and taxes	Social contributions and taxes	Social contributions and taxes	Social contributions and taxes	Social contributions and taxes
Additional pensions	Statutory for public-sector employees (civil servants); Public collective agreement; Private collective agreements	Public collective agreement; Private collective agreements	Private collective agreements	Private collective agreements	Public collective agreements; Private collective agreements	Statutory for public-sector employees (civil servants); Public collective agreements; Private collective agreements	Public collective agreements; Private collective agreements	Public collective agreements; Private collective agreements

Sources: NOSOSCO (1992, 1999); Palme and Wennemo (1998); Social Security Programs Throughout the World (1997).

Note

1 A pension reform was finally passed in June 1998, and will gradually phase out the old system as of 2001.

Why social policy reforms?

The economic and political contexts of the 1990s

Among the Nordic countries, Sweden and Finland have experienced the most critical economic problems in the early 1990s, Denmark somewhat fewer problems, while the Norwegian economy has performed exceptionally well – thanks basically to the large revenues from the oil and gas sector.

Welfare reforms during the 1990s in the *Swedish* welfare state can only be understood in the light of the financial crisis that arose from the early 1990s. Sweden lived through the worst economic recession since the 1930s. The level of unemployment soared to about 8 per cent for the years 1993–97 (excluding those on labour market programmes); the GDP declined during each of the three years 1991–93; central government budget deficits have increased substantially, and government debt as a percentage of GDP was at the level of 83–85 per cent during 1993–96 (OECD 1997d). Primarily because of unemployment and a declining GDP, social expenditure as a per cent of GDP peaked at 40.3 per cent in 1993. Sweden had a non-socialist government with a Conservative Prime Minister during 1991–94, and has had a Social Democratic government before and after.

Finland has in some ways been worse off. The Finnish economy – which in the 1980s was referred to by commentators as the successful 'Europe's Japan' – collapsed after the combined effect of international recession, the fall of the Soviet Union (dramatic fall in trade between the countries), and the political decision to link the Finnish mark to the German mark at a time when the latter was extremely solid. GDP declined in each of the three years 1991–93, but began to pick up again in the latter half of 1993. From an average unemployment rate of 4.8 per cent during the previous decade, the figure during 1991–97 has averaged 15 per cent (OECD 1997a). The budget deficit peaked at 70 per cent of GDP in 1995 (OECD 1996). High unemployment pushed social expenditure as a per cent of GDP up to the level of 37.8 per cent in 1993, but was brought down to 33 per cent in 1997. Finland had a centre-right government during 1991–95, with a Prime Minister from the Centre Party, and has since 1995 had a 'Rainbow Coalition' government led by a Social Democratic Prime Minister.

Denmark has had quite high unemployment figures since the mid-1970s, but the rate peaked at 12.8 per cent in 1993, and averaged 10.4 per cent during 1990–97 (OECD 1997b). Hence, given long-term unemployment, the change in the 1990s appeared less dramatic than in Sweden and Finland. Also, Denmark did not have to endure years of economic decline. During Europe's economic 'annus horribilis' in 1993, the Danish economy showed a solid balance of payments, foreign trade surpluses and ultra low inflation (OECD 1997b). As of 1997, unemployment is falling and the state budget for the first time in 10 years shows a surplus. Denmark had a Conservative–Liberal (Agrarian) government with a Conservative Prime Minister between 1983–93, and has since had a centre-left Social Democratic-led coalition government.

Norway has been in a Nordic world of its own. Not only is it the only country in Europe which (twice through referenda) has declined invitations to become a member of the European Union, it has also most persistently shown economic growth in every year since 1989. The average growth rate of GDP was 3.5 per cent during 1990–96, compared to the OECD average of 2.5 per cent, and the EU average of 1.7 per cent (OECD 1997a). Unemployment peaked at 6 per cent in 1993, and was down at 3 per cent (excluding those on labour market programmes) by October 1998. For the first (and only) time since 1950, the general government financial balance was in the negative in 1992 and 1993, but was well back on the plus side with an estimated surplus of 6.8 per cent of GDP – the highest in Europe – in 1997 (OECD 1997c). Norway had a Labour Party minority government between 1990 and October 1997 when a centrist minority coalition government, led by the Christian People's Party took over.

Given the above summary outline of the state of the economy, unemployment levels, social expenditure and public finances, it would be reasonable to assume that a motivation for political action to reform and modify generous social security and welfare programmes would be generated in Sweden, Finland, and Denmark, and to a lesser degree in Norway. As will be seen from the discussion below, efforts to introduce reforms in social security have been most marked in Sweden and Finland, whereas the changes in Norway and Denmark have been few and modest in both scope and kind.

While acknowledging the substantial variation concerning the welfare policies pursued, four common features can be said to characterise the political develop-ment in the area of social security: First, there is *widespread political consensus, both among political elites and the electorate, about the continued public responsibility for welfare provision.* Population surveys show highly stable patterns of support for state provided welfare, and no major political actor in any of the countries has called for state withdrawal from central spheres of social security (Ferrera 1993; Hatland *et al.* 1996). Second, there are signs of erosion concerning the traditional dividing lines between left and right in the Nordic parliaments, and *welfare reforms are being achieved through cross-cleavage compromises.*[3] In Sweden the Social Democrats, traditionally strong advocates of welfare state universalism, have intensified their close cooperation with the agrarian Centre Party on social security issues, and the 1996 decision to reform the pension system resulted from a controversial compromise with the Conservatives, the Liberals and the Christian Democrats (Palme and Wennemo 1998). The Social Democratic government has also implemented a number of cutbacks and legislative changes since taking office in October 1994. For example, and even though the party opposed the general reduction of replacement rates to 80 per cent under the Conservative-led government in 1993, it was the Social Democratic government that decided to lower the sickness benefit compensation rate to 75 per cent in 1996.

In Finland Paavo Lipponen's 'Rainbow-coalition' (Conservatives, Greens, Left-wing Alliance, Swedish People's Party, Social Democrats), has had to deal with one of the deepest economic crises in Finland's modern history. The key remedy has been unpopular cuts in a whole range of key social security benefits, only made possible through broad political compromises. Even in affluent Norway – 'the Scandinavian Kuwait' – the fear of inflation and an 'overheated economy' has brought the Social Democrats and the Conservatives closer together in matters concerning government spending in general, and expenditure on welfare in particular. It has come as a surprise though that the new minority government of October 1997 achieved parliamentary majorities in favour of significant cash benefits to families with small children not being sent to kindergartens, and significant increases in the level of minimum pensions.

Third, *the political debate over state welfare is increasingly influenced by advocates emphasising incentives to work, individual initiative and the, allegedly, detrimental effects of a comprehensive welfare state.* In all four Nordic countries there has been a shift of focus from receiving passive benefits to active participation, through rehabilitation, training and education. This shift stems partially from the experience with large budget deficits during the 1990s, a lot of which was accumulated through mass unemployment and the financing of social security schemes. But it also reflects the acknowledged need to keep or move people into regular employment. Stricter employment criteria, tightening of eligibility, and shortening of benefit periods all illustrate this shift of focus, manifested *inter alia* through the Danish labour market reform (1994), the recommendations of the 'Incentives Trap Working Party' in Finland (1996) and the various Swedish reforms in the unemployment and sickness benefit schemes. Furthermore, some aspects of the incentives debate seem *ideologically* motivated by a neo-liberal orientation towards the comprehensive welfare state. This orientation has been most evident in Finland, where the economic crisis was most badly felt, and where politicians and researchers expressed fears over the risk of developing a state-based 'dependency culture' (Heikkilä 1997).

Fourth, a *strong welfare populism* is evident with the smaller parties on both the left and the right of the political spectrum, and has proven to have some electoral appeal. Whereas the parties on the left simply seem to want more welfare policies, the 'new right' parties in Sweden (New Democracy) and Norway (Progress Party), have demonstrated a highly inconsistent political approach to social security. On the one hand they are strong advocates of general tax reduction, increase in the individual responsibility for securing welfare and private insurance arrangements, yet on the other hand they favour a substantial increase in public spending on health and pensions.

A closer look at the political variations between the Nordic countries can serve to elaborate the outline above. In Sweden the general need to reform has been acknowledged by almost all important political parties, and the reform process which has taken – and is taking – place has enjoyed support from both left and right of the political spectrum although, naturally, disagreement on exactly what kind of measures to take exists (Palme 1994). The entire election campaign in 1994 was fought over the welfare state, the public deficit and the economy. There is general agreement upon the necessity of state intervention in the sphere of social security, but there are also strong advocates for increasing the responsibility of both the family and the market. Important political differences exist – at least in principle – regarding the coverage and level of benefits and reliance on different rules of eligibility and entitlements. On these issues a clear neo-liberalistic tendency is discernible in the arguments that the benefit system works as a disincentive to work. The Conservatives, who were the leading governmental party during 1991–94, want less public insurance because they view the general level of taxation as harmful to the rate of investment and economic growth. But the party had in practice to abandon the idea of major tax cuts. The Conservatives also argue that the family should have the larger responsibility within a general framework financed by the state, while the individual should have greater opportunities to choose insurance from a set of private insurance companies.

Similar arguments were heard in the Norwegian election campaign in September 1997, especially from the Conservatives and the Christian People's Party. The Swedish Liberal Party, a government coalition partner 1991–94, actually changed its views on social security issues during that period. In opposition they favoured tax cuts, while in power they argued in favour of the maintenance of tax levels in order to protect the earnings-related basis of the social security system. Yet, reforms are necessary they claim, and they advocate a system with a stronger link between contributions and benefits, and stronger incentives for work participation. The (Agrarian) Centre Party is a traditional defender of flat-rate benefits, since the farming population has (had) little to gain from earnings-related benefits. The party has called for the strengthening of the basic security elements of the social security system, and for reducing costs through a general lowering of benefit ceilings.

The Swedish Christian Democrat Party, which entered parliament for the first time in 1991, is a strong advocate of a cash care allowance to families with children, in order to permit greater family choice in terms of child care through kindergartens, mother/fathers, *au pairs*, or other solutions. In Norway, its sister party has argued strongly along similar lines for some time, and such a scheme has been implemented (1998) after a budget compromise with the Conservatives and the Progress Party. The Swedish Centre Party defends cuts in public spending and the need for incentives, but wants to maintain major public responsibility in the area of social security. The short-lived right-wing populist party, New Democracy, which may have influenced public opinion, but otherwise played a marginal political role, favoured tax cuts, more means-testing, and a general reduction of earnings-replacement rates to 70 per cent. This is very much on a par with its populist cousin in Norway, the Progress Party.

The Social Democrats, traditional defenders of welfare state universalism, have altered their views on a number of social security issues since financial problems made their impact on Sweden in 1990–91. The party has on several occasions implemented cut-backs in schemes it previously protected from changes, as was the case with the unemployment and the sickness benefit schemes in 1996. Since 1995, its most stable parliamentary ally has been the Centre Party, and their common aim is to balance public finances by 1998 and to halve unemployment levels by 2000. By implication, the possibilities for expanding social expenditure are clearly constrained, and there is strong evidence that the Swedish Social Democratic Party has undergone a process of 'modernisation' during the upsetting 1990s.

Beyond the parties, the Swedish employers' federation has strongly argued in favour of lower replacement rates; more private providers of social insurance benefits; and a financial system that gives economic incentives to individual employers to reduce health hazards. Between 1990–96 the average tax for the average production worker rose by more than 5.5 per cent (Hansen 1997). Still there is no doubt that Swedish voters prefer a comprehensive welfare state, even to the extent of favouring tax and contribution increases to tax cuts in order to finance social expenditure (Palme 1994).

The Danish Conservative-led government 1983–93 pursued the overriding goal of keeping inflation down. The political debate before and after the 1994 election was dominated by the topic of the future of the welfare state (Borre and Goul Andersen 1997) – very similar to what happened in the Swedish election campaign in 1994 and in the Norwegian election campaign in 1997 – the difference being, though, that in Denmark the premise was how to deal with the unemployment problem and the growth in social expenditure, while in Sweden it was how to cut benefits and expenditure, and in Norway how much more of public finances ('oil money') should be put into the health system, old-age pensions and old-age care. (For an elaborated analysis and interpretation of reform developments in the Danish case, see Chapter 5 in this volume). As in Sweden, the Danish welfare state enjoys strong popular support, and there is widespread consensus on public responsibility for welfare. Yet there is some evidence of declining welfare state support in the Danish case, mainly resulting from concerns over the problems of future financing (Goul Andersen 1997).

Finnish politics in the 1990s is the politics of cuts and retrenchments in the area of social security. The struggle to regain control of public finances has led to even more dramatic policy changes than in Sweden. Social policy debate has centred around the issues of the detrimental effect of social policy on the market; of the disincentives to work, and individual initiative and on the negative effects of high taxes on willingness to work. The argument that the incentive problems were so great that they justified cuts in minimum security, quickly got their political expression: first in Lipponen's government programme in 1995 and later in the recommendations from the 'Incentive Trap Working Party', led by minister Arja Alho (Heikkilä 1997: 18). Even though the crisis in the public finances brought forth a number of critics, the popular support for the welfare state, for primary public responsibility for welfare, is still strong (Heikkilä 1997: 22).

Two phases can be singled out regarding reform measures that have been implemented to regain control of public finances and expenditure (Kosunen 1997). The centre-right government (1991–94) introduced cuts in the earnings-related sickness and unemployment benefit schemes. In 1991 public expenditure was reduced, taxes increased, and tighter fiscal policies introduced. Cuts in social benefits were spread to all schemes, and techniques of cutting have varied: modification of benefit levels, of compensation levels, of indexation of benefits, of eligibility to benefits. Thanks to these reforms, the growth of social expenditure in real terms decreased from 9.3 per cent in 1991 to 1.6 per cent in 1993. The economy gradually improved as of 1994, but still the 1995 budget reaffirmed the decision of

1992 to restore expenditure at the 1991 level. While the centre-right government avoided cutting into minimum security benefits, the 'Rainbow Coalition' government under Social Democratic leadership since 1995, has added minimum social security benefits to the 'cutting list' (pensions, sickness, family, labour market support). A government committee advocated a system of basic public services combined with private supplements, and based on its recommendations in 1996 the government implemented reforms which put an end to health insurance indexation, which tightened eligibility criteria, and reduced levels of compensation. Further cuts in public expenditure are envisioned, in order to curb indebtedness. During the period 1992–97, nearly all key benefits were subject to cuts, although the original structure of the benefit system has been preserved. The most radical changes were made in publicly funded unemployment and health insurance benefits, and in means-tested housing support.

Norway parts company with its Nordic neighbours – and European countries in general – when it comes to welfare cuts. The booming Norwegian oil economy in the 1990s has created opportunities for maintaining and developing the welfare state. Reforms in Norway are of a very limited scope: some schemes have been modified, others have been made more generous. The government and parliament have set up a 'Petroleum Fund' – to be used for investments abroad – to guarantee future financing of pensions and welfare. A government report on welfare submitted to parliament in 1994 (*'Velferdsmeldingen'*) concluded that the public system of social security was to be maintained in basically the same form as previously. But it emphasised a stronger work orientation: without a high level of employment and improved schemes for rehabilitation, job training, etc. it would be difficult to preserve the structure of the welfare system in the future. This view enjoys widespread support from the major parliamentary parties.

The Conservatives, the Centre Party and the Liberal Party want to promote private pension arrangements as a supplement to public pension schemes. The Christian People's Party is primarily concerned about care for the elderly, increased minimum pensions, and family-oriented policies (increased cash allowance for families with children). The two latter priorities were realised in 1997. The decision increased the minimum pensions by 18 per cent and introduced a flat-rate cash allowance for parents who wish not to make use of state-subsidised kindergartens/day care institutions. The Labour Party emphasises the 'work orientation' in social security matters, i.e. the importance of moving people from passively receiving benefits to active work through measures such as job training, education, etc. and the tightening of eligibility/lowering of compensation in regular transfer schemes. Special public efforts should be made for the young, sick, disabled, etc. who are especially exposed to the risk of social marginalisation and exclusion. The Labour Party sees no need to modify the sickness insurance scheme, and want the minimum old age pension to remain exempt from taxation.

The Socialist Left Party is mainly concerned with the principle of fair distribution of resources in society. It advocates a strong public sector, and counters all proposals to privatise welfare. Health services should be improved, a national plan to fight poverty should be implemented, and unemployment benefits should be made payable independent of previous work history. Survey studies indicate strong popular support for the Norwegian welfare state, and party manifestos reflect this broad support. Among Nordic welfare states, the Norwegian one is the least threatened at the dawn of a new century, and it may currently pose as the strongest representantive of the historic 'Scandinavian welfare model'. This situation is likely to persist, but might change with a consistent and permanent drop in the price of oil.

Summary review of reforms in the 1990s

If one should extract a single common denominator for the welfare development in the Nordic countries in the 1990s, it would be a *less generous welfare state*, but Norway is an important exception to the general picture. The basic structure of the welfare systems has been preserved, with the partial exception of the pension reforms in Finland (1996) and Sweden (legislated 1998). Not necessarily valid for all the four countries, and not for all schemes, there are at least five factors justifying the interpretation of decreased generosity in the field of public welfare: First, *benefit levels are reduced*, most markedly in Finland and Sweden across all social security schemes. Second, *benefit periods are shortened and waiting periods prolonged*. Third, *eligibility has been tightened* through a whole range of different measures. Fourth, a *much stronger emphasis on rehabilitation, activation, education and training* is evident. Finally, *substantial (structural) reforms in the old-age pensions systems in order to handle the increase in old-age pensioners in the next century.* Both the Swedish and the Finnish system will in the future have a much closer linkage between work history/contributions, and payments. In the future, the previously universal basic pension will only be paid if the employment-derived pension is very low or non-existent.

Perspective on the Nordic welfare states

The review and assessment made suggest that reform activity is basically motivated by socio-structural, economic or financial considerations, and much less by political visions of an alternative type of welfare state or society. Public deficits, public indebtedness, (temporary) decline in gross domestic products and high unemployment have induced substantial retrenchments of social security schemes in Sweden and Finland, and to a lesser extent in Denmark, while Norway has largely avoided both problems and retrenchment. Although all of the Nordic countries are now more open for private initiatives in the fields of health services, social care services and social insurance than before, no political party – and very few voters – favour a deconstructed welfare state. Health, welfare, social security and unemployment are on top of the list of issues of concern at election time. Neo-liberal ideas may, however, be said to have had some impact upon reform activity promoted by both non-socialist and social democratic governments, and retrenchment reforms may well induce more private and non-governmental welfare arrangements in years to come. Over time, new generations of voters will become more accustomed to a mixture of public and private welfare and social security arrangements, and thus the presently high and rather unidirectional expectations towards the state as welfare provider will most likely be lower. The effects of a gradually more economically (and politically) integrated Europe will probably be similar: the hitherto near monopolistic 'national-state' welfare provision will be challenged from the access to, and growth of, private welfare provision organised by transnational firms. A general observation is that governments have modified several social security programmes in a direction which give actual and potential beneficiaries *incentives* to be in, or find, gainful employment. The basic structures of Nordic social security and welfare systems have been maintained, normally through broad political compromises in parliament and with tolerable support from voters. Though the structures are basically solid, generosity of benefits, earnings-replacement rates and eligibility criteria have been modified substantially for some schemes in Sweden and Finland. In both Denmark and Norway, the introduction of labour market measures and reforms have actually entailed a more active welfare state concerned about training and educating the unemployed for jobs. The parental leave schemes have been significantly improved and made more generous in Norway, and in general, family- and child-oriented policies have been 'protected' against severe retrenchments during periods of financial strain. These policies have undoubtedly been conducive to maintaining relatively high (European-wise) fertility rates in the Nordic countries. All across the Nordic countries we may observe a more distinct political concern for what governments label the 'work line', which should not solely be interpreted as a reflection of the impact of neo-liberal ideology: it may just as well be interpreted to conform with a traditionally strong work ethic in the northern, Protestant territory of Europe.

Survival of the Nordic model

Given the varying economic situation in the Nordic countries during the 1990s, one may conclude that welfare state developments have been slightly divergent rather than convergent: between Sweden and Finland on one side, and Denmark and Norway on the other. But these observations should not overshadow the principal observation of persistent stability, rather solidly resting on the institutional and normative legacy of the 'Scandinavian' or 'Nordic model' or type of welfare state. We may argue that the following three elements are pivotal to this 'model'. (1) The dominant *role of the state and public sector* (including local government). Transfers and services are provided by central and local government based on rights extended to all citizens and residents. Government has taken, and still takes, fundamental charge of the security dimension of the welfare state. The importance of the state has increased in absolute terms (cf. Table 3.1). The total amount of resources in society spent on social security and welfare provision is likely to increase. (2) The principle of redistribution through general taxes, producing relatively *egalitarian distribution of income*. Values of equality are strong within Nordic societies. Contrary to the beliefs of many economists, egalitarianism can go hand in hand with economic efficiency: the Nordic countries could boast a more rapid economic growth during the period 1960–90 than many other, less equality-oriented, West European countries (Korpi 1992). Poverty in general, and among the old, is low. Development of private insurance and health and other services as complements and supplements to public arrangements are likely to create a new institutional mix of public and private welfare which will entail a socially more unequal distribution of welfare. But the value of equality still seems important for the framing of debates and decisions on matters of social security, health and welfare. (3) *Full employment* has been proclaimed to be an overall goal of Nordic governments since the Second World War, and most pronounced in Sweden and Norway (Kosonen 1996). Unemployment has since the late 1970s in Denmark, and since the 1990s in Finland and Sweden, and to a much lesser degree in Norway, emerged as a major challenge. Active labour market programmes have been initiated in all countries, and can certainly show some success, especially in Denmark in recent years. That all governments embrace the so-called 'work line' is another proof of the – at least verbal – strength of the goal of full or increased employment. But this element of the normative legacy of the Nordic 'model' may be the one which is most exposed in the light of domestic and external economic challenges.

Notes

1   We want to thank Hannu Uusitalo, Juho Saari, Mauno Konttinen, Paavo Löppönen, Niels Ploug, Joakim Palme and Irene Wennemo for assistance in providing sources, material and assessments of social policy development in Finland, Denmark and Sweden in the 1990s. Stein Kuhnle thanks participants at the European Forum seminar on 20 January 1999 for critical, constructive comments.

2   Denmark introduced labour market pensions in 1989 as part of the agreement between the labour market partners which gives the Danish system a *de facto* earnings-related element.

3   This has also to do with changes in the Nordic party system formats during the last two decades. Majority cabinets derived from a single party is now a thing of the past, the norm in the 1990s being multi-party coalitions as presently is the case in Finland (majority), Denmark (minority) and Norway (minority), or single party minority governments as in Sweden. Hence the present governments are much more dependent on parliamentary support from different sides of the political spectrum.

References

Borre, O. and Goul Andersen, J. (1997) *Voting and Political Attitudes in Denmark*, Aarhus: Aarhus University Press.
Esping-Andersen, G. (1990) *The Three Worlds of Welfare Capitalism*, Cambridge: Polity Press.
Ferrera, M. (1993) *EC Citizens and Social Protection*, Brussels: Commission of the European Community.

Goul Andersen, J. (1997) 'Changing Labour Markets, New Social Divisions and Welfare State Support: Denmark in the 1990s', unpublished paper, University of Aalborg.

Hansen, H. (1997) *Elements of Social Security in 6 European Countries*, Copenhagen: The Danish National Institute of Social Research.

Hatland, A., Kuhnle, S. and Romøren, T. I. (1996) *Den norske velferdsstaten*, (2nd edn), Oslo: Ad Notam Gyldendal.

Heikkilä, M. (1997) 'Justifications for Cutbacks in the Area of Social Policy', in M. Heikkilä and H. Uusitalo (eds) *The Cost of the Cuts*, Helsinki: STAKES.

Heikkilä, M. and Uusitalo, H. (eds) (1997) *The Cost of the Cuts. Studies on Cutbacks in Social Security and their Effects in the Finland of the 1990s*, Helsinki: STAKES.

Korpi, W. (1992) *Halkar Sverige efter?*, Stockholm: Carlssons.

Kosonen, P. (1996) 'Nordic Welfare Models in the 1990s Internal and RC19', 19–22 August, 1996, ANU, Canberra.

Kosunen, V. (1997) 'The Recession and Changes in Social Security in the 1990s', in M. Heikkilä and H. Uusitalo (eds) *The Cost of the Cuts*, Helsinki: STAKES.

Kuhnle, S. (1990) 'Den skandinaviske velferdsmodellen – skandinavisk? velferd? modell?', in A. Hovdum, S. Kuhnle, L. Stokke (eds) *Visjoner om velferdssamfunnet*, Bergen: Alma Mater.

NOSOSCO (1992) *Sosial trygghet i de nordiske land. Omfang, utgifter og finansiering 1990*, Oslo: Nososco.

—— (1997) *Social Security in the Nordic Countries: Scope, Expenditure and Financing 1995*, Copenhagen: Nososco.

—— (1999) *Sosial tryghed; de nordiske lande. Omfang, udgifter og finansiering 1997*, Nordisk socialstatistisk komite, no. 11, Copenhagen: NOSOSCO.

OECD (1996) *Economic Surveys: Finland*, Paris: OECD.

—— (1997a) *Economic Outlook*, no. 61, Paris: OECD.

—— (1997b) *Economic Surveys: Denmark*, Paris: OECD.

—— (1997c) *Economic Surveys: Norway*, Paris: OECD.

—— (1997d) *Economic Surveys: Sweden*, Paris: OECD.

Palme, J. (1994) 'Recent Developments in Income Transfer Systems in Sweden', in N. Ploug and J. Kvist (eds) *Recent Trends in Cash Benefits in Europe*, Copenhagen: The Danish Institute of Social Research.

Palme, J. and Wennemo, I. (1998) *Swedish Social Security in the 1990s: Reform and Retrenchment*, Stockholm: Ministry of Health and Social Affairs.

Ploug, N. and Kvist, J (1994) *Overførselsindkomster i Europa: Systemerne i Grundtræk*, Copenhagen: Socialforsknings-instituttet.

Social Security Programs Throughout the World (1997), Washington DC: Social Security Administration.

Sørensen, Ø. and Stråth, B. (1997) 'Introduction: The Cultural Construction of Norden', in Ø. Sørensen and B. Stråth (eds) *The Cultural Construction of Norden*, Oslo: Scandinavian University Press.

4 The Finnish welfare state in the 1990s

A long-term perspective

Matti Alestalo

The crisis

The Finnish welfare state which, in the 1980s, had been on the average European level or slightly above it in terms of social expenditure, public employment and level of taxation suddenly, in the 1990s, proved to be a burden for the shaky national economy. Because of rapidly increasing mass unemployment, the negative economic growth rates and only moderate adjustments in the major welfare schemes, the proportion of total social expenditure of the GDP rose, within a few years, from 26 per cent to 35 per cent (Table 4.1).

The crisis of the economy, the rapidly increasing budget deficit and foreign debt and the rise of mass unemployment were not accompanied by a declining total social expenditure. The exceptionally high growth in the proportion of social expenditure of the GDP can easily be explained by the increasing unemployment expenditure and the overall negative economic growth rates. At fixed prices the unemployment expenditure in 1993 was six times greater than in 1990, and its share of total social expenditure rose from 3 per cent to about 14 per cent (Table 4.2).

Table 4.1 The Finnish economy and welfare state, 1989–96

Year	GDP at fixed prices as % of previous year	Public debt as % of GDP	Unemployment as % of the total labour force	Social expenditure as % of GDP
1989	5.7	14.6	3.5	25.5
1990	0.0	14.4	3.4	25.5
1991	−7.1	22.1	7.6	30.4
1992	−3.6	40.7	13.1	34.4
1993	−1.2	57.0	17.9	35.4
1994	4.4	59.6	17.8	34.6
1995	5.0	58.1	16.7	32.7
1996	3.7	57.9	15.8	32.3
1997	6.0	55.4	14.5	30.0

Sources: *Taloudellinen katsaus* 1995; 1998; Heikkilä *et al.* 1993; *Sosiaaliturva Suomessa 1993*; Preliminary data from the Ministry for Social Affairs and Health; Kosunen 1997b: 42; *Sosiaaliturvan suunta 1998–1999*.

Table 4.2 Social expenditure in Finland, 1990–93

	At fixed prices (1990 = 100)			Per cent			
Expenditure on	1991	1992	1993	1990	1991	1992	1993
Pension security	101	101	111	40.2	38.0	38.1	37.4
Unemployment security	265	474	590	2.8	6.8	11.2	13.6
Other income maintenance	107	111	113	19.8	19.6	18.7	18.6
Services	104	101	98	37.2	35.6	32.0	30.4
Total	108	117	120	100.0	100.0	100.0	100.0

Source: *Sosiaalimenotoimikunnan välimietintö 1993*, 15.

In terms of the total social expenditure of the GDP, the Finnish record proves to be a very ambiguous one. Due to poor economic performance Finland became one of the leading welfare states in Europe – if the most commonly used indicator of the welfare state, the share of total social expenditure of the GDP, is trusted. This goes to show the unreliability of this indicator.

The welfare state became an important issue in the political, academic and public debates in the 1990s. The waves of neo-liberal ideas and policies were welcomed especially by the employers' organisations and parties on the right. But also other political forces have become more favourable to cuts and adjustments in the various welfare schemes and in the supply of public welfare services. Up until the late 1990s, in the major sectors of the welfare state only minor adjustments and cuts have been made (see Chapter 3 in this volume). However, the pressures for cuts and reductions have steadily increased and the debate on the welfare state is accelerating. The existence of almost all important forms of social protection has been questioned. Unemployment benefits, public sector pensions, private sector employment pensions, housing allowances and even child allowances have come under serious discussion and many cuts and reductions have been made (see Kosunen 1997a). Towards the end of the 1990s the economy started to expand and because of this and of the cuts and adjustments in the welfare state the proportion of total social expenditure started to decline (see Table 4.1).

Until the mid-1990s these developments were not accompanied by a decline in total social expenditure. It was not until 1993 when the expenditure growth started to decline (see Table 4.2). It has been estimated that in 1994 the total social expenditure was about 25 per cent higher than in 1990. On the other hand, according to an estimate of the Ministry for Social Affairs and Health the total social expenditure in the year 2000 will be 8.6 per cent lower than would be the case without cuts and other adjustments (Kosunen 1997b: 42). As compared to major income maintenance schemes social welfare and health care services show a declining trend (see Table 4.2). In order to offer a clear picture of the totality of social welfare and health care services the following description is based on information on the expenditure of social welfare and health care services and on the data describing the recipients and beneficiaries of these services.

The long expansion period of the social welfare and health care services seems to be over. In most of the social welfare and health care services the amount of expenditure is not increasing any more. This holds true in day care, in sickness and health services as well as in the case of institutional care for the elderly and the disabled (*Sosiaaliturva Suomessa 1993*). During the crisis years the major trend in the provision and use of various kinds of social welfare and health care services has been quite similar to that of the expenditure development. The number of children in public day care is diminishing as well as is the number of clients in the old people's homes and beds in hospitals owned by the municipalities (Stakes 1995). The expansion of the provision and use of social welfare and health care services has ended and there are a lot of downward trends.

All the main indicators give a very similar picture. Public services offered mostly by local authorities have systematically been reduced. This holds true in the case of children in public day care as well as in the major forms of institutional care and in the various kinds of home help. The major study on the municipal welfare and health care services comes to a similar conclusion. The author of the study even suggests that 'it may well be that the changes in the period 1990–94 indicate a turning point in the development . . .' (Lehto 1995).

The historical legacy of the Finnish welfare state

In order to have a full understanding of the current problems connected with the welfare state and to discuss the survival of the welfare state in Finland the past as a determinant of the present has to be taken into serious consideration. The origins of the Finnsh welfare state are deep in history and an analysis of the long-term interaction between the state and the civil society constitutes an important precondition for a full understanding of the characteristics and the problems of the current welfare state. In the discussion of the historical legacy of the Finnsh welfare state the state–society relationship as well as some important ideological backgrounds and developments should be considered.

State and society

In comparative terms, the coexistence between the state and the people has been unusually peaceful in the Scandinavian area. This has not been a result of the development of the welfare state. On the contrary, due to some important and unique historical transformations the class structure of the Scandinavian societies has made the expansion and popularity of the welfare state possible.

Without going further into history the positive role that the state played in the modernisation of Scandinavian agriculture should first be taken into consideration. In the process of agricultural modernisation the state did not develop into a 'remote, alien and demanding force outside the peasant communities', as Norwegian scholar Øyvind Østerud has described the role of the state (1978: 69–112). In the absence of feudalism the peasant ownership of land prevailed and was further completed by enclosure movements which in Scandinavia were a state intervention for the modernisation of agriculture. The strong position of peasants during the preindustrial period and the challenge of commercial agriculture is one of the major factors behind the peaceful Scandinavian development.

The relatively good position of the peasantry formed a basis for the growth of social and political movements. In the absence of large-scale rural exploitation by land-owning classes, no deep cleavage between the social groups in the countryside developed, but instead an important cultural and economic cleavage emerged between urban elites and the rural population. This cleavage became accentuated in the quest for franchise and parliamentary reform. One of the Scandinavian peculiarities has been the rise of a class of independent farmers. The class structure developed into a tri-polar model. Alongside the working class and the urban upper class and their parties and interest organisations parties and unions for agricultural producers also emerged in Scandinavian polities (see, for example, Castles 1978: 103–42).

The long-lasting domination of agriculture in Scandinavia also affected the composition of the working classes. From the very beginning the working classes had a dual character. They were composed of the rural landless proletariat and industrial workers. The unity of the two groups becomes more understandable if the strong non-urban character of early industrialisation in Scandinavia is remembered. Although the share of agricultural and rural workers and small-holding farmers has been rapidly declining during the current century and is nowadays becoming almost negligible, many workers even today have a farm or other rural origins (Alestalo and Kuhnle 1987: 3–38).

In Scandinavia, the labour movement was considered a part of the popular movements and the ascendance of the working class into the polity was a relatively easy and tranquil process. It occurred almost simultaneously with the rise of the agrarian parties and the overall opposition to the labour movements was remarkably mild. In the absence of official repression working-class movements adopted a reformist character. Social democratic parties developed into mass parties with an exceptionally strong party formation and with a high degree of unionisation. The fierce Civil War and the extensive repressive terror after it describes the exception of Finland among the Scandinavian countries (Alapuro 1985: 93–107) but during the inter-war years Finland reached the tranquil Scandinavian path.

In the absence of ethnic, religious and linguistic cleavages no major parties based on religion, language or ethnic groups emerged (with the exception of a party for the Swedish-speaking population in Finland).

It has to be emphasised that the state in Scandinavia did not develop into a coercive apparatus or into a tool of oppression in the hands of the upper classes as was the case in many parts of Central and Eastern Europe, but rather the state developed into a peaceful battleground of classes. Therefore, the nature of the state came to reflect the balance and the changes of power between classes. A political culture of social corporativism was constructed 'through fits and starts rather than according to some conscious program' (Katzenstein 1985: 190). Only in the light of this kind of development are the popular Scandinavian slogans about 'people's home', 'historical compromise' or even the 'welfare state' understandable (cf. Korpi 1978: 80–90).

'Between Manchesterism and Marxism'

As early as 1874, Yrjö Koskinen, a historian and a leader of the Finnish nationalist movement welcomed the foundation of the *Verein für Sozialpolitik* in Germany. Yrjö Koskinen was highly interested in the reformulation of the tasks of the state by the German Historical School. According to him, the 'nightwatchman state of the liberal economists' does not function as 'a means of historical progress'. 'State manifests the spirit of the nation' and promotes not only its material and economic resources but also its 'mental and moral progress'.

As in Germany, the Hegelian concept of the state became diffused with the fears caused by the Paris Commune of 1871 and by the expansion of the social democratic movement. The intervention of the state proposed by the German *Kathedersozialisten* was welcomed by Yrjö Koskinen 'with high expectations for the future'. Following the German example Yrjö Koskinen defined the proper ideological position of Finnish intellectuals to support the social reforms by the state and to stand between 'Manchesterism and Marxism' (Yrjö Koskinen 1874).

In the early 1880s the breakthrough of the Bismarckian social insurance in Germany was closely observed in Scandinavia. Laws on occupational injuries were passed in Denmark, Finland and Norway in the 1890s and in Sweden in 1901 (Kuhnle 1981: 125–50). In Finland the passing of the Act on Occupational Injuries was preceeded by a heated debate between the liberals, who stressed self-reliance, and the conservatives who supported state intervention and compulsory social insurance as a means of mitigation of the emerging class antagonism (Alestalo 1990).

But only the very early beginning was a success in Finland. The other Scandinavian countries continued to enlarge their social policy legislation at the turn of the century. In Finland, instead of an introduction of further reforms in social policy, the idea of state intervention was only extended to the relationship between the landowners and the landless population. The 'land question' came to dominate the 'labour question' in Finnish politics (Alestalo 1986: 22–28).

Independent Finland belonged to the group of new states emerging from the ashes of the First World War and from the collapse of the Russian and Austro-Hungarian Empires. Unlike her Scandinavian neighbours Finland implemented no 'social revolution' by extensive social policy reforms but tried, like the other new states within 'the western fringe of the red revolution in Russia', through a 'green revolution' of extensive land reforms to resist social upheavals and to bury the memory of the fierce Civil War (see Heaton 1966: 472). A mass of independent small-holding farms was created and farmers started to consolidate in economic, social and political terms.

Even if the establishment of the state apparatus and the introduction of some social improvements like compulsory primary schools increased state personnel and social expenditure during the inter-war years there was not a similar tendency towards social reforms in Finland as was the case in the other Scandinavian countries. It was not until the latter half of the 1930s that a more comprehensive welfare state legislation was gradually introduced by the coalition cabinet of the Agrarians and the Social Democrats. The basic difference in regard to the other Scandinavian countries was that this coalition emerged as a green–red one instead of the dominant red–green coalitions in the other Scandinavian countries. With regard to the coverage of major social security schemes and to social expenditure, Finland lagged far behind the other Scandinavian and Western European countries (Alestalo *et al.* 1985: 188–210).

The great structural transformation

As compared to the other Scandinavian countries the post-war structural development in Finland was retarded, more unbalanced and more sudden. Since the Second World War Finland's economic performance has been very rapid but fairly uneven. The pace of industrialisation and the expansion of the service sector have been very rapid and the structural transformation of the labour force has been unusually extensive. The simultaneous growth of manual and white-collar occupations differentiated Finland from the earlier industrialised countries where the growth of the number of manual workers both started and ended earlier. The expansion of public employment had an important role in this transformation.

From the very beginning of this transformation the Social Democrats tried to improve the social security of the working class. They were, however, even with the help of the Communists, unable to break the opposition of the employers and non-socialist parties. It was only after reaching compromises with the Agrarian Party and the employers that the Social Democrats could make some progress. The Agrarians favoured flat-rate schemes which they considered would best promote the needs of the large agricultural population. In the interest of employers was, above all, the reduction of the costs of labour and the control of the pension schemes by organising them into private pension funds and companies.

An extensive period of reforms started from the mid-1950s onwards. The national pensions were reformed and the introduction of sickness insurance and occupational pensions moved Finland towards the Scandinavian model of the welfare state (Salminen 1993; Kangas 1992).

Towards the Scandinavian model

Especially during the decades from the 1950s onwards there was a catching-up process whereby Finland, little by little, reached the other Scandinavian countries and the Western European countries in terms of economic performance and industrial and population structures. Finland became a part of the European affluent and structurally converging society where middle classes are expanding and the population is growing older (see Alestalo and Flora 1994).

The expansion of the welfare state is here exemplified by two simple indicators, social expenditure and public employment. Compared to the other advanced countries social expenditure in Scandinavia did not reach unusually high levels until the 1960s. Also, the inter-country variation between Denmark, Norway and Sweden was very small during the post-war years. In the 1970s and 1980s the Scandinavian countries differed from most Continental and Anglo-Saxon countries. Simultaneously, the differences within Scandinavia increased as Sweden and Denmark became the leading welfare spenders among the advanced market economies. It should be remembered, however, that in Finland and Norway the real growth of the social expenditure in the 1980s was faster than in Denmark and Sweden but the proportion of social expenditure of the GDP remained lower because of their faster overall economic growth. Towards the end of the 1980s the Scandinavian countries spent almost 25–35 per cent of their national incomes on social expenditure (Alestalo and Uusitalo 1992: 37–68).

Richard Rose shows in his historical analysis of the long-term changes of public employment in France, Germany, Italy, Sweden, the United Kingdom and the United States that until the early 1950s no great differences existed between these countries in the share of public employment. Sweden was not an exception (Rose 1985: 8–9). A similar conclusion can be reached, for example, by looking at the OECD statistics for the early 1960s (Alestalo *et al.* 1991).

But during the following three decades a massive recruitment of people into the public sector has taken place throughout Scandinavia. In the 1980s over 40 per cent of the labour force was employed by the public sector in Sweden. The corresponding figures were over 35 per cent in Denmark and about 30 per cent in Finland and Norway. In this calculation the employees of the state-owned companies are included in the category of employees in the central and local administration and services.

In all the Scandinavian countries the major part of public sector growth has been caused by the expansion of the social services. With the exception of Finland, the share of the welfare segment (education, health care and other social services) has been over 50 per cent from the late 1970s onwards. It should also be remembered that the social services became almost totally public during these years (Alestalo *et al.* 1991).

The rapid expansion of public employment in Scandinavia would not have been possible without an increased participation of women in the labour force. From the late 1970s onwards over half of the public employees have been women. The feminisation of the labour force has had a genuinely public sector character (Alestalo *et al.* 1991: 36–58).

These developments of social expenditure and public employment point out that especially during the past three decades a great expansion of public welfare has taken place in Scandinavia. In the late 1980s the Scandinavian welfare state had two cornerstones: generous social benefits and extensive public services. This also implied a decreasing inequality and an absence of or rapidly decreasing poverty (Uusitalo 1989: 77–83; Uusitalo and Ringen 1992: 69–91; Ritakallio 1994).

The survival of the Finnish welfare state

In his comparison on the coherence and complexity of the Western European welfare state models Pekka Kosonen (1994: 72–73) concludes that the Scandinavian welfare states can be characterised as ' "work societies" in the sense that there is a right as well as an obligation to work, both for men and women'. The other important characteristics of the Scandinavian welfare state model are universal social security rights and high degree of stateness in the welfare institutions (cf. also Alestalo and Flora 1994).

Kosonen's description fits the case of Finland particularly well. The Finnish welfare state can be considered as an achievement of poor small-holding farmers and workers with an almost equal standard of living. The making of the welfare state in Finland was a process based on increasing consensus among the major population groups and it resulted in the late 1980s in a universal, state-centred system with almost a world record in female participation in full-time paid work.

This perspective provides a good starting point for discussing the survival of the welfare state in Finland. Although there have been many kinds of political configurations and conflicts concerning the adaptation of the welfare state to the increased economic constraints, no serious challenge to the current welfare state has emerged. Partly, this is due to the historical legacy in which even an important part of the Conservatives share a positive approach towards a state-centred system. This legacy was enforced during the period from the early 1960s onwards when all major parties have, in one way or other, been involved in the corporatist incomes policy through which most of the welfare state reforms have been made. Perhaps even in the late 1990s Erik Allardt's somewhat ironic statement from the mid-1980s still holds true in a country where the cabinet consists of Conservatives, Swedish-speaking Liberals, Social Democrats, Greens and Communists: 'all major parties in the Nordic countries today support the social democratic prewar conception of the welfare state' (Allardt 1984: 183).

During the expansion period of the welfare state the public sector, especially the organisations of local government, has taken over many responsiblities from the households and the organisations and associations of civil society. In the present-day political discussion many voices have claimed an increase of the supply of welfare promotion through the civil society, third sector or voluntary organisations. In this discussion the positive examples have been taken from the Continental countries. Even if there are in Finland some important private sector organisations providing social welfare and health care services we have to remember that in most cases these organisations have been heavily supported by the state (Anttonen and Sipilä 1992: 447–49). In addition, it should be remembered that the services and charitable help offered by the voluntary organisations are in most cases oriented to meet the needs of well-to-do people (Wuthnow 1991: 293) and not so much the needs, for example, of old people living in the countryside of a sparsely populated country. ˋ

The role of the market as a provider of welfare and health care services is not a very prominent one in the Finnish welfare mix. In the absence of any strong input from the market and civil society the provision of welfare and health care services remains to be divided between the public sector and households. An extensive reduction in the overall scale of public services will have a direct effect on the duties of households.

In its present form, the Finnish welfare state presupposes high employment rates and constant tax revenues. In the short run the welfare state may succeed to function as a buffer for the hardships caused by the economic recession. As the major study on cuts in social security concludes: 'Our research suggests that the Finnish welfare state has been successful in preventing large population groups from sliding into poverty as a result of unemployment and the gradual vanishing of market-driven income' (Heikkilä and Uusitalo 1997: 12). But in the long run the combination of high unemployment rates, generous benefis and extensive services will certainly be a heavy burden even for a fast-growing economy.

References

Alapuro, R. (1985) 'Interstate Relationships and Political Mobilization in the Nordic Countries: a Perspective', in R. Alapuro, M. Alestalo, E. Haavio-Mannila and R. Väyrynen (eds) *Small States in Comparative Perspective. Essays for Erik Allardt*, Oslo: Norwegian University Press.

Alestalo, M. (1986) 'Structural Change, Classes, and the State. Finland in an Historical and Comparative Perspective'. Research Reports 33, Helsinki: Research Group for Comparative Sociology.

—— (1990) 'Vuoden 1895 tapaturmavakuutuslaki. Uudistus ylhäältä', in M. Peltonen (ed.) *Arki ja murros. Tutkielmia keisariajan lopun Suomesta*, Jyväskylä: Suomen Historiallinen Seura.

—— (1994) 'Finland: The Welfare State at the Crossroads', in N. Ploug and J. Kvist (eds) *Recent Trends in Cash Benefits in Europe. Social Security in Europe 4*, Copenhagen: The Danish National Institute of Social Research.

Alestalo, M., Bislev, S. and Furåker, B. (1991) 'Welfare State Employment in Scandinavia', in J. E. Kolberg (ed.) *The Welfare State as Employer*, New York: M. E. Sharpe.

Alestalo, M. and Flora, P. (1994) 'Scandinavia: Welfare States in the Periphery – Peripheral Welfare States?', in M. Alestalo, E. Allardt, A. Rychard and W. Wesolowski (eds) *The Transformation of Europe. Social Conditions and Consequences*, Warszawa: IFiS Publishers.

Alestalo, M. and Kuhnle, S. (1987) 'The Scandinavian Route: Economic, Social, and Political Developments in Denmark, Finland, Norway, and Sweden', in R. Erikson, E. J. Hansen, S. Ringen and H. Uusitalo (eds) *The Scandinavian Model. Welfare States and Welfare Research*, New York: M. E. Sharpe.

Alestalo, M. and Uusitalo, H. (1992) 'Social Expenditure: a Decompositional Approach', in J. E. Kolberg (ed.) *The Study of Welfare State Regimes*, New York: M. E. Sharpe.

Alestalo, M., Uusitalo, H. and Flora, P. (1985) 'Structure and Politics in the Making of the

Welfare State: Finland in Comparative Perspective', in R. Alapuro, M. Alestalo, E. Haavio-Mannila and R. Väyrynen (eds) *Small States in Comparative Perspective. Essays for Erik Allardt*, Oslo: Norwegian University Press.

Allardt, E. (1984) 'Representative Government in a Bureaucratic Age', *Daedalus* 113: 169–97.

Anttonen A. and Sipilä, J. (1992) 'Julkinen, yhteisöllinen ja yksityinen sosiaalipolitiikassa – Sosiaalipalvelujen toimijat ja uudenlaiset yhteensovittamisen strategiat', in O. Riihinen (ed.) *Sosiaalipolitiikka 2017. Näkökulmia suomalaisen yhteiskunnan kehitykseen ja tulevaisuuteen*, Helsinki: WSOY.

Castles, F. C. (1978) *The Social Democratic Image of Society. A Study of the Achievements and Origins of Scandinavian Social Democracy in Comparative Perspective*, London: Routledge and Kegan Paul.

Heaton, H. (1966) *Economic History of Europe*, Tokyo: Harper & Row and John Weatherhill (rev. edn).

Heikkilä, M., Hänninen, S., Kosunen, V. Mäntysaari, M., Sallila, S. and Uusitalo, H. (1993) *'Hyvinvoinnin päätepysäkillä. Aineistoa hyvinvointipolitiikkaa ja lamaa koskevaan keskusteluun'*, raportteja 128, Helsinki: STAKES.

Heikkilä, M. and Uusitalo, H. (eds) (1997) *'Leikkausten hinta. Tutkimuksia sosiaaliturvan leikkauksista ja niiden vaikutuksista 1990-luvun Suomessa'*, raportteja 208, Helsinki: STAKES.

Kangas, O. (1992) 'The Politics of Universalism: the Case of Finnish Sickness Insurance', *Journal of Social Policy*, 21: 25–52.

Katzenstein, P. J. (1985) *Small States in the World Markets. Industrial Policy in Europe*, Ithaca and London: Cornell University Press.

Korpi, W. (1978) *The Working Class in Welfare Capitalism. Work, Unions and Politics in Sweden*, London: Routledge and Kegan Paul.

Kosonen, P. (1994) *European Integration: A Welfare State Perspective*, University of Helsinki: Sociology of Law Series No. 8.

Kosunen, V. (1997a) 'Lama ja sosiaaliturvan muutokset 1990-luvulla', in M. Heikkilä and H. Uusitalo (eds) *Leikkausten hinta. Tutkimuksia sosiaaliturvan leikkauksista ja niiden vaikutuksista 1990-luvun Suomessa*, raportteja 208, Helsinki: STAKES.

—— (1997b) 'Laskusuhdanteesta leikkauksiin – muutosten taustaa', in M. Heikkilä and H. Uusitalo (eds) *Leikkausten hinta. Tutkimuksia sosiaaliturvan leikkauksista ja niiden vaikutuksista 1990-luvun Suomessa*, raportteja 208, Helsinki: STAKES.

Kuhnle, S. (1981) 'The Growth of Social Insurance Programs in Scandinavia: Outside Influences and Internal Forces', in P. Flora and A. J. Heidenheimer (eds) *The Development of Welfare States in Europe and America*, New Brunswick and London: Transaction Books.

Lehto, J. (1995) 'Kunnallisten sosiaali- ja terveyspalvelujen muutossuunta 1990-luvun alun talouskriisin aikana', in S. Hänninen, J. Iivari and J. Lehto (eds), *Hallittu muutos sosiaali- ja terveydenhuollossa*, raportteja 182, Helsinki: STAKES.

Østerud, Ø. (1978) *Agrarian Structure and Peasant Politics in Scandinavia. A Comparative Study of Rural Response to Economic Change*, Oslo: Norwegian University Press.

Ritakallio, V-M. (1994) *Köyhyys Suomessa. Tutkimus tulonsiirtojen vaikutuksista*, tutkimuksia 39, Helsinki: STAKES.

Rose, R. (1985) 'The Significance of Public Employment', in R. Rose (ed.) *Public Employment in Western Nations*, Cambridge: Cambridge University Press.

Salminen, K. (1993) *Pension Schemes in the Making. A Comparative Study of the Scandinavian Countries*, The Central Pension Security Institute, Studies 1993: 2, Helsinki: The Central Pension Security Institute.

Sosiaalimenotoimikunnan välimietintö (1993) Komiteanmietintö 1993: 24, Helsinki.

Sosiaaliturva Suomessa 1993. Sosiaaliturva 1995: 2, Helsinki: Sosiaali-ja terveysministeriö.

Sosiaaliturvan suunta 1998–1999. Sosiaali- ja terveysministeriön julkaisuja 1998: 15. Helsinki: Sosiaali- ja terveysministeriö.

STAKES. National Research and Development Centre for Welfare and Health. *Facts about Finnish Social Welfare and Healthcare.* Helsinki: STAKES.

Taloudellinen katsaus (1995) Helsinki: Valtiovarainministriön kansantalousosasto.

—— (1998). Taloudelliset ja talouspoliittiset katsaukset 5/1998. Helsinki: Valtiovarainministeriö. Kansantalousosasto.

Uusitalo, H. (1989) *Income Distribution in Finland. The Effects of the Welfare State and the Structural Changes in Society on Income Distribution in Finland in 1966–1985,* Central Statistical Office of Finland, Studies No. 148, Helsinki: Central Statistical Office of Finland.

Uusitalo, H. and Ringen, S. (1992) 'Income Distribution and Redistribution in the Nordic Welfare States', in J. E. Kolberg (ed.) *The Study of Welfare State Regimes,* New York: M. E. Sharpe.

Wuthnow, R. (1991) 'Tocqueville's Question Reconsidered: Voluntarism and Public Discourse in Advanced Industrial Societies', in R. Wuthnow (ed.) *Between States and Markets. The Voluntary Sector in Comparative Perspective,* Princeton, NJ: Princeton University Press.

Yrjö Koskinen, Y. S. (1874) 'Työväenseikka', *Kirjallinen kuukausilehti* 9: 1–9, 91–97, 195–99, 220–27.

5   Welfare crisis and beyond
Danish welfare policies in the 1980s and 1990s

Jørgen Goul Andersen

Introduction: the Danish welfare miracle?

The last decade has witnessed many claims that the European welfare states in general and the Scandinavian welfare model in particular are badly equipped to meet the challenges of globalisation and demographic change (see e.g. Rhodes 1995; Esping-Andersen 1996; Taylor-Gooby 1996). Whereas the Swedish experience could at first glance seem to lend credibility to such theories (Lindbeck 1994), a record of the Danish welfare state in the 1980s and 1990s tells quite another story. In the early 1980s, the Danish welfare state indeed faced a serious economic crisis that seemed to threathen its survival: the budget deficit of the state exploded to 11.5 per cent of GDP in 1982, and from 1979 to 1983, net state debt rose from 14 to 55 per cent of GDP. Furthermore, by 1982 the balance of payment deficit was 4.1 per cent of GDP, and foreign debts reached 34.5 per cent of GDP. In spite of economic recession and mass unemployment, inflation remained above 10 per cent.

This crisis would seem to call for major institutional adjustments of the welfare state. However, as described below, nearly all the above-mentioned problems were solved without any significant institutional change: unemployment was reduced to a low level even though income distribution became more equal; large-scale public deficits turned into a surplus in spite of considerable increase in public expenditures; and although taxes remained very high throughout the 1990s, there were few legitimacy problems among a population that came to enjoy the highest level of private consumption in the EU next to Luxembourg.

The Danish experience indicates that the economic sustainability of the welfare state has been seriously underestimated. This chapter will analyse how the problems were overcome and discuss whether they were adequately solved, as judged from a long-term perspective. Ironically, *after the recovery*, the Danish welfare state has been subject to changes that may, intendedly or unintendedly, lead to major innovations. The fact that these changes were *not* very obviously made out of economic necessity suggests that when considering the future of the welfare state, we should perhaps be less concerned with exogeneous *'challenges'* such as economic pressures and be more concerned with (endogenous) *political and institutional dynamics*. Thus, beyond serving as a test case of the sustainability of the Scandinavian welfare model, the Danish experience may also illuminate the dynamics of welfare state change.

Economic aspects: the realities of retrenchment in the 1980s

As in many other countries, the Danish economic problems caused by the oil crisis in 1973/74 were at first countered by demand-stimulating Keynesian policies and by incomes policies. Later on followed policies aimed at a 'switch' from private consumption to labour-intensive public consumption, as well as generous early exit opportunities. But all efforts seemed inefficient, and negative side effects accumulated (Goul Andersen 1997). In the autumn of 1982, the Radical Liberal Party withdrew its support for the incumbent Social Democrats and paved the way for a bourgeois government (led by Conservative Prime Minister Poul Schlüter) that remained in office until January 1993. The main aim of the bourgeois government, and its main justification among voters, was to 'reconstruct the economy'. A cornerstone was the abolition of restrictions to free capital movements and the adoption of a fixed currency policy which irreversibly institutionalised tight economic policies. As to welfare policies, the government declared a principle of zero growth in public expenditures and adopted a new budgetary system to attain this goal. Among the Danish voters who had developed a high crisis awareness (Petersen *et al.* 1987), the government's economic policies were accepted; in particular, the fixed currency attained high symbolic importance. The government's welfare policies, on the other hand, were only reluctantly accepted, as necessary in order to improve the economic situation (Goul Andersen 1988: 22–23).

Although the balance of payment was given priority over employment, the opposite happened, because of an unexpected rise in private consumption and investments. The state budget showed a surplus already by 1986 but only at the expense of an all-time-high balance of payments deficit. This forced the government to implement contractive policies (credit restrictions). Alongside a reduction of tax deductions for interest this started a recession that lasted for seven years, culminating with an unemployment rate of 12.4 per cent in 1993;[1] but at the same time, the balance of payments had improved to a surplus of 3.5 per cent of GDP. In 1993, this enabled the new centre-left government headed by the Social Democratic Prime Minister Poul Nyrup Rasmussen to adopt an expansionary policy. The economic boom that followed mirrored the mid-1980s, catalysed by lower interest rates and capital gains among houseowners and shareholders, only this time the point of departure was a large surplus on the balance of payments enabling the boom to continue.

As to welfare policies, the main goal of the bourgeois government was zero growth in public expenditure and a reduction of public employment. Retrenchment policies appeared harsh at times but a closer look on the aggregate figures tells a rather different story: from 1982 to 1992, total expenditure increased by 21 per cent in real terms (see Table 5.1). In fact, the government *did* manage to

Table 5.1 Total public expenditure, public consumption, transfers to households, and interests in Denmark, 1980–98 (per cent of GDP, and in fixed prices[1]; index 1982=100 and index 1992=100)

	Total public expenditure		Public consumption		Transfers to households		Interest on state debt	
	Per cent GDP	Index: fixed prices[1]	Per cent GDP	Index: fixed prices[1]	Per cent GDP	Index: fixed prices[1]	Per cent GDP	Index: fixed prices[1]
1980	55.6	91.8	26.7	94.5	16.6	90.9	3.9	65.0
1982	60.2	100.0	28.2	100.0	18.1	100.0	6.0	100.0
1984	59.6	106.7	25.9	99.5	17.0	100.6	9.6	170.8
1986	55.0	108.6	23.9	102.7	15.5	99.6	8.8	170.6
1988	58.7	114.1	25.7	106.1	17.3	112.6	8.0	155.8
1990	58.4	114.7	25.3	105.0	18.4	121.6	7.3	145.4
1991	59.2	116.6	25.5	104.8	19.0	126.9	7.4	148.2
1992	60.5	120.8	25.6	106.3	19.6	132.3	6.8	139.0
1992	58.2	100.0	25.8	100.0	18.9	100.0	6.6	100.0
1993	60.6	104.5	26.8	104.1	19.8	105.1	7.3	109.6
1994[2]	60.5	110.2	25.9	107.1	21.2	117.9	6.7	105.6
1995	59.0	111.0	25.6	109.6	20.3	116.5	6.5	106.7
1996	58.4	112.7	25.7	112.3	19.7	116.5	6.1	102.4
1997	56.4	112.6	25.2	114.7	18.7	113.9	5.8	99.8
1998B	55.5	112.7	25.7	118.1	18.1	112.5	5.4	94.9
Corrected 1998B[2]	53.7	109.1	25.7	118.1	18.1	101.6	5.4	94.9

Sources: Statistics Denmark, *Statistiske efterretninger, Statistisk 10 års oversigt*, various issues. Figures 1992–98 are based on the new 1995 SNA National Account System.

Notes
1 Public consumption is deflated by public consumption deflator; Capital accumulation is deflated by deflator for fixed investments; transfers are deflated by the consumer price index. Capital transfers are omitted. Public consumption is calculated net of user charges, etc. Capital accumulation is calculated less of sales of land and intangible assets.
2 Figures for 1994 and following years are not corrected for an 'artificial' increase in transfers by about 2.0 per cent of GDP, due to grossification of transfers. The corrected 1998 budget indicates how this would change the figures.

keep zero growth in public consumption except in 1984–88 and 1992, and throughout the decade 1982–92, cumulative growth in public consumption was only 6.3 per cent in real terms;[2] when the Social Democrats were reinstalled, cumulative growth amounted to 18 per cent from 1992 to 1998.[3]

Working hard to keep public consumption under control, however, the bourgeois government lost control over transfers. Transfers to households remained constant from 1982 to 1986 because of cutbacks and lower unemployment. But then expenditure exploded: from 1986 to 1989, transfers to households increased by 20 per cent in real terms, mainly because of political reforms in 1988/89 such as new systems of child allowances and students' allowances, alongside improvements of pensions, unemployment benefits and social assistance. In the following years, unemployment-related expenditures pushed the increase even further. By 1992, transfers to households had increased by 32 per cent in real terms in spite of 10 years of retrenchment. This triggered off the belief that transfers were 'uncontrollable'; however, expenses related to unemployment, early retirement and ageing only accounted for about one-half of the increase (Goul Andersen 1997), even including the improvements which the government was forced to accept in 1988/89. In short, it was political factors more than social processes in terms of ageing, unemployment and labour market marginalisation that explained the economic pressures of increasing transfers.

Despite hard efforts, the bourgeois government did not succeed in bringing expenditure down. Relative to GDP, public expenditure remained the same, and in real terms, it increased by 21 per cent. Nevertheless, at the expense of a temporary growth in unemployment, the balance of payments problem was solved without state debt getting out of control.

Institutional change: consolidating the universal welfare state

The most important fact about retrenchment in the 1980s was, however, that in institutional terms, very few changes took place. In 1982, the government had great plans for a 'bourgeois revolution'; a whole vocabulary was invented for the government's attempts to 'modernise' the welfare state. But little happened apart from the introduction of some new public management techniques and of more exit and voice opportunities in the public service sector. In practice, the decisive motive was short-term budget considerations (Jonassen 1998: 121). Proportional budget cuts was the preferred method to keep budget increases low; privatisation was often used as 'window dressing' of budgets; the idea of introducing new user charges on a broad scale was buried almost immediately; and contracting out was not carried very far (Greve 1997: 40–58; Klausen and Ståhlberg 1998). If we look at results rather than intentions, the conclusion is that the universal welfare model was consolidated from 1982 to 1992.

In spite of political promises, taxation was not significantly lowered: corporate taxes were raised from 40 to 50 per cent by 1986 and then lowered to 40 and 38 per cent from 1990 and 1992, respectively. A further decline had to wait until the Social Democratic government took over. The uniform VAT (*'moms'*) was raised from 22 to 25 per cent (as from 1988/92). Income taxes remained almost unchanged: the highest marginal income tax was raised from 70 to 73 per cent in 1982 and then lowered to 68 per cent in the 1985 tax reform, but only alongside a broadening of the tax base where the 'tax value' of interest payment was reduced to a flat rate of about 50 per cent. Already before this reform, owners' income tax deductions for taxes on real property had been abolished. Members' and employers' contributions to unemployment insurance funds were raised but unemployment insurance remained mainly state-financed. From the mid-1980s, some taxes on 'luxury goods' were reduced in order to limit border trade but otherwise adaptations, following the Single European Act in 1986, turned out to be small.

Some of the most significant institutional reforms may even be described as a continuation of a 'creeping universalism' (see Table 5.2): first, as compensation for the reduced tax deductions for homeowners, universal child allowances (amounting to nearly 1 per cent of GDP) were introduced by 1986. Next, 1988 witnessed the introduction of a generous, universal students' allowance which was now given independently of parents' income from the age of 19/20 years. Third, means-tested user charges for home help given on a permanent basis were abolished in 1991. And finally, maternity leave after birth was substantially improved, from 14 to 24 weeks from 1984/85.[4]

On the retrenchment side, average replacement rates for the unemployed declined because of a somewhat lower ceiling but maximum replacement remained 90 per cent, and eligibility criteria remained very soft.[5] The only major institutional reform (to which we return below) was the new indexation of transfer incomes introduced by 1990.

As a whole, the main history of the welfare state was one of steady improvements, only at a lower speed. But alongside tight economic policies, this proved sufficient to overcome the economic crisis of the welfare state without institutional change.

Policy effects: avoiding poverty and living with unemployment

Turning to policy effects, the most significant finding is the absence of increasing inequality and poverty in the 1980s. Relative poverty (according to the standard definition) remained by far the lowest in the EU (European Commission 1994: 139–41), and even among households in which the head of household was unemployed, only 3 per cent fell below the poverty level in 1988 (as compared to an EU average of 38 per cent and 22 per cent in the Netherlands which came second to Denmark in the ranking). Also, Denmark was among the few countries to experience *less* inequality in disposable incomes in the 1980s (Ministry of Finance 1995; Goul Andersen 1997). Inequality in primary incomes *did* increase but the redistributive effect of the welfare state increased even more (Ministry of Finance 1997: 133). Even political participation became more evenly distributed (Goul Andersen and Hoff 1995).

These findings are significant in light of the one deterioration that *did* take place: increasing unemployment. But in the first place, the tight economic policies paved the way for the 'job miracle' bringing unemployment down from 12.4 per cent to 6.0 per cent of the labour force from 1993 to 1998 (December) – by ILO definition even to a low figure of 5 per cent. And second, although there have been indices of an accumulation of serious problems among the weakest groups of unemployed (Christoffersen 1996), large groups seemed to cope surprisingly well with unemployment. For instance, in a representative survey of long-term unemployed in 1994, only 34 per cent indicated a decline in general well-being during unemployment whereas 28 per cent indicated an improvement; 44 per cent 'would welcome' a longer period without work provided that they could

Table 5.2 Major reforms under the Danish bourgeois governments, September 1982–January 1993

Time	Reform
1982	Automatic cost-of-living adjustment of wages suspended (abolished in 1987)
1982–85	Freezing of maximum amounts of unemployment benefits, early retirement allowance, and social assistance; replacement levels unchanged 90 per cent As from July 1988 extraordinarily raised by 10 per cent
1983	Special tax on pensions savings; on average, real interests above $3\frac{1}{2}$ per cent was paid as tax to the state (changed to a new tax from 1999). This was originally the proposal that forced the previous Social Democratic government to resign
1982 and later	Higher members' and employers' contributions to unemployment insurance (to cover one-third of the expenses)
1980s	Various minor changes in sickness insurance, employers' payments for sickness and first day of unemployment
1984/85	Improved maternity leave to 24 weeks after birth. Same compensation as unemployment benefits but full compensation increasingly included in collective agreements at the labour market
1987	Generous universal child allowance introduced as compensation for lower tax deduction of interests in the 1987 tax reform. Later improvements fom time to time used as compensation mechanism for various tightenings. Means-tested child benefits maintained
1988	Extraordinary regulation of old-age pension and early retirement pensions by 5 per cent (singles) or 7 per cent (married couples)
1988	Generous universal students' allowance introduced, granted independently of parents' incomes from the age of 20 (also universal but graduated for the 19-year-olds)
1991	Universal home aid: home aid free of user charges for all pensioners who are granted home aid on a permanent basis
1982–93	Highest marginal income taxes: 1982: from 70 to 73 per cent 1987: from 73 to 68 per cent Corporate taxes raised from 40 to 50 per cent from 1986; lowered to 40 per cent from 1990 and to 38 per cent from 1992 Indirect taxes: 1988: various social contributions of employers abolished and replaced by a 'labour market contribution' (AMBI) which was, in effect, a VAT in disguise; 1992: AMBI banned by the European Commission and replaced by VAT increase from 22 to 25 per cent; 1989–92: a number of taxes on various commodities from alcohol to televisions abolished or reduced in order to avoid border trade
1990	New regulation of all transfer incomes to households by annual wage for manual workers, less increasing contributions to pensions savings, etc.
1992	Introduction of new leave arrangements but based on employers' approval and replacement with unemployed
1982–93	Elements of 'New Public Management' introduced in public services

receive unemployment benefits as long as they wished; and 29 per cent 'could adapt to the situation' (Goul Andersen 1996).

No doubt, the relatively high economic security and low stigmatisation associated with unemployment at the time of interviewing played an important role. The ceiling was low (11,000 DkK per month in 1994) but a high compensation rate of 90 per cent of previous earnings secured an acceptable standard of living. In practice, right to unemployment benefits could be maintained almost infinitely until the period of support was fixed in the 1993 labour market reform to seven years, of which the last three years must be on activation, i.e. job training or education. Besides, in the high-unemployment period, control with active job-seeking was limited. Also, the integration of women on the labour market, increasingly on a full-time basis,[6] helped to alleviate the economic consequences of unemployment at the family level as there is rarely more than one person unemployed in a family. Thus, even among those who had been without ordinary employment for 10 years, a majority were homeowners, provided that they were married (Goul Andersen 1996).

The bourgeois government gave second priority to the goal of unemployment but as it maintained a generous social security for the unemployed,[7] the social costs of retrenchment did not grow to intolerable levels. In fact, it was demonstrated how a Scandinavian welfare model, contrary to some predictions, was able to live with enduring high unemployment without undermining its economic foundations and without sacrificing basic normative principles. Furthermore, as a consequence of high unemployment, the Danish society *de facto* moved further towards the 'ultimate universalism' in the shape of a sort of citizens' wage, at least in the sense that nearly anybody without paid employment was entitled to a basic income – and in the sense that the formal duty to seek employment was practised liberally.

Basically, the bourgeois government from 1982 to January 1993 consolidated the universal welfare model by slowing down the speed of social reforms and by rationalising service production. This was sufficient to overcome the economic crisis of the welfare state; with a high balance of payments surplus it was only a matter of time before increasing private consumption would bring the recession to an end and stabilise the state budget through lower costs and increasing revenues.

Adequate solutions? – Danish welfare and long-term challenges

Although the Danish welfare state recovered from immediate economic pressures, it may still be questioned whether it is able to meet future challenges. Below, we briefly consider a few such long-term challenges grouped under the headings: European integration, globalisation and employment; demographic change; and problems of controlling large-scale welfare states. These challenges affect all welfare states but in different ways, depending on institutional preconditions in different 'welfare regimes' (Esping-Andersen 1990, 1996).

To begin with *European integration*, it has sometimes been argued that this could undermine the welfare state. Now, such arguments often rest on the false assumption that the Danish welfare state is significantly more generous than other Northern European welfare states. Generally speaking, this is not the case; it is mainly institutions and priorities that are different (Goul Andersen and Munk Christiansen 1991; Ministry of Finance 1994). As to the economic requirements of the Economic and Monetary Union (EMU), similar requirements have constituted a self-imposed restriction on Danish economic policies since the mid-1980s. In a world with free capital movements, 'irresponsible' economic policies of small countries are punished by high interest rates anyway as foreign investors withdraw. Therefore it makes little difference *for economic policies* whether Denmark remains outside or eventually decides to join the common currency.

It remains to be seen whether the EMU and the common currency will entail 'spill-over' effects beyond economic policy requirements. But so far, taxation and welfare are largely outside the European agenda. Considering the difficulties of obtaining agreement over treaty changes and common rules, not to mention implementation problems, common policies do not seem likely to proceed very far. More importantly, even if common rules were possible, they would probably be guided by the underlying interest of avoiding unfair competition from 'social dumping': nobody would be interested in imposing less generous welfare on other countries. Thus the most important question is about the sustainability of the tax/welfare system in a world with open borders. In practice, this is a question of incentives and mobility of tax objects. Beginning with capital, mobility is high but incentives are small as Danish corporate taxes are around the European average. Commodity taxes are far above average but have long ago been fine tuned to limit border trade. When it comes to labour, both mobility and incentives are low. Taxes on labour (combined income taxes and social contributions) are close to European average (Lassen and Nielsen 1996); and because of very favourable support systems for families with children and the young, there are few incentives to migration for young people. Ironically, taxation of labour has nevertheless been the most important concern in debates over globalisation and taxes.

Basically, the question of European integration is just another aspect of globalisation in general. *'Globalisation'* is often regarded as a threat to the sustainability of European welfare states. However, it is a catchword with diffuse meanings. If it refers to increasing world trade it is somewhat misleading as it ignores the high international trade before 1914 (Krugman 1996; Hirst and Thompson 1996). Still, it remains that as compared to the heydays of Keynesianism, nation-states have fewer instruments to avoid unemployment. Whereas globalisation and technological change does not seem to affect aggregate employment much, it is often argued that global competition between European countries with compressed wage structures and newly industrialised countries tend to generate a low-skilled surplus population (OECD 1994). Esping-Andersen (1996) accepted this problem definition and described four strategies which he identified with his three welfare regimes: the 'liberal' strategy of lower minimum wages to expand low-productive employment; the 'conservative' strategy of exit arrangements to reduce labour supply; and the two 'social democratic' options of public service growth and of active labour market policies to enhance qualifications; to these may be added the fifth possibility of accepting unemployment as unavoidable and making the best of it (as citizens' wage proponents would have it, e.g. Offe 1996).

Apart from the 'liberal' option, Denmark has applied all of these strategies and even added a sixth one: a 'home service' arrangement with government-subsidised services for private households delivered by certified firms. This is a growing business but still employs only about 10,000 persons (1998). Since 1993, Denmark has increasingly chosen the strategy of active labour market policies. This has contributed to abolishing youth unemployment (which has always been comparatively low in Denmark) but otherwise, cost/effectiveness of active labour market policies has not been too convincing (for an overview of evaluations, see Schøler 2000; Langager 1997). Besides, the activation strategy may become extremely costly during a recession.

Although unemployment was halved from 1993 to 1998 and is now among the lowest in Europe (5 per cent by common ILO definition), it is not yet convincingly proved that it is possible to avoid unemployment and labour market marginalisation. In fact, the Danish economy has been unable to produce any long-term growth in private sector employment over the last 50 years (Table 5.3). All increase in employment has taken place in the public sector where employment has increased from about 150,000 in 1948 to about 800,000. Also, part of the explanation of the decline in unemployment in the 1990s was an increase in all sorts of exit from the labour market although this has now been reversed:[8]

- Transitional allowance (introduced in 1992; entrance closed by 1996) enabled long-term unemployed to exit from the age of 50. By 1995, 45,000 had exploited that opportunity, partly because of a hoarding effect when it was announced that the programme would be closed. By the end of 1998, the figure was 34,000 persons.
- Early retirement allowance (strongly modified from 1999) enabled people to leave at the age of 60 on conditions roughly similar to unemployment benefits (benefits reduced to 80 per cent after two and a half years). Figures increased from 102,000 in 1992 to 144,000 by the end of 1998. Also here, a hoarding effect is visible.

Table 5.3 Public and private sector employment in Denmark, 1948–92 (full-time employment, in thousands)

Sector	1948	1960	1970	1980	1999	1997
Private	1,782	1,915	1,938	1,751	1,788	1,789
Public	151	222	403	691	785	800
Total	1,933	2,137	2,341	2,442	2,574	2,589

Sources: ADAM databank; Statistics Denmark, *Statistiske efterretninger.*

- Early retirement pensions (previously disablement): from 1992 to 1998, figures increased from 257,000 to 272,000.
- Leave arrangements: parental, educational and sabbatical leave was introduced by 1992, extended in 1993 but substantially modified from 1996.[9] These rights were also granted to unemployed people who have constituted about one-half of those who are on leave. In 1998, the figure was about 40,000, one-half of the numbers in the mid-1990s.[10]

Including people on sickness benefits, maternity leave, activation programmes and long-term unemployment, some 900,000 full-time persons aged 15–66 years mainly lived on transfer income from the state by 1998. When the figure reached one million in the mid-1990s, this issue was strongly used to criticise the welfare state, and the government has been keen to reduce the figures, partly by tightenings, partly by reducing the pension age to 65 years from 1999.

Now, in the Danish case, the figures of 'inactivity' above may be seen less as a social problem than as an expansion of welfare. Economically, on the other hand, there is little doubt that the long-term dynamic effect of exit arrangements is a reduction of aggregate employment. What remains from the Danish experience, however, is the fact that even with mixed results in the fight against unemployment, the welfare system was able to alleviate negative consequences for citizenship without deteriorating the economy.

Ageing populations is another common challenge to European welfare states. However, the Danish welfare state does not seem very vulnerable to this change: fertility rates in Scandinavia are the highest in Europe, perhaps reflecting welfare provisions for working mothers. Along with immigration surplus this means that demography will change less than in most of Europe. Taking Germany as a counterpoint, population prognoses from the mid-1990s indicated that in Germany, the proportion of the population aged more than 60 years would increase to 33 per cent in 2025 whereas the estimate for Denmark was 26 per cent (Council of Europe 1996, 1997).

Next, the Danish system of universal flat-rate public pensions is not very costly. Along with housing allowances and various social benefits tied to age, the pension system does provide an exceptionally high compensation rate of nearly 100 per cent for low-income groups such as single, unskilled workers. But for medium- and high-income groups, compensation is low. Furthermore, part of the basic pension (some 40 per cent for singles) is a 'pensions supplement', means-tested on other income, e.g. from private or labour market pensions. Thus, only two-thirds of the old-age pensioners receive full pension supplement and some 15 per cent do not receive pension supplement at all (Statistics Denmark: *Statistiske Efter-retninger*).

This is reflected in experiences with pension expenditure until now: from 1972 to 1998, the absolute numbers of old-age pensioners (67 years or more) increased by 33 per cent, equivalent to an increase from 10.5 per cent to 13.3 per cent of the entire population. But adjusted for the tax reform in 1993/94, the proportion of GDP spent on old-age pensions has declined from 5.1 per cent in 1972 to 4.6 per cent in 1998 (Goul Andersen 1998: 130).[11] Calculations of the future costs of ageing diverge, depending on methods and assumptions. In 1996, the total increase including services was estimated at some 3–4 per cent of GDP around 2025 (Ministry of Finance 1996, Chapter 8). At least by comparative standards, the fear of a 'pension bomb' is exaggerated as the Scandinavian systems along with the UK are among the most 'robust' (Roseweare *et al.* 1996). A far more important challenge is to avoid labour market marginalisation before retirement – and to control public budgets.

The extent of the challenge of *controlling the public economy of large-scale welfare states* is frequently under-estimated. In fact, this is also a rather new challenge. It involves two important problems: controlling public budgets while ensuring 'value for money', and avoiding distortion effects on markets. The growth of the welfare state may explain the 'Copernican turn' among many economists, from advocating state solutions to market imperfections to advocating market solutions to state imperfections.

The challenge of controlling budgets and ensuring value for money is extraordinarily important in Scandinavian welfare states with their very large public service sectors and, consequently, with very large numbers of public employees (roughly one-third of the labour force). There is a permanent pressure for higher budgets, and in the absence of systems forcing political actors to make priorities, the sum of individual spending decisions easily adds up to larger total expenditures than desirable (Kristensen 1980; 1987). The softening of such controls does contribute to explaining the somewhat unintended increase in public expenditures after 1993. In spite of dramatically increased revenues, surplus on the state budget in 1997 and 1998 was obtained mainly by 'window dressing' – e.g. by extraordinary revenues from changing the transfer of taxes from municipalities and by selling government-owned companies (Christiansen 1999). Thus, a structural deficit on public budgets seems to remain. But this is a matter of political priorities rather than exogenous pressures; and even though political pressure for increasing public consumption is strong, it is far from uncontrollable. This was also the lesson from the 1980s.

As to welfare distortions on markets, speculations have blossomed but attempts to demonstrate such effects empirically have not been encouraging (Pedersen 1993). Disincentives of taxes have been difficult to prove; work incentives may be weak for the lower-skilled but effects on job-seeking are surprisingly small (Smith 1998; Pedersen and Smith 1995; Goul Andersen 1996: 187). Further, high unemployment protection should be seen against low job protection (Goul Andersen and Munk Christiansen 1991: 90–3, 177–80): the protection against being fired is much lower than in most European countries. This welfare mix has its shortcomings in terms of incentives for employers; but it has contributed to an extremely flexible labour market where unemployment is highly dispersed (e.g. across age groups) and where 'insider/outsider' problems are small: 'insiders' may easily become 'outsiders' if wage demands are pushed too far. This mix reflects the legacy of a small-firm society but seems well-adapted to new market surroundings where flexibility is a strong requirement.

Finally, Scandinavian welfare states act more in conformity with the market than is implied to by such terms as 'decommodification'. To repeat a classical argument, universal programmes are less likely to generate 'poverty traps' than selective ones. Besides, the very incentive to present oneself as needing or deserving may more easily lead to 'welfare dependency'.

To conclude, it is difficult to argue that the challenges associated with European integration, globalisation, ageing and the side effects of welfare should constitute any threat to the survival of the Danish welfare state. On the contrary, it seems well-prepared for nearly any conceivable external challenge. But even though external challenges are manageable, this does not prevent political actors from making changes. Rather than looking for economic pressures, we should look for *political logics* that determine the future of the welfare state – political logics that are closely related to the institutional set-up of the welfare state.

New dynamics and new trajectories

One question is whether it will be possible to maintain the Danish welfare model. A second question is whether it is desirable. And a third question – on which we shall focus here – is whether it is likely. This may depend on public opinion and on political will of the major parties (both seem rather favourable). But to an even larger degree, it may depend on intended or unintended changes that may evoke new dynamics. Decison-makers are not always fully aware of the long-term policy path dynamics that may follow from short-term decisions, and institutional change may sometimes be antecedent to both elite and mass opinion. From this point of departure, we may briefly address a few of the major institutional changes in the 1990s.

As in other countries responsive to OECD recommendations, the most significant change is perhaps the *active line in labour market policies*. By European standards, Denmark pursued an active strategy already from around 1980 but much more based on social rights and less aimed at control. At that time, the government in fact came close to entering a citizens' wage trajectory. Eligibility criteria to unemployment benefits were soft, the works test was liberal, and in theory, only occasional employment was required to maintain unemployment benefits almost indefinitely until the age of 50 where transitional allowance was offered. When new leave arrangements (parental, educational and sabbatical leave) were introduced in 1992 and improved in 1993, this could also have become the beginning of a new policy path. These arrangements became popular among the younger generations, and vested interests preventing a reversal could easily have developed.

However, this contributed to a backlash, not least among the government coalition partner, the Radical Liberals, which began to speak loudly about un-controllable transfers, 'dependency culture' – and against the idea of a 'citizen wage' that had in fact been introduced to the Danish public by one of the party's own prominent figures in the 1970s. Instead of citizens' wage, the idea of 'activation' expanded forcefully. A modest beginning was taken with a labour market reform in 1993 which defined the maximum unemployment period to seven years (plus up to two years on leave) but at the same time divided the unemployment period into two, the last period being an activation period of three years. In this period, the unemployed should be on permanent activation and did not gain the right to a new period on unemployment benefits.

Two years later this was significantly tightened as part of an agreement over the state budget with the Conservatives which in fact constituted a second labour market reform. Entitlement to unemployment benefits was restricted to five years, of which three years should be on permanent activation. Eligibility became somewhat restricted. And for people aged less than 25 years, unemployment benefits could be obtained for only half a year before they have to accept 18 months of education on highly reduced benefits. People on social assistance can receive support for only six months before having an 'individual plan of action' and subsequent activation.

This 'active line' was interpreted as a considerable success as it turned out that most young unemployed were able to find a job in order to avoid activation. Also, activation itself has been a success for some groups. And more generally, people who run the risk of losing unemployment benefits seem surprisingly able to find a job.[12] No doubt, economic prosperity has also contributed to the apparent success. In an agreement over the 1999 state budget but with the acceptance of the unions, the maximum period of unemployment was reduced to only four years, with activation after one year. At the same time, the early retirement allowance was tightened: access was reduced by requiring 25 years of contributions, now in the shape of a large but voluntary contribution targeted to early retirement; besides, people were given strong incentives to stay in the labour market at least until the age of 62 years. In addition to this 'third labour market reform' in 1998, a new law of social assistance was implemented. It was based on a 'communitarian' notion of integration by work and imposes a 20 per cent cut for those who refuse to accept activation. The practical implementation effects, however, are not yet fully clear. But the 'active line' marks a break away from 20 years' unemployment policies, in particular with its significant stress on duties. So far, possible effects on social integration or on stigmatisation are more or less unknown, and theoretical interpretations in terms of 'workfare' or 'enabling state' are divergent (Torfing 1999; Jensen 1999). It also remains to be seen how this new (and expensive) system may work under a recession.

Whereas there is little doubt that the active line has constituted a self-reinforcing departure from the past, the *path-breaking potentials of a tax reform* in 1993 were *not* exploited. The 1993 tax reform introduced a new tax called 'labour market contributions' but labelled 'gross tax' by the political opposition. It is a formally earmarked (and deductible) social contribution, paid overwhelmingly by wage earners and only to a negligible extent by employers. Until now, the Danish tax system has been unique in Europe as it is almost entirely based on income taxes rather than a mix of income taxes and social contributions/or employers' taxes. Formally, the new tax system marked an approach to other European tax systems although it was a strange hybrid.

But harmonisation was hardly among the government's dominant motives which were unclear but appear to have been much more tactical. Apparently, the government had hoped to make taxes less visible (it even sought to remove the 'gross tax' from the printed tax accounts) and it may also have hoped to improve re-election chances. But in retrospect, decision-makers would describe the main motive as a broadening of the tax base by reducing the tax value of deductions for interests and other expenses. Thus, in 1993 and in a subsequent reform in 1998, 'fiscal welfare' has been substantially reduced. On the other hand, the prospects of a new trajectory involving some approach to a Bismarckian system withered away. The idea of earmarking was finally given up when it would have forced the government to lower the 'labour market contributions' and the label 'gross tax' gradually became accepted even by the government. In the new tax reform in 1998 (presented as an economic package), the idea of increasing labour market contributions further was given up while other ways were found to reduce the tax value of deductions for interest payments.

Apart from broadening the tax base, the main changes are a lowering of marginal income taxes at all levels (the highest marginal tax rate was reduced from 68 per cent in 1993 to about 62 per cent in 1998, including the 'gross tax'). In return, taxes on energy, water and electricity – so-called 'green taxes' – have been raised (as commodity taxes are already the highest in the EU, this marks a further deviation from any EU harmonisation of tax systems). Finally, property tax was abolished as part of the 1995 budget agreement with the Conservatives. As municipal taxes have increased, the lowering of income taxes for small incomes has been less than intended but Danish income taxes are far more progressive than in most EU countries. Even though the high VAT and the new green taxes are regressive, the redistributive effect of the tax/welfare system increased during the decade of bourgeois government, and this seems to have continued with the two tax reforms in 1993 and 1998. At any rate, apart from broadening the tax base and increasing green taxes, the Danish tax system has not been fundamentally changed. It remains unique as the single European tax system where social contributions are negligible.

Finally, *the pension system is undergoing rather fundamental change.* In the 1960s, Denmark failed to introduce income-related superannuation schemes as in Sweden and Norway, mainly because the rank-and-file members of the labour movement preferred the citizenship-based, flat-rate pensions. However, catalysed by governments' willingness to support any form of private savings that might improve Denmark's chronic balance of payments deficits, a dual pension system gradually emerged where two-thirds of the population had no pension coverage other than their basic ('people's') pension. Now, in the early 1980s, basic pensions (and various supplements) had been improved to a level where the compensation rate was coming close to 100 per cent for single, low-income wage earners. To illustrate the replacement level, more than 60 per cent of all old-age pensioners (67 years or more) are homeowners. But partly because this was not really recognised, partly because of fears of the future 'pension bomb' which at that time seemed threatening, the unions made collective agreements with employers on a (formally private) 'labour market pension'.[13] In the 1990s, this was extended to nearly all collective agreements. At the same time the bourgeois government had made one single institutional change which was important in the long run: wage increases devoted to pensions were excluded from the annual regulation of old-age pensions and other transfers.

In combination with means-testing of pensions supplements, the Danish flat-rate pension will be lower in future and supplemented by an income-related pension. Besides, increasing incomes from other pensions may serve as arguments for abolishing various subsidies targeted to pensioners as a category. Thus in the 1998 budget, housing allowances for pensioners were substantially reduced, in particular for better-off pensioners. Being a 'functional equivalent' of public income-related superannuation schemes, it is noteworthy that Danish labour market pensions are without any maximum and that coverage is far from universal. The system is only gradually implemented; collective agreement in 1998 raised contributions to 5.7 per cent (as against 10–15 per cent for white collar groups who already have a pension scheme). When fully implemented, the Danish pension system seems likely to become a unique hybrid between a universal, a residual and a corporatist model. From the government's point of view, the system has the additional advantage that pension contributions are not counted as taxes, unlike obligatory social contributions. Ironically, this rather fundamental change was never really imagined or discussed during 50 years of debate about the future of the pension system. It must be acknowledged, though, that basic pensions remain quite generous by comparative standards and that the new system will not mature until the middle of the next century.

To conclude, unlike the bourgeois governments in the 1980s, the Social Democratic government since 1993 has introduced (or accepted) welfare innovations in two fields: in the field of unemployment where a 'communitarian' principle of workfare has been introduced, although so far in a moderate version, and in the field of pensions where trade unions made their own pensions policy. Finally, as in many other countries, the government has introduced a tax reform which reduces marginal taxes and broadens the tax base but without fundamental changes. These changes, of course, have some relation to the national and international debates over challenges to the welfare state but they can hardly be considered 'necessary' adaptations. Several courses of action or inaction were possible. As to intensified activation, the government has explicitly stated that it does not pay from a narrow economic point of view but is aiming more at the goal of social integration. As a final characteristic, all these changes took place without much public discussion. The labour market reforms of 1995 and 1998 were introduced as part of a compromise over the government's budget for the next year, and the 1998 tax reform was masked as an economic package.

Conclusion

The first lesson to be learnt from the Danish experience in the 1980s is that it was possible to overcome a severe economic crisis of the welfare state without fundamental changes. Unintendedly, the 'Social Democratic' model was in fact consolidated. All that was needed was a slow down of the speed of reforms and a willingness to impose strong controls on public spending. In spite of retrenchment, the 1980s remain almost one long story of improvements of welfare, especially in the field of transfers. What remains of structural imbalances on the state budget is explained by the rapid expansion of public services from 1992–98. This chapter has not discussed whether sufficient 'value for money' is provided by the Danish welfare model. But it is not possible to point to any exogenous factors that seriously could undermine its economic foundations. The major economic challenge is endogenous rather than exogenous: insufficient budget controls can make the welfare state vulnerable if prosperity should suddenly come to an end. Besides, high costs of activation could prove counterproductive in such a situation.

The second lesson is that economic challenges and innovation are independent, crosscutting variables. Under bourgeois governments aiming at something like a 'bourgeois revolution' in the 1980s, the Danish welfare state survived severe challenges without any significant innovations, by means of more tight budgetary controls. In the economic prosperity of the 1990s, welfare expenditures have been allowed to increase at a quite rapid speed but here we have witnessed more far-reaching institutional changes than in the 1980s, mainly in terms of 'active line' labour market policies and pension policies. Thus we are tempted to conclude that the main prospects for change do not stem from economic pressures. They stem from political choice – but not always from fully *conscious* political choice. Rather than the 'crisis literature', we must turn to theories of political coalitions, party strategies, 'garbage-can' theories of political decision-making, theories of the formation of elite ideas and discourses, and finally to theories of intended and unintended 'path dynamics' of policies to foresee future changes to the Danish welfare state.

Notes

1 Originally, competitiveness and economic growth in the private sector was seen as the means to fight unemployment. But from 1988/89, philosophies changed towards the ideas of supply-side economics: unemployment came to be seen as a structural problem rooted in market distortions (disincentives, inflexibility, etc.). In accordance with this diagnosis, few initiatives were taken against rising unemployment.

2 Due to the 'Baumol effect' (Baumol 1967), public consumption nevertheless remained quite high as a percentage of GDP. For instance, in spite of economic growth from 1987 to 1991 alongside declining public consumption in real terms, public consumption as a percentage of GDP in fact increased.

3 As user charges and fees, etc. increased by 50.0 per cent from 1982 to 1992 and by 31.9 per cent from 1992 to 1996 (in 1980 prices), the production value of public consumption increased more.

4 Maternity allowances are equal to unemployment benefits but full compensation is most often ensured in collective agreements between employers and trade unions.

5   Average wage–benefit replacement ratio was lowered from about 0.70 to just below 0.65 (Pedersen *et al.* 1995: 41). Until 1966, replacement ratio was about 0.45 but then increased to a peak of 0.75 in 1972/73.

6   Working at slightly reduced hours remains popular, but according to the standard definition of full-time employment as 83 per cent of normal working hours, part-time employment has almost disappeared. Among 30–39-years-old women, the proportion of part-time employed declined from 35 per cent in 1982 to 7 per cent in 1997. This marks a 'second phase' of labour market integration following the 'first phase' from 1965 to 1982 when housewives disappeared and part-time employment exploded.

7   This must be seen in relation to the extremely liberal rules with regard to firing people, see also pp. 73–5.

8   Sources: Statistisk 10 års oversigt, S.E. Social Sikring og retsvæsen (various issues). S.E. Arbejdsmarked (various issues) AMS: Efterlønsstatistik; Nyt fra Danmarks Statistik.

9   Parental leave has mainly become an extension of maternity leave as compensation level has been reduced from 80 per cent of maximum unemployment benefits to 70 per cent in 1996 and 60 per cent in 1997. Municipalities may provide additional compensation but this has become rare.

10 The extension of leave arrangements in 1993 was motivated by the wish to improve unemployment (also for re-election purposes). Later, it was rationalised as a new philosophy of work and welfare.

11 This calculation is based on the most conservative assumptions but does not include a correction for a change in the pension system in 1984. However, the conclusion that old-age pensions have declined relative to GDP is robust to any combination of correction and assumptions.

12 At least for the 26 weeks necessary to begin a new unemployment period; it is usually not difficult to find a job, e.g. as a taxi driver or as a cleaning assistant.

13 An additional explanation may be the interests of the trade unions in controlling collective funds as the idea of economic democracy was finally buried in the 1980s.

References

Baumol, W. J. (1967) 'Macroeconomics of Unbalanced Growth', *American Economic Review*, 57, 2: 415–26.

Cameron, D. (1978) 'The Expansion of the Public Economy: A Comparative Analysis', *American Political Science Review*, 72, 4: 1243–60.

Christiansen, P.M. (1999) *Ej blot til pynt? Om budgettets politik og politikernes budget*, Aalborg: Rockwool Foundation/Aalborg University Press.

Christoffersen, M. N. (1996) 'Opvækst med arbejdsløshed. En forløbsundersøgelse af to generationer født 1966 og 1973', Publication 96:14, Copenhagen: Danish Institute of Social Research.

Council of Europe (1996, 1997) *Recent Democratic Developments in the Member States of the Council of Europe*, Strasbourg: Council of Europe.

Esping-Andersen, G. (1990) *The Three Worlds of Welfare Capitalism*, Princeton, NJ: Princeton University Press.

—— (1993) *Changing Classes*, London: Sage.

—— (1996) 'After the Golden Age? Welfare State Dilemmas in a Global Economy', in G.

Esping-Andersen (ed.) *Welfare States in Transition. National Adaptations in Global Economies,* London Sage.

European Commission (1994) *Employment in Europe, 1994.* Danish ed. 1995.

Gaasholt, Ø. and Togeby, L. (1996) *I syv sind,* Aarhus: Politica.

Goul Andersen, J. (1988) 'Vælgermosaik', Working Paper, Centre for Cultural Research, University of Aarhus.

—— (1992) 'De arbejdsomme danskene. Om Skatteplagede danskeres arbejdsvillighed og fleksibilitet', in E. Petersen *et al., De trivsomme og arbejdsomme danskere,* Aarhus: Department of Psychology/Aarhus University Press.

—— (1996) 'Marginalisation, Citizenship and the Economy: The Capacities of the Universalist Welfare State in Denmark', in E. O. Eriksen and J. Loftager (eds) *The Rationality of the Welfare State,* Oslo: Scandinavian University Press.

—— (1997) 'The Scandinavian Welfare Model in Crisis? Achievements and Problems of the Danish State in an Age of Unemployment and Low Growth', *Scandinavian Political Studies,* 20, 1: 1–31.

—— (1998) 'Velfærdens veje i komparativt Perspektiv', *Den jyske historiker,* 82 (December 1998): 114–38.

Goul Andersen, J. and Munk Christiansen, P. (1991) *Skatter uten velfærd. De offentlige udgifter i international belysning,* Copenhagen: Jurist- og Økonomiforbundets Forlag.

Goul Andersen, and Hoff, J. (1995) 'Lighed i den politiske deltagelse', in M. Madsen, H.J. Nielsen and G. Sjöblom (eds) *Demokratiets mangfoldighed. Tendenser i dansk Politik,* Copenhagen: Forlaget Politiske Studier.

Greve, C. (1997) 'Fra ideologi til pragmatisme? Træk af forvaltningspolitikken for privatisering i Danmark 1983–1996', in C. Greve (ed.) *Privatisering, selskapdannelser og udlicitering. Et politilogisk perspektiv på udviklingen i Danmark,* Aarhus: Systime.

Hirst, P. (1997) *Globalisering, demokrati og det civile samfund,* ed. Kaspersen, L. B., Copenhagen: Hans Reitzels Forlag.

Hirst, P. and Thompson, G. (1996) *Globalization in Question: The International Economy and the Possibilities of Governance,* Cambridge: Polity Press.

Hoff, J. (1993) 'Medborgerskab, brugerrolle og magt', in J. Andersen *et al. Medborgerskab. Demokrati og politisk Deltagelse,* Herning: Systime.

Inglehart, R. (1990) *Culture Shift in Advanced Industrial Societies.* Princeton, NJ: Princeton University Press.

Jensen, P. H. (1999) 'Activiation of the Unemployed in Denmark since the Early 1980s: Welfare or Workfare', CCWS Working Papers 1/1999, Aalborg University: Department of Economics, Politics, and Public Administration.

Jonassen, V. (1998) *Dansk socialpolitik 1708–1998: Menneske, økonomi, samfund – og social arbejde,* Aarhus: Den sociale Højskole.

Klaussen, K. K. and Ståhlberg, K. (eds) (1998) *New Public Management in Norden,* Odense: Odense University Press.

Kristensen, O. P. (1980) 'The Logic of Political Bureaucratic Decision Making as a Cause of Governmental Growth', *European Journal of Political Research,* 8: 249–64.

—— (1987) *Væksten i den offentlige sektor: Institutioner og politik,* Copenhagen: Jurist- og Økonomiforbundets Forlag.

Krugman, P. (1996) *Pop Internationalism,* Cambridge, MA: MIT Press.

Langager, K. (1997) 'Indsatsen over for de forsikrede ledige. Evaluering af arbejdsmarkedsreformen I', Publication 97: 20, Copenhagen: National Institute of Social Research.

Lassen, D. D. and Nielsen, S. B. (1996) 'Er skattebyrden højere end i andre europæiske lande?', paper, Economic Policy Research Unit, Copenhagen Business School.

Lindbeck, A. (1994) *Turning Sweden Around.*, Cambridge, MA: MIT Press.

Ministry of Finance (1994) Budgetredegørelse 1994 (ch. 1), Copenhagen: Ministry of Finance.

—— (1995) *Finansredegørelse 1995.* Copenhagen: Ministry of Finance.

—— (1996) *Finansredegørelse 1996.* Copenhagen: Ministry of Finance.

—— (1997) *Finansredegørelse 1997.* Copenhagen: Ministry of Finance.

Nationalbanken (1996) *Statens låntagning og gæld, 1996.* Copenhagen: Nationalbanken.

OECD (1994) *The OECD Jobs Study. Evidence and Explanations,* 1–2, Paris: OECD.

Offe, C. (1996) 'Full Employment: Asking the Wrong Question?', in E. O. Eriksen and J. Loftager (eds) *The Rationality of the Welfare State,* Oslo: Scandinavian University Press.

Pedersen, L., Pedersen, P. J. and Smith, N. (1995) 'The Working and the Non-working Populations in the Welfare State', in G. V. Mogensen (ed.) *Work Incentives in the Danish Welfare State,* Aarhus: Aarhus University Press/The Rockwool Foundation Research Unit.

Pedersen, P. J. (1993) 'The Welfare State and Taxation in Denmark', in A. B. Atkinson and G. V. Mogensen (eds) *Welfare and Work Incentives. A North European Perspective,* Oxford: Clarendon Press.

Pedersen, P. J. and Smith, N. (1995) 'Unemployment and Incentives', in G. V. Mogensen (ed.) *Work Incentives in the Danish Welfare State. New Empirical Evidence,* Aarhus: The Rockwool Foundation Research Unit/Aarhus University Press.

Petersen, E., Kristensen, O. S., Sabroe, K.-E. and Sommerlund, B. (1987) *Danskernes tilværelse under krisen, I-II,* Aarhus: Aarhus University Press.

Petersen, J.-H. (1990) 'The Danish 1891 Act on Old Age Relief: A Response to Agrarian Demand and Pressure', *Journal of Social Policy,* 19, 1: 69–91.

Regeringen (1993) *Ny kurs mod bedre tider.* Copenhagen: The Danish Government.

Rhodes, M. (1995) 'West European Welfare States in the Global Economy', paper, Manchester: Department of Government and Florence: EUI.

Rold Andersen, B. (1993) 'The Nordic Welfare State Under Pressure: The Danish Experience', *Polity and Politics,* 21, 2: 109–20.

Roseweare, D., Lebfritz, W., Fore, D. and Wurzel, E. (1996) 'Ageing Populations, Pension Systems and Government Budgets: Simulations for 20 OECD Countries', Economic Department Working Papers 168, Paris: OECD.

Schøler, S. (2000) 'En oversigt over evalueringer af arbejdsmarkedspolitikken i Danmark', Arbejdsnotat 1/99, Aalborg University: CCWS, Deptartment of Economics, Politics and Public Administration.

Smith, N. (1998) *Arbejde, incitamenter og ledighed,* Aarhus: Aarhus University Press/Rockwool Foundation Research Unit.

Statistics Denmark (various years) *Statistiske efterretninger. Social sikring og retsvæsen,* Copenhagen.

Taylor-Gooby, P. (1996) 'The Response of Government: Fragile Convergence?', in V. George and P. Taylor-Gooby (eds) *European Welfare Policy. Squaring the Welfare Circle,* London: Routledge.

Togeby, L. (1987) 'Notat om børnepasningsdækningen i de nordiske lande' (mimeo). Aarhus: Department of Political Science, Aarhus University.

Torfing, J. (1999) 'Workfare with Welfare: Recent Reforms of the Danish Welfare State', *Journal of European Social Policy,* 9, 1: 5–28.

Van Stenbergen, B. (1994) *The Condition of Citizenship.* London: Sage.

6 Exploring the sustainable limits of public expenditure in the British welfare state[1]

Richard Parry

Introduction: sustainability from Conservative to Labour governments

The British General Election of 1 May 1997 produced the biggest-ever election victory for the Labour Party. Labour regained political power after 18 years, but it was much less clear that they would pursue the reinstatement of any socialist welfare state project. Influenced by the examples of Bill Clinton in the United States and Paul Keating in Australia, Labour had concluded that their route to power lay in the projection of fiscal safety to middle-class and skilled working-class wage-earners with families. This involved an appropriation of some aspects of Thatcherism – 'toughness', encouragement of work and respectable families, retention of earnings rather than their redistribution. This was in line with the personality of Tony Blair, Labour's leader. Like Clinton, Blair is generally progressive but seems to have a cautious streak and is happy to present a changing selection of policies framed by trusted advisers to win voter appeal. While an impressive example of political communication, Labour's approach now lacks ideological content or strong roots in the prior history of the party.

These cautious tendencies ensure a continuation of an important argument under the Conservative government – on the level of public demand on the national economy. The governments of Margaret Thatcher (1979–90) and John Major (1990–97) tried to roll back the state, and did deregulate industrial policy. But in social policy they preserved a structure of flat-rate state pension and benefits, income support for those without resources, and a largely free, non-billed National Health Service.

Recent academic argument on the sustainability of the British welfare state (such as Pierson (1994)) has placed great stress on the durability of public support for at least some welfare programmes, especially those whose impact had diffused throughout the class structure. Hence, in this view, the Thatcher project despite efforts was not in most areas able to make great headway in its attempt to retrench the welfare state. This does indeed provide an explanation for the continuing high level of welfare expenditure in the national economy. It had been assumed that Labour's return to power would remove constraints on support for welfare being expressed in new or more expensive policies. But there is an alternative hypothesis:

that policy-making on welfare is set on economic grounds relatively autonomously of interest and opinion structures. In this approach, on the public opinion side, survey evidence favouring pro-welfare sentiments reflects an aspiration independent of factors having a decisive influence on electoral choice; and on the governmental side, spending on welfare becomes dependent on permission from the guardians of the national economy – the Treasury and its ministerial head, the Chancellor of the Exchequer. The way that this permission has been granted or withheld in recent British social policy is the focus of this chapter.

The Treasury, uniting the functions of finance, economics and budget ministries, has long served for the Labour Party as a symbol of the repeated frustration of the party's hopes in government. Therefore Labour's initial period in office has provided an important case study. The background to it is the way that the values of the Treasury have fallen into some sort of concordance with those of what the party calls 'new Labour'. From 1992 Labour's economic policies were in the hands of Gordon Brown, Blair's 'older brother' figure who decided not to oppose Blair for the party leadership in 1994 but whose intellect and grasp of economics surpasses his leader's, producing a strong but potentially uneasy relationship.

On 2 May 1997, he entered the Treasury for the first time as Chancellor of the Exchequer and was greeted by the spontaneous applause of officials as he walked up the main staircase of the building. Such a welcome, though useful, was not orchestrated by senior management as the then Permanent Secretary (chief civil servant), Sir Terry Burns, was keen to point out (Burns 1997). But here it seems very likely that he and his senior colleagues shared in this enthusiasm, which is not just a matter of professional satisfaction at managing the transition to a new government. The probability is that most Treasury officials concurred with the basic philosophy of 'new Labour', which came to office with a commitment to adopt an approach closely in line with the mission and objectives of the Treasury as these had evolved over the past five years.

The background to Labour's expenditure strategy

Against all the comparative evidence, public expenditure in Britain has been conceptualised as a problem by both main political parties – by the Conservatives as part of a pro-private sector philosophy, but also by Labour as part of its efforts to be fiscally responsible and to appeal to the tax-cutting instincts of voters. The evidence (Table 6.1) shows that the ratio of public expenditure to Gross Domestic Product (GDP) in Britain fluctuated according to the economic cycle during the years of Conservative rule but did not fall markedly. After a panic in 1975–76, when the ratio rose to a post-war peak of nearly 50 per cent, the Labour government of 1974–79 reduced it sharply under pressure from the International Monetary Fund and left office with real terms expenditure little higher than when it entered. The Conservative record was one of much stronger real terms growth (35 per cent over the Thatcher and Major governments).

The most meaningful aggregate has been the so-called General Government Expenditure (X) which excludes privatisation proceeds. This fell below 40 per

Table 6.1 The long-term record on public expenditure in the British economy

	Control total (from 1992–93) %GDP	General %GDP	Government expenditure (X) real terms, £bn	GGE[a] %GDP
Labour				
1974–75 (first year)		46.7	227.2	48.8
1975–76 (peak)		47.2	227.9	49.3
1979–80 (last year)		42.4	229.6	43.9
Conservative				
1982–83 (peak)		45.5	242.7	47.3
1988–89 (trough)		38.0	255.8	37.8
1992–93	38.25	43.4	291.3	42.9
1993–94 (peak)	37.5	43.2	297.2	43.2
1994–95	36.4	42.7	306.3	42.5
1995–96	35.8	42.3	301.5	42.7
1996–97	34.5	40.9	307.9 (price base)	41.1
Labour				
1997–98	33.2	39.2	304.4	39.8
1998–99 (est.)	33.0	39.2	308.9	39.9

Source: HM Treasury (1998a table B24, 1998b table 3.1).

Note
a   General government expenditure. GGE(X) is the best measure as it excludes privatisation
    proceeds.

cent during the boom of the late 1980s but then rose to over 43 per cent in 1992 as
tax receipts fell off during the recession, producing a public sector deficit which
peaked at nearly 8 per cent of GDP in 1993–94. The deficit then fell to below the
Maastricht reference level, and in its last Budget (November 1996) the
Conservative government adopted a target ratio of public spending to GDP of
under 40 per cent. These figures are consistently about 5–6 percentage points
less than the EU average, though the lead is less marked when transfer
payments are excluded. EU evidence also suggests that the low level of direct
taxation of British social benefits closes most of the gap with European
comparators when net spending is considered (European Commission 1998:
10). Spending on health is notably low in Britain, because of the government's
position as supplier and financier of about 85 per cent of health spending.
Government claims that spending was increasing in real terms every year,
and by cumulatively large amounts (see Table 6.1) diverted the debate away
from voter demand for services and suggested that these increases were a
political or economic problem.

   What are the implications of these figures for the 'sustainability' concept? Even
in its least favourable years, the state of the British fiscal balance has elicited little

political rhetoric about any crisis of welfare. Successful European economies run much higher levels of public sector activity and tax-benefit transfers. Expenditure in Britain is influenced by strong top-down mechanisms, the effective absence of demarcated funding for pensions or health, and the dependence of sub-national government on central funds (local government raising less than 20 per cent of its own revenue). Expansions of welfare expenditure on the French or German model by levying increased contributions to cope with rising costs or demands would not happen. From 1993, top-down management was operationalised by the device of the 'control total' which covered 85–90 per cent of public spending (excluding debt interest and cyclical (unemployment-related) social security). The Cabinet agreed the total (in cash terms) for the financial year forthcoming on 1 April in the previous summer and autumn, and these were then allocated between departments by a Cabinet committee on public expenditure chaired by the Chancellor of the Exchequer (known as EDX under the Conservatives and PX under Labour). Once they are announced in the budget they cannot be amended by parliament or re-opened by ministers. The British approach is explicitly top-down, in line with the centralising bias of the British state. Resisting breaches of the control total became an end in itself, and the mechanism for expressing public demand for taxing and spending is suppressed. In the 1992 election, the Labour opposition presented a programme of tax rises and increased spending. After that election was lost, Labour moved closer to the Conservative position that income tax rises were politically untenable and that the ambitions of spending departments had to be contained. In the process, Labour's notion of sustainability started to approximate to that of the Treasury.

Recent themes in the Treasury's approach to social policy

The British Treasury stands at the heart of British government and has grown in importance as economic policy has come to dominate British politics (see the major accounts by Heclo and Wildavsky (1974) and Thain and Wright (1995) and the recent ones by Corry (1997) and Chapman (1997)). It is characterised by a keen political awareness and a preparedness to engage in candid debate with politicians. Its chief minister – the Chancellor of the Exchequer – has become second only to the Prime Minister in authority and influence and it has a second minister in the Cabinet – the Chief Secretary to the Treasury, who is in charge of public expenditure. After the First World War, it won the right of referral about all government business and became the centre of control of public administration. After the Second World War, it used the importance of managing the exchange rate and the balance of payments to assert its primacy, and a 'pro-growth' spin-off, the Department of Economic Affairs (1964–69), had a short life. Other 'central' departments and units have been seen off, and the Prime Minister's own staff has never developed a serious capability to rival the Treasury's economic analysis. However, despite the lack of such capacity at No. 10 Downing Street, in the last resort that is where political authority resides, making the state of mutual confidence with No. 11 (the residence of the Chancellor) an important indicator of the stability of the government. Nigel Lawson's resignation as Chancellor in 1989, closely followed by that of Alan Walters, the special adviser appointed by Prime Minister Margaret Thatcher to second-guess Lawson's economic policies, emphasised the centrality of the Prime Minister–Chancellor relationship and the political risks if it went wrong (see Lawson's superb memoirs (1992)).

Organisational developments have taken forward the Treasury's readiness to get involved in micro-economic practice. In 1995 the Treasury put itself through a major internal reorganisation after the Fundamental Expenditure Review conducted by Jeremy Heywood (a middle-ranking and fast-rising official, from 1997 in Tony Blair's private office) and Colin Southgate (who chairs the EMI music business and now the Royal Opera House) (HM Treasury 1994). Through a combination of a self-denying mentality, a wish to set an example to other departments, and an interest in theories of delayering and empowerment, the Treasury lost 25 per cent of senior management posts and sought to live on even thinner staffing than before. In addition, the Treasury sought to set up internal dynamics in its spending function, in which organisational form followed objectives (Parry *et al.* 1997).

The Treasury's role has also been enhanced by a concern to appraise public sector activity and relate it to modern needs, rather than just drift with an incremental pattern of expenditure. A series of fundamental reviews of departmental programmes, known as the 'Portillo reviews' after their initiator as Chief Secretary in 1993, Michael Portillo, opened up departmental programmes to systematic scrutiny – a process in which the Treasury spending teams participated actively. The new ethos of public sector managerialism let them promote value for money as a universal device for intervention, reaching a peak in the unpublished (but leaked) 1996 paper *Strategic Considerations for the Treasury 2000 to 2005*, in which a small group of younger Treasury officials set out the likely policy developments that would influence the Treasury's organisation in the years ahead, and when leaked (*The Times* 17 June 1996) was misinterpreted as a clumsy grab for hegemony on the Treasury's part. Considering how its organisation might have to change under a Labour government was part of the Treasury's extensive preparation for the election (Burns 1997).

What has been clearly established over the recent past is the legitimacy of the Treasury's overall role in policy-making across government as it affects the workings of the economy (Deakin and Parry 1993). The Treasury's aims, mission and objectives are now set out formally (in the Treasury's annual public expenditure plans and elsewhere) and assert that the Treasury has views of its own which go beyond pursuing the economic policy of the government of the day. Under the Conservatives the overall aim was 'to promote rising prosperity based on sustained economic growth' (HM Treasury 1997b: chart 1A). These objectives were the Treasury's expression of what they took to be a consensus, capable of surviving a change of government, on the market-based nature of the economy. They run counter to the Beveridge idea of the government as the primary actor in the welfare state.

In Labour's summary objectives in their 1997 election manifesto, there is a concordance of language and approach: 'we will provide stable economic growth with low inflation, and promote dynamic and competitive business and industry at home and abroad'. This is flanked by 'we will help build strong families and strong communities, and lay the foundations of a modern welfare state in pensions and community care', but the spending pledges imply redistribution rather than increase: 'we will increase the share of national income spent on education as we decrease it on the bills of economic and social failure' and, for the NHS, 'reducing spending on administration and increasing spending on patient care'. Leaving to one side the implicit conceptualisation of social security as 'the bills of economic and social failure' (a very Treasury-friendly idea) we can note a convergence of strategy here which even before Labour took office implied a radical departure from the party's traditional faith in state action and corresponding distrust of the Treasury. It was no surprise when Labour's stated aim for the Treasury was set as 'to raise the rate of sustainable growth, and achieve rising prosperity, through creating economic and employment opportunities for all' – a slightly different emphasis from the Conservatives, but within the same conceptual world (HM Treasury 1998c: chart 1A).

The inheritance: the context of public finances

On public expenditure, Labour inherited a basically favourable economic climate but a Conservative proposition (held but not usually implemented during their 18 years of government) that the public sector should not encroach any further on the economy. By the last Conservative year (1996–97) education and health were stable as a share of GDP. Health was at 5.4 per cent, up from the 4.6 per cent when the Conservatives had entered office and education had fallen from 5.4 per cent to 4.9 per cent over the same period. In contrast, social security had shown strong underlying growth which, with the impact of the recession, had taken it from 10.2 per cent in 1990–91 to 13.1 per cent in 1993–94. The economic recovery and changed policies had started to reduce these shares even before Labour took office, and all three of the ratios fell in 1997–98 (HM Treasury 1998b: table 3.4).

The Conservatives' 1996 Budget planned for modest real terms growth in the two years from 1996–97 to 1998–99 but behind the likely rise in GDP. Therefore the issue facing Labour was whether to associate themselves with a Conservative strategy that was fiscally cautious but implied a further squeeze on social expenditure in the economy, or to take the opportunity of a recovering economy to expand social policy in line with voter preferences and the party's own traditions. Labour's decision to choose the first of these approaches in its initial period in office was a crucial indicator of the way that the 'Treasury line' had come to dominate British social policy.

Labour's election mantra was that it had no uncosted expenditure commitments. Its seven economic pledges in the manifesto were: fair taxes; no risks with inflation; strict rules for government borrowing ('over the economic cycle' not borrowing to fund current expenditure and maintaining a 'stable and prudent' level of public debt); stick to planned public spending allocations for the first two years of office; switch spending from economic failure to investment (by spending reviews); tax reform to promote saving and investment; a welfare-to-work Budget within two months after the election (actually a day late). The key decision was the acceptance of Conservative departmental spending plans until 1999, and the provenance of this pledge reveals much about the approach of the Labour Treasury.

Labour's tax and spend pledge

Labour was under strong pressure in late 1996 and early 1997 to decide whether it wished to continue the policy on which it had fought previous elections of allowing taxation and spending to drift upwards, in response to the party's own instincts and opinion survey evidence that the electorate wished public services to be improved. While there had been some interest in raising the top rate to 50 per cent, the announcement by Gordon Brown on 20 January 1997 that the rates would not be increased during the first Labour term was in line with the worldwide downward pressure on headline income tax rates. It left vast scope for revenue enhancement through the tax relief and indirect tax systems, as Brown did in his first Budget by removing tax exemptions for pension funds.

What was surprising was the decision announced in the same speech to accept Conservative spending plans by department as well as in aggregate and for 1998–99 as well as 1997–98. The logic was that the new Labour ministers would not spend their first year discussing how to spend more money, but would rather work out with their civil servants how to reorder their existing budgets in order to fit them with Labour's priorities (Brown 1997: 7–8). Subsequent press interviews by Brown made it clear that he was seeking to break away from the annual cycle of bidding for more money. Labour's stated rationale for this approach was that the high level of public sector deficit during an upswing in the economic cycle left them no alternative. But the primary effect of Brown's strategy may be seen as not so much to stick to Conservative plans, but to find some device for neutralising the natural tendencies of any new left-of-centre government to use public expenditure in pursuit of its objectives. Similar pressures, though resisted less rigorously, faced Lionel Jospin in France in 1997 and Gerhard Schröder in Germany in 1998.

The Treasury's interpretation of the rational choices facing politicians suggested to them that new governments could not enter office without spending pledges which would then be promoted by both departmental ministers and their civil servants. This had been the experience of the Labour governments of both 1964 and 1974 (especially in respect of pensions and housing) when it had taken two painful years before financial orthodoxy was reasserted. The 1964 Labour government was the final flourish of the attempt to manage the economy and manipulate domestic demand in a context of fixed exchange rates and vulnerability to balance of payments crises. In 1974 the Treasury and its ministers became detached from the rest of the government but eventually prevailed in 1976 once

Prime Minister James Callaghan agreed with his Chancellor Denis Healey that cuts in the public sector deficit insisted upon by the International Monetary Fund were inescapable. What is remarkable is that the latter periods of both governments were the most successful recent periods of containing public expenditure in real terms. The post-devaluation squeeze of 1968, and the cash limits of 1976, overachieved their purpose and left the overall record of the governments as an uncomfortable roller coaster. No Labour government has in practice been able to assert a consistent, distinctive spending philosophy over that of the Treasury. The difference with Labour's 1997 Treasury team (Brown and his Chief Secretary Alistair Darling) is that they sought to make a virtue out of necessity and establishing a reputation for fiscal rectitude – to reassure the markets – and synoptic control – to dominate the spending departments – right from the start.

Labour's initial impact at the Treasury

Chancellor Gordon Brown and Chief Secretary Alistair Darling are both from a Scottish presbyterian background. They are epitomes of the cautious, correct politician, serious and intelligent about the job and preferring to formulate clear policies within small groups of trusted advisers. Brown brought with him into the Treasury a quartet of special advisers – Ed Balls, Ed Miliband, Andrew Maugham and personal 'spin doctor' Charlie Whelan – and they provided a bridge between pre- and post-election policy formation which cuts across the official Treasury to a greater extent than seen under previous Chancellors. The distribution of the advisory function between officials and special advisers was the main transition issue within the Brown Treasury, rather than any dispute about policy content. As *The Economist* put it, 'this is leading to some chaos. Mr Brown sweeps through with his entourage of political trusties leaving would-be allies among officials out in the cold' (5 July 1997). In the summer the civil servant who was the Chancellor's Press Officer left when it became clear that her role had been diminished, and the position of the Permanent Secretary Sir Terry Burns seemed insecure; he eventually took early retirement in 1998.

The Labour Treasury made a dramatic start when on 6 May it transferred power to set base interest rates to a new monetary policy committee of the Bank of England. This decision was only revealed to Treasury officials the day after the election, despite their extensive contact with Brown's team during the campaign (Burns 1997). Then on 22 May it announced the transfer of the Bank of England's role on financial services supervision to an enlarged version of the present Securities and Investments Board (to be known as the Financial Services Authority). These decisions had no direct bearing on public spending, but they did reveal a strategic vision of the place of a modern finance ministry, inspired by American and German models – the role of an Alan Greenspan or Hans Tietmeyer to be the guardian of interest rates and reassure the markets, leaving the finance ministry politicians less exposed.

The interest rate policy was just compatible with the manifesto commitment to 'reform the Bank of England to ensure that decision-making on monetary policy is

more effective, open, accountable and free from short-term political manipulation', but the way it was done was in the tradition of Treasury 'bouncing' of
government into rapid action under the guise of market sensitivity – in short, not
open, accountable and free from short-term political manipulation. The new
monetary policy committee raised interest rates at its first meeting and continued
to do so well into 1998 before the economic slowdown prompted cuts; the
likelihood is that its access to only the one instrument, rather than the range of
responses available to government, would cause interest rates to err on the high
side in the long term.

The financial services decision was a countervailing surprise, effectively
dividing the Bank of England rather like the Treasury–Department of Economic
Affairs split of 1964. It replaced the present informal system of managing errant
financial institutions with a much more rigid structure. It was not foreshadowed
in the manifesto as, normally, major policy decisions of this kind might be
expected to be. Again, the decision-making technique was that of the omnipotent
Treasury, cutting back on the Bank as a correction to the extended role on interest
rates it had gained.

This style unites a traditional approach of the Treasury to that of the Brown
team, carried through from Opposition – to formulate a policy within his close
circle and then use the authority of the office to drive it through with the
minimum of discussion. Blair signalled his confidence in Brown by allowing him
to chair the Cabinet's Economic Affairs Committee (usually done by the Prime
Minister) as well as the Public Expenditure Committee. In practice, Brown
seemed to prefer his regular one-to-one meetings with the Prime Minister as his
source of advice.

When Brown's first Budget came on 2 July 1997, it offered a fairly optimistic
picture of the public finances and confirmed that the hard-to-forecast variable is
income, not expenditure. The main thrust of the Budget was the pursuit of fiscal
stability through a more rapid contraction of the deficit than had seemed likely
before. The Public Sector Borrowing Requirement was already falling more
rapidly than forecast because of buoyant tax revenues. It was now given a major
push downwards to be little more than half the projected level in 1997–98 and only
a third in 1998–99 (Table 6.2). The control total for 1996–97 came out at £260.4 bn,
£0.2 bn less than forecast in the November Budget, and receipts were £286.3 bn
against a forecast of £280.9 bn. The income tax yield was £76.5 bn against the
£71.8 bn forecast, showing how buoyant it can be when the economy is doing well.
Because of its squeeze on spending at a time of healthy GDP growth, Labour was
in a position to do better than the Conservatives in meeting the latter's target of
bringing public spending to less than 40 per cent of GDP; it was set to be under 39
per cent by the time the new Labour plans started in 1999 (Table 6.2).

The strategy of not having a spending round created a data gap. Because this
Budget did not alter departmental control totals, they were implicitly read over
from the 1996 Clarke Budget. Moreover, Brown abolished not just the 1997
spending round but also the 1997 unified Budget: there was a 'pre-Budget
statement' in November floating some policy initiatives by not providing much

Table 6.2 Labour's inheritance of improving public finances 1996–98 (figures in billion £)[1]

	Government	*1996–97*	*1997–98*	*1998–99*
Control total	CON 96	260.6	266.5	274.0
	LAB 97	**260.4**	**266.4**	**273.6**
	LAB 98	*259.8*	*264.1*	*274.9*
Cyclical social security	CON 96	14.3	14.1	14.0
	LAB 97	**14.3**	**13.7**	**14.0**
	LAB 98	*14.0*	*12.8*	*13.0*
Central government debt interest	CON 96	22.2	24.8	24.0
	LAB 97	**22.3**	**24.6**	**24.4**
	LAB 98	*22.0*	*24.3*	*24.6*
Accounting adjustments	CON 96	10.3	9.2	10.0
	LAB 97	**11.4**	**10.1**	**10.7**
	LAB 98	*12.2*	*11.0*	*12.2*
General government expenditure (X)	CON 96	322.0	307.4	324.7
	LAB 97	**308.4**	**315.3**	**324.7**
	LAB 98	*307.9*	*312.6*	*326.5*
Ratio of GCE (X) to GDP	CON 96	41.25	40.0	39.0
	LAB 97	**41.0**	**39.5**	**38.75**
	LAB 98	*40.9*	*39.2*	*39.2*
GGE after privatisation receipts and adjustments	CON 96	308.5	319.0	327.0
	LAB 97	**309.0**	**319.4**	**331.3**
	LAB 98	*309.1*	*317.1*	*332.5*
Central government receipts	CON 96	280.9	299.4	315.0
	LAB 97	**286.3**	**308.3**	**327.2**
	LAB 98	*286.4*	*313.1*	*330.1*
PSBR after adjustment	CON 96	26.4	19.2	12.0
	LAB 97	**22.7**	**10.9**	**4.0**
	LAB 98	*22.7*	*2.6*	*2.3*

Source: HM Treasury (1996 table 5.3, 1997c table 2.4, 1998a tables B3 and B24).

Note
1 The table displays figures for the following governments: Conservative, November 1996 (CON 96); Labour, July 1997 (LAB 97); Labour, March 1998 (LAB 98).

new spending data, and the main Budget reverted to its traditional March date. Clarke had plans for 1999–2000, and projections of aggregates through to 2002–03, but all that Brown provided was a table of illustrative assumptions for given tax rates and economic variables, not for choices on the level of public spending (HM Treasury 1997c: table 4.7). Brown sought to demonstrate that he was meeting his golden rule of not borrowing to pay for current consumption; he did not draw attention to the contraction of the public sector in the economy that more than matched the plans of his predecessors and could only imply an inability of the public sector to meet likely demands for health, education and income maintenance.

The improving economic picture that Labour had inherited continued to improve. By the time of the March 1998 Budget virtually all the aggregates had improved compared with the 1997 estimates. Receipts were up markedly, expenditure down. The Public Sector Borrowing Requirement for 1997–98 shrunk to £2.6 bn. In the event, the control total for 1997–98 turned out to be even less than estimated at £262.6 bn, allowing some of the unspent money from that year to be reallocated to 1998–99 (HM Treasury 1998e: table 1).

Labour's welfare to work policies

The Budget was presented as the launch of a 'modernisation' (a favourite Labour word) of the entire welfare state. In practice, it turned out to consist principally of the promised 'welfare-to-work' strategy, which bears some resemblance to earlier workfare strategies. By targeting those aged 18–25 and unemployed for six months, and withdrawing their benefit unless they accept a training place, the policy in effect raised the age of the majority for a right to income maintenance from 18 to 25. The age of 25 is of little significance sociologically, being above the age at which education will normally have been completed and family and housing responsibilities may have been taken on. Hardship cases are defined narrowly, and they will receive only 60 per cent of the benefit level.

While the benefit restrictions are under the government's control, the provision of jobs or training places relies on the private and voluntary sectors – especially through the diversion of public money to employers to take on the young or long-term unemployed. While the intentions have won wide support the instruments (summarised in Table 6.3) are less secure. The dangers that this approach will in effect subsidise or displace existing jobs have been understood since the 1970s and creates a risk of an imbalance, with funds being released fairly freely for welfare-to-work (especially to the young unemployed) but constrained tightly elsewhere in the public finances (in fact, during the first year of the measures money was reallocated away from the young unemployed and towards the older unemployed and the disabled).

The notion of the policies being 'funded from the windfall tax' was cosmetic. It was a temporary (£2.6 bn in each of 1997–98 and 1998–99), general tax on privatised firms rather than an expression of monopoly or windfall status. Moreover, the tax is used not just to fund welfare to work but also the so-called New Deal for Schools, which is an extra £300 m a year of schools capital expenditure designed to correct the years of minimal funding for this in the normal education budget. What is significant is that welfare-to-work spending financed by the windfall tax, a much lesser annual sum because it is to be spread over a longer period, is not counted in the control total. The government, resting on its manifesto approach, was reluctant to embody welfare to work in any way as a normal part of public expenditure during its first term. This meant that Brown

Table 6.3 Welfare-to-work measures in Britain

£	Peak annual expenditure	Total expenditure 1997–2002
£60 per week to employers for 6 months for taking on a 16–25-year-old out of work 6+months	830	3,150
£ per week to employers for 6 months for taking on those out of work 2+ years	100	350
Advice, training, day and after-school child care for lone parents	60	200
Help for disabled and those on incapacity benefit		200

Source: HM Treasury (1997a table 2.1).

had both a 'brand' and a source of money to pursue his own social policy. In his March 1998 Budget he took forward this approach by an ambitious new fiscal instrument – a 'Working Families Tax Credit' to maintain the incomes of households in work and replace Family Credit, a social security benefit. This expressed Brown's view that income tax credits were a politically acceptable way of providing incentives to enter and remain in work (Deakin and Parry 1998). Child benefit was also increased, a response to the vote of 47 Labour MPs in December 1997 against the removal of premiums on benefit for new lone parents – an implementation of a Conservative policy included in their spending plans. This vote had alerted the government to the uncertain acceptability of their strategy to their supporters, though in the end the decision of principle to end special help to lone parent households was asserted.

The outcome of the comprehensive spending reviews

Despite his declared intention of following Conservative plans, Brown was happy to inject additions of expenditure to health, education and social security for 1997–98 and 1998–99 on four occasions, his Budgets of July 1997 and March 1998, and his pre-Budget statements of November 1997 and November 1998. This was done by using shortfalls in expenditure on other programmes, allocating the expenditure reserve, and using windfall tax money. In July 1997 education and health were boosted by 6 and 3 per cent respectively for 1998–99. In both of the years, last-minute additions to health spending were used to avert pressure on the service during the winter. Pensioner households were provided with extra money to help with fuel bills.

These additions compromised but did not overturn Labour's intention to have a disjunction in policy in April 1999. Before that, there was in principle no departure from Conservative plans, public spending was falling to under 40 per cent of GDP, there was no argument in the ministerial public expenditure committee, and there was a demarcation of spending on new Labour policies from those that were inherited. Afterwards was a zero-based reconstruction of public expenditure on Labour principles based on full spending reviews and constrained only by a commitment to a low public sector deficit and no increases in income tax rates. The public expenditure system as it had evolved represented a compromise between incremental and zero-based budgeting which was politically realistic and could be sustained on a multi-year basis. Now, we were to have a 'big bang' in which Labour declared itself on public expenditure 15 months after entering office. Managing this process depended on the success of the Comprehensive Spending Reviews which were undertaken in the year up to July 1998.

Labour's spending reviews were a continuation of the Treasury technique of fundamental review to gain leverage over policy and expose what are seen as complacent and self-interested spending department approaches. The Portillo reviews from 1993 and the associated senior management reviews let the Treasury into policy debate within departments. It is difficult to see how the identification of issues and spending demands could have been much different under Labour, even if the conclusions drawn might be, and the status of the reviews as a simultaneous whole government exercise will focus decision-making. The official line was an exhortation of the 1970s zero-based budget approach and gives little credit to the difficulties of these exercises.

When the terms of reference of the reviews were announced on 24 June 1997 they were not to a consistent format – there was a mention of a zero-based approach in some but not all, some quotes from the Labour manifesto (health), some pledges to redefine objectives to make them consonant with government priorities, some analytical in approach (housing), others fairly empty. An interesting feature were the seven cross-departmental reviews, some chaired by the Treasury. What was also striking was the abbreviated timescale – departments were to present early findings in September and October 1997, and detailed proposals by November in preparation for a comprehensive review by the PX Cabinet committee in spring 1998. In the event, this proved optimistic. The Social Security review proved very difficult, and there were so many leaks about likely cuts that the interim report was not shown to ministers until Tony Blair had taken control of the policy process in December 1997 by chairing a new Cabinet committee on welfare reform. But through a great effort inside the Prime Minister's Office and the Treasury the reports were brought together in time for a summary version to be published in July 1998. Along the way it was decided to set budgets for most departments (but not social security) for the three years from 1999–2000 and set a new control aggregate of 'Total Managed Expenditure', close to general government expenditure and reabsorbing cyclical social security. An Economic and Fiscal Strategy (HM Treasury 1998d) set 'golden rules' about borrowing only to invest and made it clear that any spending increases were to be within a framework of control and austerity.

The results of the Comprehensive Spending Reviews represented a real injection of new expenditure into Labour's favoured areas, health and education.

Between 1999 and 2002, education was set to rise by 5.1 per cent annually in real terms, and health by 4.7 per cent (HM Treasury 1998f: chart 1). Over the whole life of the government, these increases are less impressive but still a perceptible boost – health up by 18 per cent and education by 19 per cent; the relative loser was social security at 6 per cent (HM Treasury 1998f: tables 2 and A3). The government had decided to turn away from the containment of public expenditure below 40 per cent of GDP and allow it to settle at 40–41 per cent for the rest of the parliament. Constraints were imposed on the use of this money. Departments have been made to enter into 'Public Service Agreements' incorporating hundreds of performance indicators (HM Treasury 1998g). And even though resources were increased there was a limit to radical reform, as the failure of Frank Field's exercise to reform welfare indicates.

Mobilising resources for the welfare state: Frank Field's approach

Labour MP Frank Field, a former Director of the Child Poverty Action Group, has become the keeper of Labour's conscience on comprehensive, Beveridgean welfare as opposed to the targeted, means-tested approach favoured by the Treasury. Field won general respect for his ability and imagination as Chairman of the House of Commons Social Security Committee (which like all such committees had a Conservative majority until 1997 but produced generally non-partisan reports). In 1995 he had suggested a radical 'stakeholder's insurance scheme' (Field 1995) which would mobilise self-interest and private finance. In an article written hours before he was unexpectedly appointed by Blair as 'Minister of State for the Reform of Welfare' at the Department of Social Security, Field put the dilemma of British welfare neatly:

> The British electorate want high Continental benefit levels with low American tax rates. There is no way this dream can be met. With taxpayers unwilling to pay more for better services, the control of the services needs to be handed over to the taxpayers themselves. New forms of collective provision, which have nothing to do with state provision, will need to be urgently considered. Such reforms would go beyond controlling the welfare bill. They should be considered as rebuilding intermediate institutions which form the very basis of a pluralistic democracy.
>
> (*Sunday Telegraph*, 4 May 1997)

Field's only practical suggestion in this article for 'unlocking the welfare budget', as he put it, was to finance student grants privately, but he had the previous year recommended the greater use of National Insurance contributions to fund much more of unemployment insurance, the Health Service, and long-term care (Field 1996). This manifesto may have won him a place in Blair's government but it was not easy to take further in a short-term economic context. It suggests that people must face up to the cost implications of the welfare they are demanding, and then organise and pay for the service through the most efficient public or private channels (for instance, by demarcating health service financing from the rest of taxation and levying contributions necessary to maintain the assessed needs of the service). Such an approach might well involve a higher *de facto* income tax as the only way of getting more money into the system, but this is proving more and more difficult politically for Labour.

The Field review proved difficult to carry forward because Field's approach ran counter to the less universalistic, more targeted strategy of the Treasury. Field, working at one remove from the Comprehensive Spending Reviews, produced a draft Green (consultative) paper on welfare reform in autumn 1997, but its publication was held up until March 1998 after the Budget as the government grappled with the philosophical implications it raised. The document was a disappointment (Department of Social Security 1998a). It set out very few proposals even in a tentative form, instead providing an analysis to show why the welfare state was no longer achieving its purpose, why reform was necessary and what the measures of successful reform might be. Field's position within his department weakened and he finally resigned in July 1998, with Alistair Darling moving from the Treasury to become Secretary of State for Social Security. Brown said in an interview, 'he [Field] said his proposals involved redistribution. That would mean people had to pay more taxes' (*Daily Mail*, 31 July 1998).

In late 1998, Darling produced his policy proposals. Widows' and incapacity benefits were to be made more means-tested and an interview as a gateway to benefit was to be made compulsory for all new benefit claimants of working age, irrespective of their contributions record (Department of Social Security 1998b). More importantly, a pensions proposal called for the abolition of the State Earnings-Related Pension Scheme (after a transitional period) in favour of a flat-rate pay-as-you-go State Second Pension for low earners; others outside occupational schemes were to be given fiscal encouragement, but not compelled, to take out a stakeholder pension on Field's model (Department of Social Security 1998c). By modern standards the degree of comprehensive provision mandated by government was low, and the proposals were seen as a victory for Treasury thinking concerned with immediate impact on expenditure and reluctant to impose obligations on employers and the state.

Conclusion: the Treasury's power-base in welfare reform

The Treasury's position under Brown became very strong in 1997. He was the first Chancellor since Nigel Lawson to have a clear sense of a wider role for the Treasury in setting priorities for the government as a whole. As a friendly critic, John Lloyd, put it in *The Times*, 'he conceives of the Treasury as the headquarters of an industrial conglomerate, with subsidiaries quaintly entitled the Departments of Education, Health, Social Security, Trade and Industry. He shares the view of his fellow countryman Adam Smith that the economy is an interrelated matrix of activities' (4 July 1997). Lloyd's 'holding company' image is one already held, with criticism and concern, by finance staff in the spending departments.

Much depended on Brown's personal relationship with the Prime Minister, which weakened in January 1998 when a new biography (based on interviews with Brown and his staff) suggested that Brown remained resentful at not becoming party leader ahead of Blair (Routledge 1998). A government reshuffle in July 1998 disfavoured Brown's allies, and the decision to reinforce the Cabinet Office, reporting directly to the Prime Minister, with new units on cross-departmental issues, was a potential weakening of Treasury authority. In compensation, the Treasury was pursuing a social policy of its own on the interface between welfare and work through the New Deal and fiscal instruments. The emphasis on financial stability in the new government's headline objectives, which in earlier Labour administrations took years to assert over the manifesto-backed claims of ministers in spending departments, has been present from the start.

The sustainable level of public expenditure is a concept that Labour has been slow to explore. They are not committed to any particular level of expenditure and seem to be evading the issue by placing faith in the capacity of existing money to be reallocated within existing aggregates in accordance with Labour priorities. The improving fiscal position of 1997–98 facilitated this approach within the aggregate Conservative plans that were maintained, and faced Labour with the possibility of public expenditure falling to well below 40 per cent of GDP. Their response was to agree to clear real terms increases in social expenditure for the rest of their term of office, carefully hedged at Treasury insistence with emphases on long-term investment, fiscal stability and performance targets. The economic slowdown of 1999 did call into question this relaxation of spending discipline, and it remained to be seen whether a retrenchment exercise would eventually be forced on the Blair government as it had on his Labour predecessors.

Labour's emphasis is on public spending as a means to an end – a self-reliant ethical socialism in a society nourished by the notion of inclusion through hard work. This harmonises well with the philosophical approach of the Treasury and has reinforced Treasury scepticism about the sustainability of increased public spending on the lines traditionally associated with left-wing governments. Increased welfare expenditure has made only a conditional return, on the Treasury's own terms and autonomous of the structures of political and social support for it. At the moment there is no suggestion that the government is prepared to move to the average European level of transfers from taxes and contributions into welfare expenditure; the avoidance of tax increases has become the principal constraint on social policy. By associating itself with the Conservative argument that such levels are not sustainable in Britain, Labour is making the survival of the welfare state in Britain a continuing issue.

Note

1   Research into 'The Treasury and Social Policy' was carried out with the support of the Economic and Social Research Council through a grant in their Whitehall programme (L 124 25 1004). Nicholas Deakin of the University of Birmingham has been co-researcher of this study and his contribution is gratefully acknowledged.

References

Brown, G. (1997) 'Responsibility and Public Finance', speech 20 January.

Burns, Sir Terence (1997) 'Preparing the Treasury for the Election', Frank Stacey Memorial Lecture, 1 September.

Chapman, R. (1997) *The Treasury in Public Policy-Making*, London: Routledge.

Corry, D. (ed.) (1997) *Public Expenditure: Effective Management and Control*, London: The Dryden Press.

Deakin, N. and Parry, R. (1993) 'Does the Treasury have a Social Policy?' in R. Page and N. Deakin (eds) *The Costs of Welfare*, Aldershot: Avebury.

—— (1998) 'The Treasury and New Labour's Social Policy' in E. Brunsdon, H. Dean and R. Woods (eds) *Social Policy Review 10*, London: Social Policy Association.

Department of Social Security (1998a) *New Ambitions for our Country: a New Contract for Welfare*, London: The Stationery Office, Cm 3805.

—— (1998b) *A New Contract for Welfare: Principles into Practice*, London: The Stationery Office, Cm 4101.

—— (1998c) A *New Contract for Welfare: Partnership in Pensions*, London: The Stationery Office, Cm 4179.

European Commission (1998) *Social Protection in Europe 1997*, Luxembourg: Office for Official Publications of the European Communities.

Field, F. (1995) *Making Welfare Work: Reconstructing Welfare for the Millennium*, London: Institute of Community Studies.

—— (1996) *How to Pay for the Future*, London: Institute of Community Studies.

Heclo, H. and Wildavsky, A. (1974, 2nd edn 1981) *The Private Government of Public Money*, London: Macmillan.

HM Treasury (1994) *Fundamental Review of HM Treasury's Running Costs: a Report to the Chancellor of the Exchequer by Sir Colin Southgate, Jeremy Heywood, Richard Thomas and Suzanne Cook*, London: HM Treasury, mimeo.

—— (1996) *Financial Statement and Budget Report*, London: The Stationery Office, HC 60.

—— (1997a) *Public Expenditure Statistical Analyses, 1997–98*, London: The Stationery Office, Cm 3601.

—— (1997b) *Chancellor of the Exchequer's Smaller Departments: the Government's Expenditure Plans 1997–98 to 1999–2000*, London: The Stationery Office, Cm 3617.

—— (1997c) *Financial Statement and Budget Report*, London: The Stationery Office, HC 90.

—— (1998a) *New Ambitions for Britain: Financial Statement and Budget Report*, London: The Stationery Office, HC 620.

—— (1998b) *Public Expenditure Statistical Analyses 1998–99*, London: The Stationery Office, Cm 3901.

—— (1998c) *Departmental Report of the Chancellor of the Exchequer's Departments*, London: The Stationery Office, Cm 3917.

—— (1998d) *Stability and Investment for the Long Term: Economic and Fiscal Strategy Report 1998*, London: The Stationery Office, Cm 3978.

—— (1998e) *Public Expenditure 1997-98 Provisional Outturn*, London: The Stationery Office, Cm 3988.

—— (1998f) *Modern Public Services for Britain: Investing in Reform. Comprehensive Spending Review: New Public Spending Plans 1999–2000*, London: The Stationery Office, Cm 4011.

—— (1998g) *Public Services for the Future: Modernisation, Reform, Accountability*, London: The Stationery Office, Cm 4181.

Lawson, N. (1992) *The View from No 11*, London: Bantam Press.

Parry, R., Hood, C. and James, O. (1997) 'Reinventing the Treasury: Economic Rationalism or an Econocrat's Fallacy of Control?', *Public Administration*, 75, 3: 395–415.

Pierson, P. (1994) *Dismantling the Welfare State*, Cambridge: Cambridge University Press.

Routledge, P. (1998) *Gordon Brown: the Biography*, London: Simon and Schuster.

Thain, C. and Wright, M. (1995) *The Treasury and Whitehall: the Planning and Control of Public Expenditure 1976–93*, Oxford: Clarendon Press.

Much Treasury documentation is available at http://www.hm-treasury.gov.uk

7   Welfare without work?

Divergent experiences of reform in Germany and the Netherlands

Anton Hemerijck, Philip Manow and Kees van Kersbergen

The continental, Bismarckian welfare state, to which the Dutch and German welfare states belong, comes closest to what Titmuss (1974) has called the industrial achievement–performance model of social policy. The specific characteristics of this type of welfare state regime have had a strong impact on the precise form and character of the predicament of the welfare state as well as on the possibilities of reform and chances for survival.

The response to the 'crisis' of the welfare state in Germany and the Netherlands – at least initially – was very similar. In both countries socioeconomic response patterns, particularly towards unemployment, were characterised by the attempt to reduce the supply of labour via early retirement, relatively generous disability pensions and the discouragement of female labour force participation. The predicament of these continental welfare states could be correctly epitomised as 'welfare without work'. However, since roughly the mid-1980s the adjustment paths of both countries have started to diverge considerably. This chapter is an attempt to explain these divergent adaptive dynamics and focuses on causes and mechanisms of the political responses to the 'welfare without work' crisis in Germany and the Netherlands.

After justifying the German–Dutch comparison, we give a stylised account of the 'welfare without work' pathology in the continental welfare state. We then illustrate the divergent paths of adjustment in both countries. In the next section, we argue that both welfare states are characterised by an intimate link between various social and economic policy domains; they are 'tightly coupled'. The main issue for welfare reform under conditions of tight coupling is how the various interdependencies are politically managed. Here, we find crucial differences between the Netherlands and Germany. In two separate case analyses (see pages 115–24) we elaborate and substantiate this finding. The conclusion summarises the result and discusses some broader implications.

A German–Dutch comparison

Germany and the Netherlands are interesting and appropriate cases to compare because their welfare state regimes (continental, see van Kersbergen 1995; Esping-Andersen 1996; Castles and Mitchell 1993; Huber and Stephens 1997), economic governance structures (sectorally coordinated or organised, see Soskice 1990; Kitschelt *et al.* 1999), and industrial relations systems (intermediate, see OECD 1997: 63; OECD 1994; Iversen 1998) are very similar. Moreover, the welfare states of both countries can be characterised as 'tightly coupled' (see below), indicating that the policy domains of industrial relations, macroeconomic policy, labour market policy and social security are highly interlinked.

Given the independent monetarist status of macroeconomic policy and the lack of an active labour market stance, however, the *core* linkage in the Dutch and German welfare states revolves around the nexus between the sphere of industrial relations and the system of social security. The commitment to open trade, combined with the disinflationary mission of the central bank gives organised interests little room to abuse their public status and organisational powers for cartelistic and protectionist purposes. It has also hindered Keynesian deficit spending or strategic currency depreciation for stimulating the economy. Collective bargaining predominantly takes place at the sectoral level (OECD 1994: 175–77). The coverage of collective bargaining is high, co-ordination between trade unions and employers' associations and practices of codetermination are considerable. The level of industrial conflict is low, but when it occurs, it is highly organised.

Both German and Dutch industrial relations are deeply entrenched in a complex institutional framework of which the system of social security is an integral part. The policy domains of industrial relations and social security are linked, even to the extent that they form a particular configuration of complementary and self-supporting policies and institutions. They are indeed 'tightly coupled'. Because the systems of social security are predominantly financed out of payroll contributions from workers and employers, the substantive interdependency between industrial relations and social security is particularly strong.

One of the upshots of such tight coupling between the sphere of capitalist production and the sphere of social protection is that welfare reforms have often safeguarded the particularist interests of unions and employers' associations. Their interests primarily result from the fact that the welfare state can serve as an institutionalised support structure for the social partners, allowing them to externalise the costs of economic adjustment onto the social security schemes. This common cost externalisation has given rise to a specific adjustment path in which the welfare state functions as a 'productivity whip', because social insurance contributions impose considerable non-wage costs on labour. However, the welfare state also functions as an 'inactivity trap', because it generously provides various pathways into non-employment. This implies that finding a balance between productivity and inactivity is fundamentally a *political* task.

Given the striking similarity of the institutional set-up of both the welfare state and the economic governance structure in Germany and the Netherlands, and given the different adaptive dynamics that recently are found in both countries, we argue that it is necessary to 'build a micro logic into existing models of welfare regimes' (Mares 1996: 3; see Naschold and de Vroom 1994) by looking at the production–protection interface. Our claim is that the distributive effects on central political actors, particularly employers and unions, of the specific linkages between the welfare state and the production regime strongly influence the *prospects for* and *dynamics of* welfare reform. To understand why the adjustment paths of both countries differ, we first analyse the features of the continental model in general and then look at the inner working of each model in particular.

The pathological spiral of welfare without work

A crucial feature of the achievement–performance model of social policy is the strict adherence to the insurance principle. This implies that entitlements follow the income distribution generated by the market. As a result, the welfare state puts a premium on steady working careers, benefits workers with relatively high skills and incomes and discriminates against part-time work and female labour force participation.

The lack of a basic pension tends to add to this. If pension entitlements follow strictly the length and level of previous contributions, workers are unwilling to engage in part-time work or to move in and out of work for shorter periods of time. Such welfare state-induced rigidities support full-time, life-long employment. The norm of the 'standard worker family' (Esping-Andersen 1996: 76) stands in the way of significant job creation in the service sector and of the proliferation of more flexible employment patterns.

The steady erosion of stable employment relations without corresponding changes of the social insurance provisions results in a process of slow, incremental disentitlement. Simultaneously, job creation in the service sector is very meagre. Hence, the number of people who never will be really integrated into the 'old order' of the standard employment relationship increases significantly, whereas the number of people that drop out of this old order increases.

The main beneficiaries of the continental welfare state have been the male skilled workers in the manufacturing sector and specific occupational groups such as civil servants, miners and farmers, for whom special laws apply. The labour force in continental welfare states is 'comparatively very masculine, and very protected' (Esping-Andersen 1996: 76). Since pensions are status-oriented and should enable people to maintain their standard of living during retirement, there is usually no gradual transition from work to retirement. Employers have no interest in creating part-time jobs that would allow for a slower passage to retirement. Correspondingly, labour unions have no interest in engaging in the struggle for part-time employment. A variety of generous disability pensions stimulate early labour market exit.

The clear-cut boundary between work and retirement is one of many reasons why early retirement is so attractive for employers who seek to downsize their workforce without stirring up major unrest within the firm. The many possibilities for early retirement have been extensively used in times of economic downturn. Using the old age insurance as an instrument of industrial adjustment has yet another rationale. It is an implicit form of wage flexibilisation if wages follow seniority. At the same time, it can have the beneficial side-effect of leading to an improvement of skills within a firm, since firms then can hire young workers who have been trained in the most advanced technologies.

A stylised account of the interplay between a high wage production regime and the continental welfare state goes something like this. Under increased competitive pressure, firms can only survive if they are able to increase labour productivity. This is most commonly achieved by raising the productivity levels of workers through high quality vocational training and education, labour-saving investments and by laying off less productive or 'too expensive', mostly elderly workers. Under the principle of traditional breadwinner family dependence, the latter strategy drives up taxes and payroll social security contributions. The productivity whip, in turn, puts pressure on wage costs, which provides new ground for reassessing the remaining workforce in terms of their level of productivity, most likely leading to another round of dismissals. As a result, a virtuous cycle of productivity growth changes into a vicious cycle of high wage costs, the dismissal of less productive workers, and increases in social security contributions. These necessitate further productivity increases in competitive firms as a result of which another round of reductions in the workforce begins and so on.

This, then, leads to the pathological spiral of 'welfare without work'. Jobs disappear in sectors where productivity increases stagnate and prices of goods and services cannot be easily raised. Moreover, if service sector salaries are linked to wage developments in the exposed sector, the interactive logic frustrates job growth in the labour-intensive public and private services sectors, especially at the low end of the labour market. In other words, a crisis of inactivity gives rise to the emergence of a new class of non-employed, low-skilled, permanently inactive, welfare-dependent citizens. These citizens are unable to gain access to the formal labour market, because of the prohibitively high costs of job creation, which is a direct consequence of the transfer-based and payroll-financed system of social security. A new cleavage between labour market insiders and outsiders emerges.

The labour market effects of this particular interplay between production and social protection are the following:

- overall low employment and high structural unemployment (see Figures 7.1 and 7.2);
- low female participation rates (see Table 7.1);
- declining participation of older workers (see Table 7.2);
- underdevelopment of part-time jobs (see Table 7.3);
- below average job growth in the service sector.

Low employment, high unemployment, short working hours, high labour costs and unfavourable population dependency ratios are the result of the interplay between the productivity whip and the inactivity trap. These have important repercussions for the welfare state. While the economy may be perfectly able to maintain and restore its international competitiveness because of high productivity, with the passing of time, it proves unable to defend welfare state objectives of high levels of employment and social protection.

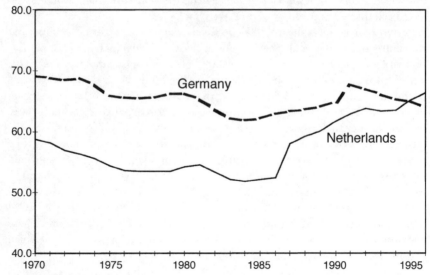

Figure 7.1 Employment ratios in the Netherlands and Germany, 1970–96. Source: OECD,
1997: Statistical Compendium (Labour Force Statistics), calculations by the
MPIfG and OECD, 1997: *Employment Outlook*, p. 163.

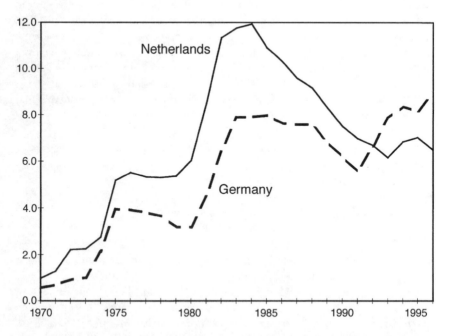

Figure 7.2 Unemployment in the Netherlands and Germany, 1970–96. Source: OECD, 1997:
Statistical Compendium (Labour Force Statistics), calculations by the MPIfG.

Table 7.1 Labour force participation rates by sex in Germany, the Netherlands and USA, 1973–95 (percentage)

	Men				Women				Total[a]			
	1973	1983	1993	1995[b]	1973	1983	1993	1995[b]	1973	1983	1993	1995[b]
Germany	89.6	82.6	81.2	80.3	50.3	52.5	61.8	61.3	69.4	67.5	71.7	71.0
Netherlands	85.6	77.3	78.7	79.1	29.2	40.3	56.0	58.9	57.6	59.0	67.5	68.8
United States	86.2	84.7	84.7	85.0	51.1	61.9	69.0	70.7	68.4	73.2	76.8	77.8

Source: OECD (1996: 196–97).

Notes

a Defined as the total labour force divided by the working-age population.
b Secretariat estimates based on OECD *Economic Outlook*, No. 59, June 1996.

Table 7.2 Labour force participation rates of older workers in Germany and the Netherlands, 1960–95 (percentage)

		Men 55–64	Women 55–64	Total 55–64
Germany	1979	66.9	28.4	44.0
	1983	63.1	26.3	41.8
	1990	57.7	26.4	41.6
	1995	54.5	31.3	42.8
Netherlands	1979	65.3	14.4	38.6
	1983	54.2	14.4	33.3
	1990	45.7	16.7	30.8
	1995	42.3	18.6	30.3

Source: OECD (1996b: 187–89).

Escaping the pathology?

However, the incidence of part-time work in Germany and the Netherlands (Table 7.3) and the development of unit labour costs between 1970 and 1996 in both countries (Figure 7.3) indicate that the trend towards increasing unemployment and declining labour force participation is not irreversible.

It is fair to say that the key to the relative success of the Dutch model is the 'job miracle'. Job growth has been 1.6 per cent per year since 1983, which is four times the average of the European Union. The Netherlands has succeeded in having cut the unemployment rate during the past decade by more than half, from almost 14 per cent in 1983 to just over 6 per cent in 1997, that is to say well below the 11 per cent average for the European Union. However, when we look at labour force participation rates, the Netherlands seems to have merely caught up with the OECD average, just reaching above the German level for 1996 (see Figure 7.1).

On the other hand, the once highly acclaimed performance of the 'Modell Deutschland' has worsened substantially over the past decade or so. German unemployment is very high (see Figure 7.2), job creation and overall employment have been very low. Because social policy promotes labour market exit, the ratio between welfare state contributors and recipients has become increasingly unfavourable (see Esping-Andersen 1996). Hence, even steady efforts for cost containment have not brought social insurance contributions significantly down (see Schmidt 1998: 154; BMA 1998; Alber 1998a, b). In fact, the costs put onto labour by the welfare state have increased in the recent past.

The Dutch experience seems to indicate that there is still considerable scope for modernising the welfare state without undermining the normative ambition of high levels of employment and social protection. At the same time, the German *Reformstau* (literally: reform jam) with respect to high and persisting levels of unemployment and non-employment seems to be the classic example of the dead-end street into which the continental social policy model of labour supply reductions and the maintenance of the 'family or productive wage' has led (see also Scharpf 1997).

Table 7.3 Incidence and composition of part-time employment in Germany, the Netherlands and USA, 1973–95 (percentage)

| | Part-time employment as a proportion of employment | | | | | | | | Part-time employment as a proportion of total employment | | | | Women's share in part-time employment | | | |
| | Men | | | | Women | | | | | | | | | | | |
	1973	1983	1993	1995	1973	1983	1993	1995	1973	1983	1993	1995	1973	1983	1993	1995
Germany	1.8	1.7	2.9	3.6	24.4	30.0	32.0	33.8	10.1	12.6	15.1	16.3	89.0	91.9	88.6	87.4
Netherlands[a]	—	6.9	15.3	16.8	44.0	50.3	64.5	67.2	—	21.2	35.0	37.4	—	78.4	73.7	73.6
United States[b]	8.6	10.8	11.0	11.0	26.8	28.1	25.5	27.4	15.6	18.4	17.6	18.6	66.0	66.8	66.0	68.0

Source: OECD (1996b: 192).

Notes
a Break in series after 1985
b Break in series after 1993.

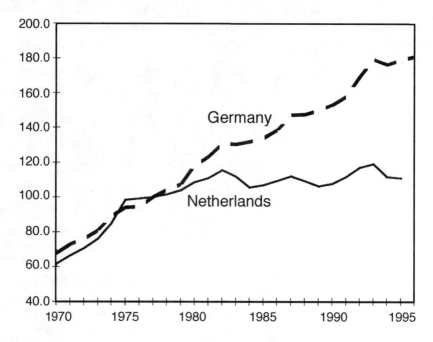

Note:
The comparison of unit labour costs should be interpreted with caution. It may overstate changes in competitiveness, since unit labour costs are only a (small) part of overall costs and value added.

Figure 7.3 Unit labour costs in the Netherlands and Germany, 1970–96 (in national currency; 1977 = 100). Source: Bureau of Labor Statistics, 1997, http://stats.bls.gov, calculations by the MPIfG.

These considerations justify the focus on the different dynamics of crisis and reform in two continental welfare states. While unification certainly has posed a massive external shock to the German model, the predominant response pattern comprising massive early retirement and the radical reduction of female labour force participation conforms very much to the picture associated with the continental welfare state. If Germany is now undergoing a crisis comparable to the Dutch predicament in the late 1970s and early 1980s, the question is how and under what conditions a continental welfare state is capable of finding a way out of the 'welfare without work' dilemma.

Similarities and differences: tightly coupled welfare states

The continental welfare state is characterised by an intimate link between the policy domains of macroeconomic policy, industrial relations, social security and labour market policy. Although fundamentally engaged in the tasks of meeting and stabilising the material needs of their citizens, these policy areas vary in substantive policy content and are governed according to different rules of policy-making.

Tightly coupled welfare states entertain strong interdependencies between the different policy areas. The unique features of the linkages between the policy domains shape path-dependent trajectories of policy change. Policy change is likely to proceed – if at all – in a sequential-diachronic rather than parallel-synchronic way. Policy adjustments in one area require consecutive changes in neighbouring policy domains. One of the reasons is that efficiency gains won in one area tend to incur efficiency losses elsewhere.

The crucial issue in the tightly coupled continental welfare state is how policy interdependencies and policy interfaces are *politically* managed. Here lies a critical difference between Germany and the Netherlands. Bargaining coordination in the Netherlands is 'overt coordination' defined as the 'centralised concertation of bargaining rounds among the peak associations of business and labour' (possibly in cooperation with the state) (OECD 1994: 175). Conversely, German industrial relations reveal a pattern of 'covert coordination', relying mainly on the 'pace-setting role of bargaining in key sectors' (ibid.) without substantial state involvement. Hence, the analysis of reform dynamics in social policy has to take into account the structure of industrial relations. Although the Netherlands and Germany are usually classified as being sectorally coordinated market economies, the logics of coordination differ substantially.

In both countries social policy belongs to a corporatist complex in which the state cannot intervene autonomously, but is bound to a negotiated consensus with organised labour and capital. Organised labour, capital and the state, however, have different degrees of autonomy. While the economic response pattern of both countries resembles each other much (a similar 'policy content'), the institutional context within which the relevant political actors can choose and coordinate their strategies to overcome the 'welfare without work' dilemma is different. This variation in the degree of autonomy of the social partners and the state is likely to have important consequences for negotiated social policy reform. A more detailed analysis of the two cases will highlight this.

The Netherlands: corporatist resurgence, political crisis and reform

Again the era of corporatism

In the Netherlands the initial policy response to the first oil shock was expansionary and resulted in wage hikes and soaring inflation. By the mid-1970s the experiment with Keynesian reflation was aborted. A fixed exchange rate to the Deutschmark was adopted. The centre-right coalition (Christian democrats and conservative liberals, 1982–86) threw its support behind a deflationary programme. Although the 'hard currency policy' provided for greater macro-economic stability, it also implied that changes in the international political economy had to be met by voluntary wage moderation and productivity increases.

The shift to restrictive macroeconomic policy pushed up the level of unemployment to unprecedented levels. With unemployment soaring at a post-war record, the trade union movement, having lost almost 20 per cent of its membership in less than a decade, was in no position to wage industrial conflict. After a decade of failed tripartite encounters, based on Keynesian premises, the new coalition's entry into office was crowned by a bipartite social accord. With the so-called Accord of Wassenaar (December 1982), the unions recognised that only a higher level of profitability would lead to a higher level of investment, which was considered essential for job creation and the reduction of unemployment. This path-breaking accord marked the resurgence of corporatist adjustment on the basis of a commonly understood 'supply side' diagnosis of crisis (Hemerijck and van Kersbergen 1997; Visser and Hemerijck 1997).

The accord inaugurated an uninterrupted period of wage restraint up until the mid-1990s. All agreements since 1982 have reconfirmed the need for wage restraint. Nominal wage increases have fallen to zero and since the 1980s the anticipated increase in inflation has been the basis for sectoral negotiations. Only in 1992 and 1993 did the average negotiated wage increase exceed the inflation rate by half a percentage point. Estimations are that over 40 per cent of job creation in the last decade must be contributed to prolonged wage moderation. Keeping wages down is defined as the strongest instrument in the Dutch strategy of industrial adjustment (Centraal Plan Bureau 1995: 268) and a remarkable degree of social and political consensus is organised in its support.

While wage restraint in itself helps to preserve and create jobs, an additional pay-off was required to make corporatist adjustment tangible for trade union rank-and-file. Over the last decade the average working week has been brought down from 40 to 37.5 hours. In those sectoral agreements, in which a reduction of the working week was negotiated, wage increases have been smallest. The process of across-the-board labour time reduction has shifted gradually towards part-time work as the main tool for redistributing work. Between 1983 and 1993 the share of workers with part-time jobs (less than 35 hours per week) increased from 21 to 35 per cent. Part-time jobs particularly meet the increased labour supply of married women.

In the 1990s we observe an important shift in emphasis, whereby wage restraint was increasingly compensated by lower taxes and social contributions and facilitated by improved public finances as well as a broader tax base through the creation of more jobs in domestic services. This helped to maintain spending power and boosted domestic demand. The avenue of substantially reducing the working week was continued by way of encouraging part-time work, endorsed by the social partners.

Although the appreciation of the Guilder has made exports more expensive, the overall decline in wage costs has practically been capable of compensating competitive losses. Moreover, monetary policy has stimulated a low level of inflation, which, in turn, has had a favourable effect on domestic wage trends.

What is more, wage moderation has had a favourable impact on employment in sectors that produce mainly for the domestic market, rendering low-wage, labour-intensive production more profitable.

The political dynamic of the renaissance of corporatism in the Netherlands is structured around regular consultations between government and the 'social partners'. Although the state plays a considerably less dominant role in collective bargaining, there is still extensive political power. The Minister of Social Affairs and Employment has the authority to declare collective bargaining agreements legally binding for all workers and employers in a certain branch of industry as a whole. This provision remains a treasured policy instrument and is crucial for securing economy-wide wage restraint. It also implies the power to declare (parts of) collective agreements not generally binding. In other words, politics still has considerable influence in industrial relations, but in a more indirect manner. Employing a so-called 'shadow of hierarchy' (Scharpf 1993), governments have been effective in encouraging labour and capital to reach agreements that concur with their central political goals.

Welfare with *work*

Organised capital and labour, under the shadow of hierarchy, have managed to find a mutually rewarding solution to problems of economic adjustment. It consisted of a pay-off between wage moderation and labour time reduction. The return to responsive corporatism, however, was in the first instance perversely facilitated by a general lenience or even permissiveness in the social security system. Prolonged wage moderation and industrial reconstruction were compensated through the welfare state, via a generous labour exit route for less productive, mainly elderly workers. Eventually, a crisis of inactivity spilled over into a general crisis of governability in the social security system, which then prompted major institutional changes.

The political crisis of the Dutch welfare state revolved around the disability scheme, which increasingly became an instrument for early retirement and industrial restructuring. A very broad definition of disability, the incorporation of labour market opportunities into the calculation of the degree of disability, and high replacement rates (80 per cent) were distinctive features of the scheme. A unique property concerned the institutional organisation of responsibilities and control. Sickness pay and disability benefits were administered by so-called Industrial Boards. These were largely responsible for examining the health of employees for whom their employers pay sickness contributions directly to the appropriate board. However, a remarkable deficiency in the transparency of medical assessments concurred with economic incentives for employers to use the sickness and disability schemes as a convenient procedure for 'firing' redundant, particularly older workers and avoid social friction at the same time. Paying a sickness benefit for one year and then letting the disability scheme take over was calculated as in many ways a much cheaper option than maintaining a redundant worker on the regular payroll. Medical doctors could interpret the labour market clause of the scheme generously, employees and the unions appreciated that the disability scheme guaranteed generous benefits until retirement, and the government had found an additional early exit instrument. In fact, the combination of the low threshold for entitlement, the blurring of social and occupational risks, and the generous level and duration of benefits explain why the disability scheme became a major method for reducing the supply of labour. The unanticipated yet inevitable result was a steep rise in the number of recipients and the exhaustion of the scheme's financial resources (see Hemerijck and Kloosterman 1995).

The disability scheme became a welfare trap: once officially recognised as partially disabled, a worker acquired a permanent labour market handicap. The Industrial Boards interpreted the labour market consideration in such a way that if productivity was below the wage level a worker would be considered fully incapacitated to work. It was simply assumed that discrimination in the labour market would prevent such a person from finding another job.

In 1987, the second centre-right government (1986–89) enacted a structural reorganisation of the system of social security. Replacement rates were cut down from 80 to 70 per cent, entitlements were restricted, indexation was cancelled and the duration of disability and unemployment benefits was shortened. Moreover, the labour market consideration of the disability scheme was repealed. However, these and similar measures had little effect on spending because the number of social security beneficiaries continued to rise. One of the reasons for the failure of the reform was that the weak prominence of the state in the social security system prevented the mobilisation of sufficient power to override the incentives to misuse the disability scheme for labour market reasons. As a result, institutional change stalled and the number of people receiving disability benefits approached one million in the early 1990s.

In this context of predicament, the centre-left government (Christian democrats and social democrats, 1989–94) proposed to introduce a more radical reform in order to discourage the misuse of sickness and disability benefits and to close off other labour market exit routes. The proposal was highly controversial, politically risky and met with stiff resistance. In 1991 nearly a million people demonstrated against the reform in what was probably the largest protest demonstration in the Netherlands ever. The Labour Party experienced a haemorrhage of its membership and of electoral support. The social democrats were largely held responsible for what the electorate saw as an attack on established rights. At the 1994 elections the party was punished with a historic defeat.

Notwithstanding popular resistance and obstruction by the trade unions, the reforms were enacted. Among the most important measures were an age-related reduction of replacement rates, a shortening of the duration of the benefit, medical re-examinations of beneficiaries, more stringent rules in general and a tougher definition of disability which forces beneficiaries to accept all alternative 'normal' jobs.

The reform endeavours of the government were critically enhanced by the results of a series of public inquiries into the causes of the crisis of social security.

These studies essentially revealed that social security was being misused by individuals, employers and firms, the Industrial Boards, the unions and local governments for purposes of industrial restructuring. In particular, the political control over the practices of the Industrial Boards was diagnosed as having failed consistently, because in the tripartite constellation of the body of control, political actors had very little power. The most problematic aspect in the institutional design of the social security system concerned the ambiguous distribution of power and responsibility. The major recommendation was that the implementation of social security ought to be monitored by a government agency that could operate fully independently of the 'social partners' and their bipartite Industrial Boards. The system was reorganised in this vein and an independent body of control was installed.

The restructuring of Dutch social security by the liberal-social democratic government (social democrats, conservative liberals and social liberals, 1994–98) revolved around two dimensions of reform: (1) the introduction of financial incentives through the partial privatisation of social risks and social policy administration; and (2) a fundamental redesign in the institutional structure of the administration of social security.

The pathbreaking reforms in the Dutch system of social security concern the status of the social partners in the administration of social insurance arrangements. Old corporatist institutions were dismantled and replaced by independent supervisory institutions, and only one separate, tripartite institution was created for the implementation of social security legislation. The full privatisation of the administration of social insurance is scheduled for the year 2000. With the introduction of independent supervision and the creation of market incentives in the administration of social security, the government believes to have laid down institutional preconditions for more effective social policy implementation in the sphere of sickness and disability insurance.

Since the majority of social security reforms only went into effect after 1992, it is too early to assess the precise impact. Recent data, however, show a reduction in social spending. More salient developments were decreasing sickness absenteeism and a drop in the number of disabled persons, from a peak of 925,000 in 1994 to 861,000 in 1995, although the figures for 1998 indicate again a rise in disability. While in the 1980s the Dutch welfare state seemed to have gone furthest on the continental path of 'welfare without work', the crisis of inactivity, especially with respect to the lenient disability scheme, has accelerated reform efforts. The major result is the institutional breakthrough that is weakening the entrenched resistance against change of the unions and the employers. With the upcoming revision of the organisation of social security, the 'social partners' are forced to accept political supervision and control over social security. Nevertheless, it has to be stressed that the disability rate remains comparatively high and that the scheme still hides unemployment.

Resistance to change and failed reform in Germany

Wage restraint and covert coordination: the road into crisis

The principle of *Tarifautonomie* (autonomy of employers and unions in collective bargaining) rules German industrial relations. Collective bargaining does not take place in 'the shadow of hierarchy', but in 'the shadow of the independent Bundesbank'. The German central bank – strictly committed to a non-accommodating monetary policy – has historically proven its eagerness to punish instantly any inflationary wage settlement by 'retaliatory interest rate increases' (Soskice *et al.* 1998: 41). This lesson was painfully learnt by the unions in the mid-1970s (see Scharpf 1987). Within this system of 'institutionalised monetarism' (Streeck 1994: 118; see Hall 1994) wages and working conditions are set through sectoral collective bargaining, in which the metalworker union, the IG Metall, usually takes the lead. Pilot agreements in key branches and regions of the metalworking sector serve as a point of reference for the rest of the sector, and are taken over by other branches as well. Wage demands usually remain within the limits set by increases in productivity plus the rate of inflation. Wage demands thus essentially mirror the publicly announced growth in the money supply to which the Bundesbank commits itself each year, taking into account exactly these two factors: 'the expected growth of real productive potential and "unavoidable" inflation' (Streeck 1994: 123). Other unions are eager to reach wage settlements not below this landmark wage deal of IG Metall.

However, given the considerable productivity gains in manufacturing, the compressed wage structure in the German economy (see Streeck 1997) and the relatively high minimum wage defined by the level of social assistance, even economically responsible wages in the manufacturing sector are usually too high to allow for significant job growth in the lower labour market segments, in particular in the service sector. However, the high wage–high productivity strategy was viable as long as the welfare state could take care of (the limited number of) those excluded from the labour force and as long as the strong performance of the German export industry led to a relatively high employment level in the manufacturing sector.

Central concertation has no real place and rationale within this framework of covert economic coordination (Flanagan *et al.* 1983: 276). The dominant macroeconomic paradigm in post-war Germany, the social market economy, ascribes to the state a role restricted to the provision of a regulatory framework within which the market may unfold its beneficial effects for society. Thus, Keynesianism could never really take hold in Germany (Allen 1989). The same is true for corporatism understood in the traditional sense as a nation-wide, tripartite political exchange, comprising wage restraint, a commitment to full employment and business cooperation. In spite of the broader public and scholarly attention that was paid to such attempts at central economic co-ordination like the Concerted Action, or more recently the Solidarity Pact (*Solidaritätspakt*; Sally and Webber 1994) or the *Bündnis für Arbeit* (Alliance for Jobs; see Lehmbruch 1996; Bispinck 1997), these coordinating efforts either failed or simply affirmed what unions, employers and the state would have done anyway.

The *Konzertierte Aktion* was essentially a symbolic exercise. Also the more recent attempts at economic coordination are far from representing a German style neo-corporatism and had rather mixed results. It is true, the main thrust of the Alliance for Jobs initiative *was* the attempt to strike a political package deal, including issues of social policy and collective wage bargaining (Bispinck 1997). However, such package deals cannot address the profound dilemma of productivity and inactivity in the German model, as long as the central union demand in exchange for wage restraint is *to maintain* generous levels of entitlements in unemployment and pension insurance in order to guarantee an easy exit into non-employment.

Thus, the problematic predominance of labour supply reductions as the standard response to economic crises essentially remains in place. Yet, it is particularly this policy that is part of the negative spiral of labour shedding, high non-wage labour costs, low employment, the financial crisis of the welfare state and the incentive for firms to increase productivity through further downsizing of the workforce.

Any reform of the pathologic interplay between the system of industrial relations and the system of social protection would have to begin with a reform of the collective bargaining system itself. However, this is not feasible under the principle of *Tarifautonomie*. Moreover, the German system lacks the institutional preconditions to strike broad package deals *across* different policy domains. Unions are sectorally fragmented, their umbrella organisation, the DGB, is weak, and the business community is heterogeneous. Employers' representatives are incapable of making binding agreements on the reduction of overtime work or the creation of new jobs, the two central union demands in the *Bündnis für Arbeit* initiative (Lehmbruch 1996; Bispinck 1997). Last but not least, the state is almost absent as a manager or moderator of industrial relations.

The dynamics of crisis and reform in the German model follows a pattern of steady erosion and permanent incremental adjustment. However, with a strong export orientation and an above-average employment share of the manufacturing sector, Germany's economy had been faring well. It was not until after unification that employment in the exposed sectors dropped dramatically. This was caused by the disappearance of the exposed sector in the GDR and by the drop in West German employment to a level reached in 1985. Since 1992 unemployment has been rising. Confronted with the challenge of unification, the system of industrial self-government proved to be inadequate.

When the unification boom was soon followed by a substantial slowdown of the economy in 1992, the Kohl government called both unions and business associations to the bargaining table. The government wanted to ensure that the supply of vocational training met demand, that the unions agree to moderate wage settlements in the West, that the adjustment of Eastern wages to the Western level is delayed and that the business community commits itself to higher investments in the new *Länder*. The metalworkers union was quick to promise wage restraint. However, with respect to adjustment of Eastern wages to Western levels, IG Metall refused to compromise. Unions feared the breakdown of the high wage regime in the West if major wage inequalities between the old and the new *Länder* persisted. In 1991 business and labour had agreed to raise wages in the Eastern *Länder* to the Western level by 1994. While productivity still differed considerably between West and East, the unification boom had led to wage settlements that had a further negative impact on the economic restructuring in the East in subsequent years (see Sally and Webber 1994: 21–22). The deteriorating rate of exchange between the Deutschmark and other major currencies aggravated this situation. Thus, the twin threat to jobs due to a strong currency and generous wage increases intensified the unification crisis that resulted from the breakdown of the East European export markets and the sudden exposure to intensified competition under conditions of high wage costs and a low level of productivity. Unemployment soared in the eastern *Länder*: 15 per cent in 1996 and almost 20 per cent in 1997.

The same pattern can be found in the union initiative in late 1995 for an Alliance for Jobs. The government proposed to cut welfare spending, to raise the retirement age, to introduce higher contributions from patients and to liberalise employment protection rules. The unions made wage restraint conditional on the maintenance of the current level of entitlements, especially unemployment and pension insurance. No bargaining was possible. In spite of the resistance of the unions and political opposition, the government in 1996 introduced most of the proposed welfare cuts anyway and the Alliance for Jobs died a quick death.

The ambivalence of reform

Emphasising the resistance of unions to major social policy reforms, however, may distract from the fact that both the government's stance towards welfare reform and the position of the employers has been ambivalent. Since the German production model is highly dependent on the compensating capacity of the welfare state, cutbacks do not translate necessarily into cost advantages for firms and thus into an increase in their international competitiveness (Manow 1997). In fact, these even entail the risk of reducing the competitive advantages of firms if they coincide with industrial strife, with a weakening of union capacity to control their members, or with the erosion of the solidarity between employers which collective bargaining at the industry-sector level forces upon them. The failed codetermination reform in the 1980s (see Wood 1997), the unclear position of employers on opening clauses in collective bargaining and on the reform of the traditional territorial wage treaties (*Flächentarifvertrag*), and the spectacular failure of sick pay reform in 1996 made clear that the employers, too, were hesitant to change the model of social policy and industrial relations. Being well aware of the increasing costs and of the positive payoffs that the existing system imposes on and offers for firms, employers are regularly undecided whether to call for major reforms or basically to stay with the status quo. Crucial is that the costs and benefits of reforms are unevenly distributed among small and big enterprises, and among firms in the exposed and the sheltered sector. Moreover, there is no arena in which side payments or package deals could be balanced between losers and winners.

Employers' interest in the maintenance of the supportive role that the welfare state plays for the high trust production regime has different implications for different social policy domains. While an agreement about the urgency of health reforms was comparatively easy to achieve among the social partners, profound reforms of insurance schemes with a closer relation to the labour market, particularly pensions and unemployment benefits, have never been a high priority for the business community. German employers as well as the unions supported the pension reforms of 1989 and 1997, but only under the condition that the most important pathways into retirement would stay open (see Kohli *et al.* 1991). Therefore, early retirement and disability pensions were conspicuously excluded from major reforms, in spite of broad concern over the extensive misuse of these provisions for the modernisation of large enterprises. The 1997 pension reform started to tackle the disability pension issue, but gradual changes in the retirement age and the partial introduction of actuarial cuts on pensions drawn earlier than at the age of 65 were supposed to not come into force before 2001, when the demographic changes will also begin to affect the labour market in the form of a growing scarcity of labour.

The tight coupling of the German model of production and social compensation has had substantial consequences for the trajectory of German unification as well. The complete transfer of the industrial relations system and of the production model from the West to the East meant that the compensatory elements of the German welfare regime had to be transferred as well. Given that the establishment of the West German model of industrial relations in the new *Länder* was to a great extent the responsibility of the social partners (see Lehmbruch 1996), the functioning of the production model would have been critically endangered by an incomplete transfer and would have entailed high political risks.

Given the tight nexus between the welfare regime and the production model the government is faced with a dilemma. Either welfare reforms that are not in the interest of the social partners are sabotaged during the implementation stage, as had been the case with the reform of early retirement in the 1980s (see Mares forthcoming), or state interventions have detrimental effects on the German system of production as a whole, as had been the case with the sick pay reform. Thus, for an understanding of the reform dynamics in the 1990s, it is just as important to understand which reforms have been avoided as it is to know which reforms have been enacted. In any case, the state has largely abstained from hurting organised capital and labour. Political actors were aware that this would only have worsened the unification crisis, both in political and in economic terms. And last but not least, unification demonstrated that the welfare state does offer the opportunity for cost externalisation to the central state as well. Especially the pension and unemployment schemes bear a considerable part of the massive West-to-East transfer payments that occurred in the wake of unification (see Bundesbank 1996). Moreover, to the economic advantages of social peace come the political benefits. It is in the central government's interest that the severe effects of the unification crisis are compensated by the welfare state.

Reforms in German old-age insurance demonstrate its two conflicting economic functions. On the one hand, the pension system is an important instrument for easing the transition from work to retirement, for reducing unemployment among older workers and for enabling employers to adjust their workforce to economic cycles in a relatively flexible, inexpensive and 'painless' way. On the other hand, the high cost of pensions increases non-wage labour costs and intensifies the pressure on firms to dismiss workers. Reform efforts, therefore, focus on older workers, since they gain relatively high seniority wages and enjoy relatively strict employment protection rules. Early retirement, then, allows for both the increase of productivity and the import of new skills through the 'rejuvenation' of the workforce. Moreover, it allows for a higher flexibility in a firm's wage structure and personnel policy (see Gatter and Schmähl 1996).

Disability pensions and pensions because of long-term unemployment are the two major roads into early retirement in the German pension scheme (see Jacobs *et al.* 1991; Jacobs and Schmähl 1989; Gatter and Schmähl 1996). Both were reformed very half-heartedly in the 1980s and 1990s despite a constant decrease in the retirement age and despite the growing strain on pension finances caused by this. Therefore, the pension reforms of the last 15 years were no solution to the precarious state of the German pension system.

The failed or at least mixed reform record in the pension and early retirement complex is also the result of the government's ambivalent stance towards profound welfare reform and of the division of interests between employers with regard to economising on early retirement benefits. Small and medium firms as well as the handicraft sector are highly critical of the large employers' practice of externalising the costs of rationalisation and modernisation onto the social insurance schemes. While they supported the attempt of the Labour Ministry to curb early retirement (see Mares forthcoming) this attempt ultimately failed, not least because the government followed this strategy only half-heartedly. Unions were divided with regard to the best strategy to lower unemployment. While the IG Metall put its main thrust on the struggle for the 35-hour week, the more moderate IG Chemie preferred measures that would reduce labour supply by lowering the retirement age. Neither on the employers' side, nor on the unions' side could institutions outbalance these internal divisions of interest. Every clear reform would have triggered the emergence of a cross-class alliance between unions and employers of either camp. But since the government itself followed an indecisive strategy, employers and unions continued to pick their preferred choice out of a rich variety of options that exist for the transition from work to retirement.

Conclusion

We have compared two similar social systems of production and welfare state regimes. The Netherlands and Germany are usually put into the same box of sectorally organised market economies with a typically continental social policy model. This is justified by the striking similarity of the institutional features of the production system and of the welfare regime in both countries. The socio-economic response patterns in both countries with respect to the economic crisis have also been similar. A supply side policy of labour force reductions via early retirement and disability pensions, and low female labour market participation rates were characteristic.

However, the subsequent *political* response patterns to the welfare-without-work crisis were very different. Our main finding is that the political management of the many interdependencies between the sphere of production and the sphere of protection in both tightly coupled welfare states differs critically. While management has been overt and deliberate in the Dutch case, the German system of covert coordination did not allow for issue-linking and a sequential reform dynamic.

Our analysis points to four broader implications. First, in substantive terms the Dutch case shows that the pathological welfare-without-work equilibrium is not inevitable for continental welfare states. Although radical welfare reform is difficult, it is not impossible. Second, theoretically the German–Dutch comparison reveals that an understanding of the adaptive dynamics in tightly coupled welfare states depends critically on an analysis of both the economic and the political effects of the production–protection interplay. In tightly coupled welfare states, in which the social security system very much belongs to a corporatist complex, the investigation into the different trajectories of welfare state reforms necessitates the study of the system of industrial relations. Third, while the welfare states of Germany and the Netherlands can be argued 'to survive', they not only do so very differently, but also with contrasting socioeconomic and political outcomes and divergent prospects. Finally, the analysis indicates that a German import of the 'Dutch model' is unlikely, because reforming the welfare state by increasing political control over the implementation of social policy and over collective bargaining presupposes a radical break with the 'German model'. However, as the Dutch experience shows, in the 'struggle for survival' radical departures from path-dependent routes cannot be excluded.

References

Alber, J. (1998a) 'Der deutsche Wohlfahrtsstaat im Licht international vergleichender Daten', *Leviathan*, 26, 2: 199–227.

—— (1998b) 'Recent Developments in Continental European Welfare States: Do Austria, Germany, and the Netherlands Prove to be Birds of a Feather?' Paper presented at the 14th World Congress of Sociology, Montreal, 29 July.

Allen, C. S. (1989) 'The Underdevelopment of Keynesianism in the Federal Republic of Germany', in P. A. Hall (ed.) *The Political Power of Economic Ideas*, Princeton, NJ: Princeton University Press.

Bispinck, R. (1997) 'The Chequered History of the Alliance for Jobs', in G. Fajertag and P. Pochet (eds) *Social Pacts in Europe*, Brussels: ETUI.

BMA (Bundesarbeitsministerium) (1998) *Statistisches Taschenbuch*, http://www.bma.de/.

Bundesbank (1996) 'Zur Diskussion über die öffentlichen Transfers im Gefolge der Wiedervereinigung', *Monatsberichte der Deutschen Bundesbank*, H. 10: 17–31.

Castles, F. G. and Mitchell, D. (1993) 'Worlds of Welfare and Families of Nations', in F. G. Castles (ed.), *Families of Nations: Patterns of Public Policy in Western Democracies*, Aldershot: Dartmouth.

Centraal Plan Bureau (1995) *Centraal Economisch Plan 1996*, The Hague: CPB.

Esping-Andersen, G. (1996) 'Welfare States Without Work: the Impasse of Labour Shedding and Familialism in Continental European Social Policy', in G. Esping-Andersen (ed.) *Welfare States in Transition. National Adaptations in Global Economies*, London: Sage.

Flanagan, R. J., Soskice, D. W. and Ulman, L. (1983) *Unionism, Economic Stabilization, and Incomes Policies*, Washington: The Brookings Institute.

Gatter, J. and Schmähl, W. (1996) 'Vom Konsens zum Konflikt – Die Frühverrentung zwischen renten- und beschäftigungspolitischen Interessen', in Bremer Gesellschaft für Wirtschaftsforschung (ed.), *Massenarbeitslosigkeit durch Politikversagen?* Frankfurt a/ Main: Peter Lang.

Hall, P. A. (1994) 'Central Bank Independence and Coordinated Wage Bargaining: Their Interaction in Germany and Europe', *German Politics and Society*, 31: 1–23.

Hemerijck, A. C. and Kloosterman, R. (1995) 'Der postindustrielle Umbau des korporatistischen Sozialstaats in den Niederlanden', in W. Fricke (ed.) *Jahrbuch Arbeit und Technik 1995. Zukunft des Sozialstaates*, Bonn: Verlag J. H. W. Dietz.

Hemerijck, A. C. and van Kersbergen, K. (1997) 'A Miraculous Model? Explaining the New Politics of the Welfare State in the Netherlands', *Acta Politica*, 32 (Autumn): 258–80.

Huber, E. and Stephens, J. D. (1997) 'Welfare State and Production Regimes', Paper prepared for the conference on 'The New Politics of the Welfare State', CES, Harvard, Cambridge MA, 5–7 December.

Iversen, T. (1998) 'Wage Bargaining, Hard Money and Economic Performance: Theory and Evidence for Organized Market Economies', *British Journal of Political Science*, 28, Part I: 31–61.

Jacobs, K. and Schmähl, W. (1989) 'The Process of Retirement in Germany: Trends, Public Discussion and Options for its Redefinition', in W. Schmähl (ed.) *Redefining the Process of Retirement. An International Perspective*, Berlin: Springer.

Jacobs, K., Kohli, M. and Rein, M. (1991) 'Germany: the Diversity of Pathways', in M. Kohli, M. Rein, A. Guillemard and H. van Gunsteren (eds) *Time for Retirement. Comparative Studies of Early Exit from the Labour Force*, Cambridge: Cambridge University Press.

Kitschelt, H., Lange, P., Marks, G. and Stephens, J. D. (1999) 'Conclusion: Convergence and Divergence in Advanced Capitalist Democracies', in idem (eds), *Continuity and Change in Contemporary Capitalism*, Cambridge: Cambridge University Press.

Kohli, M., Rein, M., Guillemard, A. and van Gunsteren, H. (eds) (1991) *Time for Retirement. Comparative Studies of Early Exit from the Labor Force*, Cambridge: Cambridge University Press.

Lehmbruch, G. (1996) 'Crisis and Institutional Resilience in German Corporatism', paper prepared for presentation at the 8th International Conference on Socio-Economics, SASE, Geneva, 12–14 July.

Manow, P. (1997) 'Cross-class Alliances in Welfare Reform – A Theoretical Framework', paper presented at the conference on the 'New Politics of the Welfare State', CES, Harvard, Cambridge MA, 5–7 December.

Mares, I. (1996) 'Firms and the Welfare State: the Emergence of New Forms of Unemployment'. WZB Discussion paper, FS I 96–308, Social Science Research Center, Berlin.

—— (forthcoming) 'Business (Non)co-ordination and Social Policy Development: the Case of Early Retirement', in P. Hall and D. Soskice (eds) *Varieties of Capitalism*.

Naschold, F. and Vroom, B. de (eds) (1994) *Regulating Employment and Welfare. Company and National Policies of Labour Force Participation at the End of Worklife in Industrial Countries*. Berlin: de Gruyter.

OECD (1994) *Collective Bargaining: Levels and Coverage, Employment Outlook*, Paris: OECD.

—— (1996a) *OECD Economic Surveys 1995–1996: Netherlands*, Paris: OECD.

—— (1996b) *OECD Employment Outlook*, Paris: OECD.

—— (1997) 'Economic Performance and the Structure of Collective Bargaining', in *Employment Outlook*, Paris: OECD.

Sally, R. and Webber, D. (1994) 'The German Solidarity Pact: a Case Study in the Politics of the Unified Germany', *German Politics*, 3, 1: 18–46.

Scharpf, F. W. (1987) *Sozialdemokratische Krisenpolitik in Europa*, New York: Campus.

—— (1993) 'Co-ordination in Hierarchies and Networks', in idem (ed.), *Games in Hierarchies and Networks. Analytical and Empirical Approaches to the Study of Governance Institutions*, Frankfurt a/Main: Campus.

—— (1997) 'Employment and the Welfare State: a Continental Dilemma'. MPIfG Working Paper, 97/7, Max Planck Institute for the Study of Societies, Cologne.

Schmidt, M.G. (1998; 2nd edn) *Sozialpolitik in Deutschland. Historische Entwicklung und internationaler Vergleich*. Opladen: Leske + Budrich.

Soskice, D. (1990) 'Reinterpreting Corporatism and Explaining Unemployment: Coordinated and Uncoordinated Market Economics', in R. Brunetta and C. Dell'Aringa (eds) *Labour Relations and Economic Performance*, London: Macmillan.

Soskice, D., Hancké, B., Trumbull, G. and Wren, A. (1998) 'Wage Bargaining, Labour Markets and Macroeconomic Performance in Germany and the Netherlands', in L. Delsen and E. de Jong (eds) *The German and Dutch Economies. Who Follows Whom?*, Berlin: Physica.

Streeck, W. (1994) 'Pay Restraint Without Incomes Policy: Institutionalized Monetarism and Industrial Unions in Germany', in R. Dore, R. Boyer and Z. Mars (eds) *The Return to Incomes Policy*, New York: Pinter.

—— (1997) 'German Capitalism. Does it Exist? Can it Survive?', in C. Crouch and W. Streeck (eds) *Modern Capitalisms*, London: Sage.

Titmuss, R. (1974) *Social Policy: An Introduction*, London: Allen & Unwin.

Van Kersbergen, K. (1995) *Social Capitalism. A Study of Christian Democracy and the Welfare State*, London and New York: Routledge.

Visser, J. and Hemerijck, A. (1997) *A Dutch Miracle: Job Growth, Welfare Reform and Corporatism in the Netherlands*, Amsterdam: Amsterdam UP.

Wood, S. (1997) 'Weakening Codetermination? Works Council Reform in West Germany in the 1980s', WZB Discussion Paper, FS I 97-302. Social Science Research Center, Berlin.

8 Implementing major welfare state reforms

A comparison of France and Switzerland – a new-institutionalist approach

François-Xavier Merrien and Giuliano Bonoli

Introduction

Under strong economic and financial pressures, all welfare states are pushed to reform their inherited regime of social protection. Nevertheless, during the 1980s and 1990s, some countries have been more successful than others in implementing reforms. Studies have demonstrated that the level of resistance varies from country to country as does the capacity to implement reforms. A number of studies have convincingly shown that the politics of restructuring and retrenchment are fundamentally different from the politics of welfare expansion (Pierson 1994, 1996). Institutional constraints that exert a powerful influence on the anticipation of actors, their collective mobilisation capacity, and whether they can exert a 'veto power'. In others words, institutions make reform and retrenchment policies possible, partially possible, or impossible. To argue that institutions have an impact on political life, is not sufficient.

The first kind of 'new institutionalism' overlaps with the approach known as the 'state centred approach'. According to this school (Evans *et al.* 1985; Skocpol 1993), the more the state is differentiated from civil society, the stronger it and its capacities are. The degree of bureaucratisation and centralisation of a country determines the capacity of the state to formulate and implement policies (state capacities).

The results of this research raise a number of issues. It is essential to distinguish the ability to invent public policies from the ability to implement them. A state can be strong in developing new measures but weak in getting them accepted (Merrien 1990). Furthermore, the implementation capacity of a programme by governments depends on the one hand on the degree of horizontal integration, and on the other hand on the degree of vertical integration (Pierson 1994). The degree of horizontal integration refers to the degree of power concentration at the national level. Theoretically, a centralised government holds more power than a federal government. A centralised government can make decisions without having to negotiate with peripheral powers.

Vertical integration relates to the concentration of power. In terms of implementation capacity, most studies highlight the superiority of strictly parliamentary regimes (Weaver and Rockman 1993). Implementation capacity is inversely related to the number of veto points that governments have to deal with when developing new measures. The concentration of power reduces the number of veto points (Immergut 1992). A parliamentary government with a stable majority is better able to resist interest group pressure.

This sort of explanation facilitates our understanding of the differing capacities of governments for action. Nevertheless, it does not allow us to understand why a theoretically strong government can fail to impose reforms. It concentrates too much on formal political institutions. Policy-makers also have to convince organised interests and society at large. From this perspective, it seems essential to consider the capacity of the state to achieve neo-corporatist compromises.

A strong state with strong institutional resources can be weak if unable to get its objectives accepted. Strong centralisation can prompt collective action, which reduces the scope for compromise in public policy (Birnbaum 1982). A corporatist political system with strong civil society might have a greater capacity to act than a strongly bureaucratised state (van Waarden 1992).

One should not, however, disregard other institutional variables covered by the concept of 'welfare state regimes' (Esping-Andersen 1990). Institutional configurations of welfare states can favour or impair given reforms. It is more difficult to retrench insurance-based programmes than tax-financed ones (Pierson 1994). The former are strongly supported by the public. Insured persons consider benefits as a right. Opposition to losses in social insurance is strong if these programmes are managed by beneficiaries or if beneficiaries are well organised. A strong government is relatively weak in imposing losses if welfare arrangements are of a Bismarckian or corporatist kind.

By looking at recent outcomes of some major welfare reforms in France and Switzerland, we will attempt to highlight the weight of different institutional factors that shape implementation capacity. During the 1990s, France and Switzerland have been confronted with similar socioeconomic pressures relating to unemployment, ageing, rising health expenditures and public deficits. Both countries have made significant efforts to modify their social policy and curb budgets deficits. The results of these efforts have varied.

Our study shows that, even if important, governmental institutions are not the only institutional factors affecting the ability to impose changes in social policies. A fuller explanation requires that other factors are taken into account, such as the nature of political welfare regimes and ideological discourses and practices that are the legacy of the past.

Reform capacity of welfare states and institutional structures

The cases

In many respects France and Switzerland are very different countries. Their state structures (strong vs. weak), their political regimes and their standard patterns of policy-making are significantly different.

France is characterised by a unitary and semi-presidential/parliamentary regime, a strong state, and a weak, but protest-oriented, civil society. The Swiss political system has four main characteristics: a 'grand coalition' government, federalism, direct democracy and corporatist liberal arrangements. Switzerland is a federation of cantons united by a two-chamber government. The cantons are highly autonomous and each has a constitution. Regulation of financial and organisational resources between the confederation and the cantons operates at three levels: delegation of traditional tasks (civil law and penal code, public health, police, traffic, etc.), new obligations for cantons accompanied by financial support from the confederation, and, thirdly, cooperation (federal legislation implemented by the cantons).

In international comparisons, the Swiss political system is generally qualified as a typical case of consensus democracy (Neidhart 1970; Kriesi 1995), even if it is less true today (Papadopoulos 1997). A key factor behind the development of consensual policy-making is the availability of the referendum to dissatisfied minorities.

A constant concern for politicians and policy-makers is to avoid the possibility that some dissatisfied groups might call for a referendum on a bill.[1] When a bill is finalised, it is presented to the parliament by the government. This procedure is repeated in each of the two chambers of parliament (Papadopoulos 1997). After the acceptance of a bill by both chambers, there is a 90-day deadline to call for a referendum. Switzerland is also considered a partially neo-corporatist country, as trade unions are fragmented, employers' associations are more centralised and organised and informal network arrangements are highly asymmetrical (Katzenstein 1984).

With regard to the relationship between state and civil society structures, France is almost the inverse of Switzerland. There, the political system is characterised by a strong centralisation of power and a weak civil society (Badie and Birnbaum 1983).

Since 1958, both the parliament and the president have been elected directly. Prime ministers are chosen from the dominant party by the President. Normally, the President is the one who decides the orientation of government policy. But, in times of *cohabitation* (1986–88; 1993–95; 1996–), that refers to a situation in which the President of the Republic and the Prime Minister belong to two opposite parties, it is in fact the Prime Minister who determines the general orientation of government policy.

The French state has long played the role of motor for social and economic development (Cohen and Bauer 1989). Some consequences of this role are a strong bureaucratisation, and the management of the state by a few top civil servants educated in the '*grandes écoles*' (Suleiman 1976; Bourdieu 1991).

On the other hand, civil society, the labour movement in particular, is weak and fragmented. At around 10 per cent, the unionisation rate is the lowest in OECD countries. This is a result of slow industrialisation and the tradition of trade unionism characterised by anarcho-trade unionism (Rosanvallon 1988; Mourriaux 1992). And since the end of the 1960s, the percentage of union members has not stopped decreasing, from 22 per cent in 1970 to 19 per cent in 1980 and from 12 per cent in 1988 to 9 per cent in 1994. If there are between 15 and 20 per cent of union members in the public sector, it represents between only 4 per cent and 7 per cent in the private sector (Mourriaux 1992).

Moreover, the labour movement is divided into rival organisations that reflect long-standing ideological cleavages. The oldest federation of trade unions is the CGT (Confédération Générale du Travail, 20.5 per cent of votes), leaning towards communism and inclined to protest. The CGT-FO (Confédération Générale du Travail – Force Ouvrière, 11.7 per cent of votes) is the result of a split from the CGT in 1947 because it did not share its communist orientation. The second largest union is the CFDT (Confédération Française Démocratique du Travail, 20.4 per cent). It is the result of a division within the Christian labour movement. It was characterised by radical socialism in the 1970s but has become more moderate since the early 1980s. Finally, the CFTC (Confédération des Travailleurs Chrétiens) is what remains of the Christian labour movement.

Employers are organised into two different confederations. The CNPF (Centre National du Patronat Français) represents large companies, although there are strong internal divisions between different economic sectors. The CGPME (Confédération Générale des Petites et Moyennes Entreprises) represents small businesses.

Social policies

The two countries also have different welfare arrangements. France is considered to be a conservative-corporatist welfare state. Switzerland shows a strong inclination for the social insurance model, but the effect of federalism and direct democracy is to limit the scope of programmes. For this reason, Switzerland trails behind other countries in Europe with regard to welfare expenditures (Gilliand and Rossini 1995).

Switzerland

It is not easy to classify the Swiss welfare system into the Esping-Andersen model. The Swiss welfare state is mainly an occupational welfare state (Bismarckian). It lags behind other rich countries in Europe on welfare expenditures (Bonoli 1997; Gilliand 1990). The three main social insurance programmes run by the Federal government – health insurance, the basic pension insurance scheme and unemployment insurance – exemplify the specific features of the Swiss welfare state. All have been reformed in recent years.

Health insurance

Switzerland still constitutes an exception in Europe in not having a public health insurance scheme. The Forrer Law leading to the establishment of a health insurance scheme was presented to the parliament in 1899. But a coalition of the medical profession, the anti-welfarist right and existing mutual societies subjected it to a referendum and the law was rejected. As a consequence, Swiss policy-makers had to search for alternatives that would be able to survive a referendum challenge (Gilliand 1990; Immergut 1992).

In 1910, a law establishing the basis of the current health care system was adopted. It was a rather minimalist arrangement. Until 1994 membership was not compulsory by federal law, but a majority of cantons had already introduced this requirement. The law prescribes a minimal level of coverage in terms of reimbursed treatments and drugs (basic insurance), which must be granted by mutual societies in order to qualify for public subsidies. Premiums paid by insured persons are their main source of funding, however. These premiums are unrelated to earnings or income, and are uniform for members of the same fund and in the same canton. As a result, they affect large families and those on low income in particular, although there are income-based subsidies. In addition, premiums can vary between funds, and, until 1994, between insured persons within the same fund. However, the most significant variations are between cantons.

Old-age pension insurance

As with health insurance, legislation for old-age pensions was hampered by the use of referenda. A basic pension scheme was accepted by Swiss voters as late as 1948. The scheme (AHV/AVS), which has been amended a number of times since then, is universal in its coverage. It is financed through contributions of employees and employers and receives a state subsidy equal to 19 per cent of outlays. There is no ceiling on contributions, but pension levels can vary between a floor and a ceiling. Replacement rates vary between 40 and 100 per cent on an average income, and even lower for higher incomes. The scheme is thus fairly redis-tributive.

A tax-funded income-based pension supplement that is slightly higher than social assistance was introduced at the federal level in 1965. And, in 1982, occupational pensions, as a second tier of pension funding, became compulsory for employees with earnings above a certain limit (about 50 per cent of average earnings).

Unemployment insurance

The principle of a non-compulsory unemployment insurance was introduced into the Swiss constitution in 1947. But by 1975, only 22 per cent of employees were covered by an insurance (Gilliand 1988). The new Federal Law on Compulsory Unemployment Insurance (LACI) came into effect in 1984. The scheme is financed by contributions from employers and employees. The benefits granted amount to 70 per cent of the last salary for those unemployed without children and 80 per cent for those with dependent children (up to a maximum).

Until the recession of the 1990s, the unemployment rate remained very low, below 1 per cent. Three main reasons explain this situation. On a general level, we can emphasise the existence of a large social consensus in favour of negotiated solutions (what is called the 'work peace') and the existence of a dual system of education in which apprenticeship is the main part. The third reason relates to the existence of a strict migration policy. The use of a strict migration policy is a long-standing characteristic of Swiss policies to control the labour market (Bonvin 1996).[2]

France

The French model is of the Bismarckian type. Social rights are based on work. Compared with other countries, withholding taxes for social benefits are high; withholding of (direct) income taxes is low and the level of indirect taxes is high. More importantly these mandatory taxes weigh heavily on employees (social security contributions are withheld from the gross salary of each employee).[3]

The Social Security Plan of 1945 sought to create a truly universal package of benefits that was uniform, unified and centralised. Aside from universality, almost all the other objectives failed either because of lobbying by special interest groups who wanted to maintain their advantages (workers and miners, railroad workers and civil servants) or because of those who refused the principle itself (shop-keepers, artisans, farmers). For these reasons, the Social Security System is divided among professional programmes. Management of the system is for the most part balanced (representatives of labour unions and employers) but on major issues, the state has the last word (Catrice-Lorey 1982).

Compared to other countries, the French system of protection may appear less complete, less universal than others[4] and more centred on the preservation of the status quo than on income redistribution. However, French people show a considerable and persistent support of their fragmented welfare system.

Welfare crisis and reforms in Switzerland and France

To a number of observers, European welfare states are affected by a severe crisis. In many countries, 'social protection is frozen in a past economic order and . . . incapable of responding adequately to new risks and needs' (Esping-Andersen 1996). The viability and fairness of welfare states are being questioned. Some argue that welfare states undermine the market economy. A second group of arguments focuses on the negative consequences of public deficits. A third group focuses on the failure of old welfare arrangements to protect new needs (social exclusion, family problems). These criticisms are inextricably interconnected. For these reasons, most of the new social policies in continental Europe during the 1990s are not simply retrenchment policies. They combine different measures of retrenchment and expenditure cuts with measures aimed at protecting more adequately some segments of the population (the poor, women). The French and Swiss governments wished to limit the growth of social expenditures but they also wanted to reform the welfare system in order to respond to new needs.

Switzerland

Unlike in other European countries, deficits, unemployment and poverty in Switzerland remained extremely low throughout the 1980s. Consequently, there was little pressure for reforming social insurance schemes. The situation, however, changed dramatically in the early 1990s when the recession arrived and unemployment rose to unprecedented levels in Swiss post-war history, although an unemployment rate of 4.6 per cent might be low by European standards. In addition, there was the problem of increasing health care costs, which led the government to adopt cost-containment measures by issuing emergency decrees.

Overall, the recession of the 1990s marked a watershed in the development of the Swiss welfare state, which until then was in a phase of expansion, albeit in part still catching up with its European counterparts (Fragnière and Greber 1997). The change in attitude towards welfare is particularly obvious if one looks at the three major reforms of the mid-1990s.

Health policy

Pressure for change in the health system intensified towards the late 1980s when health care costs increased dramatically, leading to rising health insurance premiums. There were no incentives within the health care system to exert a downward pressure on costs.

In response to public dissatisfaction, the federal government enacted emergency legislation aimed at containing health care costs in 1991 and 1992. Such legislation cannot be delayed by a referendum. The main measures included a freeze on doctors' and hospitals' fees for 1993 and 1994, the equalisation of premiums between men and women and between individuals of different ages, a compensation system between mutual funds with different age and gender structures and a charge of 10 Sfr. per day for hospital stays. The measures were relatively successful. Both decrees were temporary. However, some of these measures were incorporated into the health insurance reform of 1994.

Perhaps the most remarkable innovation of the new law is the attempt to create a competitive market between mutual funds. With the new legislation, individual funds are able to negotiate with providers directly, and thus, it is hoped, to negotiate lower fees by introducing competition between providers as well. Second, the previous legislation did not oblige mutual funds to accept new customers. Thus, affiliation could be refused if applicants were considered 'bad risks.' The new law also includes provisions that allow customers to switch between different mutual funds without risking coverage. Finally, it introduced a mechanism for inter-fund compensation in order to equalise the competitive position of mutual funds with different age and gender structures. This system implies actuarially-determined cash transfers from funds with a lower proportion of 'bad risks' to funds with a higher one.

A second important change concerned targeting of subsidies towards those on low incomes. Under the new law, subsidies are increased for and targeted at those on low incomes. In practical terms, this change implied the withdrawal of subsidies to mutual funds and the introduction of individual means-based health insurance grants.

Since its implementation in 1996, the new law has become controversial. During 1996 and 1997, premiums increased on average between 6 and 7 per cent, which was far above the rate of inflation. A major problem seems to be the fact that plans to set up a competitive market have been undermined in a number of ways by a majority of mutual funds, which were largely against the introduction of the new law. First, instead of increased competition there has been a massive wave of mergers of mutual funds over the last few years. It also seems that mutual funds have been rather reluctant to disseminate information with regard to new opportunities available to customers. Third, the new law concerns only the basic compulsory insurance. Mutual funds can, for a premium supplement, offer additional coverage, which might include a single room in a hospital, dental care, or alternative medicine. Additional provision of this sort is treated differently. For example, funds can still refuse affiliation for additional coverage to those representing 'bad risks'. Finally the new provision has to deal with the problem of 'customer inertia'. The government has acknowledged that the new legislation is not yet producing the expected outcomes.

Despite these problems, the government maintains that it is too early to assess the effectiveness of the 1994 health insurance reform and has so far refused to take corrective action.

Pension reform

The overall aim of the 1995 pension reform (the 10th AHV/AVS revision) was to introduce gender equality in the basic pension scheme. Under previous legislation, a married man would receive a 'couple pension' corresponding to 150 per cent of his pension entitlement, regardless of the contribution record of his wife. In other words, a married woman would lose her entitlement to a pension, this being replaced by a supplement to her husband's benefit. In addition, there were no contribution credits for raising children or taking care of relatives. The existence of this gender-based discrimination was widely regarded as inadequate, especially after the adoption of a constitutional article on gender equality in 1981.

Preliminary work on the reform started in 1979, but it was only in 1990 that a bill was finally presented to parliament. The 1990 pension bill was seen by many – mainly unions and feminist movements – as disappointing. It was intended that married couples would continue to receive a 'couple pension' as before, except that it would be possible to draw it separately, i.e. on request, each partner would receive half of the total pension. The bill did not include provision for the equalisation of retirement age (then at 65 for men and 62 for women), as that was also regarded as unconstitutional after the adoption of the 1981 amendment on gender equality.

The 1990 pension bill soon came under attack from women's organisations for failing to take a more far-reaching approach to gender equality. It was suggested that individual contributions paid by partners should be added, divided by two, and counted separately for each of the two spouses. Such a system became known by the name of 'splitting'. All the proposals argued for the introduction of contribution credits for couples with children, and for those with other caretaking responsibilities.

The original bill was substantially modified by parliament. The modified bill also included the controversial measure of raising the retirement age for women from 62 to 64. The proposal was made by a right-wing dominated parliamentary commission. In response, the Federation of Swiss Trade Unions called for a referendum. But the bill survived the referendum and became law in 1995.

Unemployment policies

During the 1990s, the unemployment rate rose sharply. Restrictive migration policies no longer appeared as appropriate solutions to the unemployment problem. Confronted by this new situation the Federal Council adopted several Federal Urgent Decrees (AFU)[5] aimed at a quick adaptation of the legislative provisions. Thus the maximum duration of benefit entitlements progressively increased to 400 working days. The notion of suitable work appears in the law and the unemployed person must accept any job with a salary amounting to at least 70 per cent of the last wage. The contributions were also modified and increased to 3 per cent of the payroll.

In spite of these measures, the number of long-term registered unemployed increased regularly. The phenomenon meant a much greater financial burden for both the federal unemployment insurance and the cantons and communes, which had to take charge of the social assistance expenses. After 18 months' negotiations among the cantons, political parties, social partners and a great many other professional, economic and social institutions, and after a long debate, parliament adopted the second partial revision of the LACI (*Loi sur l'Assurance Chomage et Insolvabilité*) in June 1995.

The new legislation constitutes a turning point from a rather passive policy to an active one. The entitlement to passive benefit payments has been considerably reduced. Afterwards benefit payments are linked to the entry into an active labour-market programme. The maximum duration of benefits is 520 days. The participation in an active programme does not generate any more new periods of entitlement to federal benefits, as was the case previously. If no active programme is available, the unemployed person is entitled to receive benefit payments for 80 more days.

In 1997 the Federal Council tried to reduce the level of benefit payments. A referendum was launched and in September 1997 the Swiss people refused the resolutions adopted by the Federal Council. For the second time in one year – the first was the rejection of the revised labour law in 1996 – federal authorities were defeated in a popular voting.

Reforming social policies in Switzerland

The debate on welfare retrenchment and restructuring is fairly new in the Swiss political arena. Until the recession of the 1990s, there was an overall consensus on the desirability of maintaining the existing arrangements and structures. With the recession and increasing government and social insurance deficits, political pressure in favour of welfare changes has mounted. The three major reforms of 1994–95 cannot be qualified purely as retrenchment policies. Rather, while savings are central to all of them, each also includes elements of expansion and improvement such as the introduction of pension credits for caretakers, a new income-based 'health insurance grant' and longer entitlement benefits for the unemployed, even if combined with active mandatory measures.

This combination of retrenchment and expansion within a single piece of legislation can be seen as a strategy developed by the right-wing parliamentary majority in order to make cutbacks more acceptable to the electorate (Bonoli 1997). Such a strategy can secure the adoption of cutbacks to a wider extent than would be possible otherwise within the context of a standard consensual approach. Funding reductions do not have to be agreed upon, but can be enforced and combined with compensation measures for dissatisfied groups. Often, the result is legislation that comprises elements able to attract support from very different sectors of the electorate. In addition, the combination of divergent measures in a single reform provides advocates of retrenchment with a relatively large scope for blame avoidance for unpopular cuts. Another view is that right-wing parties sharing a conservative or liberal conception of the welfare state are obliged to take into consideration the conceptions supported by the other parties. Policies tend to be moderate in order to be acceptable to all coalition members. Even if the three dominant parties of the right or centre-right can impose the adoption of controversial measures, they are generally very cautious. Acts can be subjected to referendum. Swiss policy-makers have to find political ways of implementing changes in the context of a political system that gives 'veto points' directly to the people (Immergut 1992).

France

During a 30-year period after the Second World War, France has experienced economic modernisation, increase in purchasing power, a relative reduction of social inequalities and a slow and progressive reduction of poverty. One might call this the birth of a vast income-earning society ranging from the average worker to upper management whose style of life continues to differentiate them from each other, but much less than in other times, and who share the security of vested employment.

The economic crisis of the 1970s was particularly brutal. Industrial growth, which had been the locomotive of economic development, became negative starting in 1975 and translated into substantial loss of employment. In 1968, the rate was as low as 1.7 per cent, increasing to 8.1 in 1982, and, after some fluctuation, reaching 12.6 per cent in 1994.

The crisis has had a significant impact on France's ability to finance its relatively large welfare state. The traditional state's ability to ensure growth based on Keynesian economic policies was limited by the independence of economies and rejected as a principle by new economic orthodoxy. And, from the end of the 1970s, economic policies of successive administrations became characteristically orthodox. Control of inflation and monetary supply took undeniable precedence over employment (Jobert 1995).

Increasing deficits

In addition, the foundations of the traditional welfare state are themselves shaken by structural changes (Bourdelais *et al.* 1996). From a medical standpoint, health insurance has been faced with a chronic deficit while during the economic crisis, mandatory withholding of taxes for health insurance no longer covers expenditures. The reason is that the French health system has allowed uncontrolled use of medical goods and services.

For more than a decade, the French government has been trying to control the level of social expenditure (9.5 per cent of GNP) in the field of health policy (the Beregovoy Plan of 1983, the Seguin Plan of 1986) without much success except in controlling the budget of the hospitals. The deficit increased to 27.3 billion francs in 1993, to 31.5 billion francs in 1994, and to 34 billion francs in 1995.[6] The reason is the implicit coalition of the two main social actors: users of the systems (the patients) and practitioners, each of them having the power to mobilise votes or unrest (Kervasdoué 1996).

The system of retirement benefits based on redistribution of income has fallen victim to the increasing disproportion between active (working) and inactive (non-working) members of the population. In 1993, the deficit reached 39.4 billion francs. Rationalisation efforts meanwhile allowed it to be reduced to 12.7 billion in 1994 and to 13.2 billion in 1995. But forecasts for the future are alarming.

The deficit of the social security system has been chronic for several years: 56.4 billion in 1993, 55.9 billion in 1994, 62 billion in 1995. Public business deficits and the deficits of the special social funds of these businesses must be added to the deficits of the social security system. Thus in 1994, the deficit of the SNCF (National Railway Enterprise) climbed to 175 billion francs.

By themselves, these deficits are not catastrophic. Some economists emphasise that they primarily result in weakening economic growth (OFCE 1995; Dehove and Théret 1996). But successive governments of France, both socialist and conservative, desire to show their goodwill towards European integration. The Maastricht Treaty requires France to reach commonly agreed upon objectives. Major efforts to adapt are thus required.

During the 1980s and the 1990s several attempts have been made to restore the financial viability of the system, which, like those of other European countries, is affected by the twin pressures of rising demands and insufficient growth of revenues. Measures adopted in this context have included retrenching funds as well as measures aimed at increasing state revenues, such as increases in compulsory contributions and a new tax, the Contribution Sociale Généralisée (CSG) (Bonoli and Palier 1997).

The 'Juppé Plan'

Towards the end of summer 1995, the political situation was favourable, if not ideal, for a major reform. The government had an overwhelming majority in parliament. The next general election was almost three years away and the presidential election was scheduled for 2002. In addition, the adoption of austerity measures could be justified by the need to comply with the requirements for the European Economic and Monetary Union.

The content of the plan was kept secret until the day it was presented to parliament. The 'Plan for the Reform of Social Protection', or the 'Juppé Plan' for short, was presented to parliament on 15 November 1995. It was a declaration of intent covering all areas of social security. It provided an agenda for the implementation of a number of measures. It was mainly devoted to finding a solution to social security deficits and responding to new needs without negative effects on employment. Some of the measures were already specified in detail (Bouget 1998). Its main points were:

- Introduction of a universal health insurance scheme.
- Reform of public sector pension schemes.
- Partial transformation of financing mechanisms of social security.
- Taxation of family benefits.
- A new tax on all revenues.
- A constitutional amendment to allow parliament to vote on a social security budget (*Droit Social* 1995, 1996).

The plan was viewed by French and international commentators as a major restructuring of the social security system. It was not *per se* a retrenchment programme. Some measures, such as the introduction of a universal health insurance scheme and a new way to finance health insurance, could be qualified as equity measures. It did in fact contain a number of measures that were bound to be extremely controversial. Obviously, the reform of public sector pensions was one of these. There were also a number of structural changes. This was the case, for instance, with the tabling of a constitutional amendment allowing more power to parliament, the increase in the use of taxation in financing, as opposed to employment-related contributions, and the introduction of a universal health care scheme.

Unsurprisingly, the reactions to the Juppé Plan were mixed. First, among the unions, the CGT and FO condemned the whole programme, and called a one-day strike in the public sector. Other trade unions took a less radical position. The CFDT agreed with much of what was said in the plan, with the exception of public sector pension reform. Some renowned intellectuals like Touraine and Rosanvalon approved the programme of reform, others – with Bourdieu at their head – were radically against the plan. The socialists were divided. The line adopted by the Socialist Party under the leadership of Lionel Jospin, was to attack the method of the government's approach, rather than the content of the plan. It was, in fact, not too far from what the socialists had been arguing for in the past. In contrast, employers were satisfied with the proposed measures.

The protest movement

The protest movement started a few days later, on 24 November 1995. Initially it was mainly employees of the national rail company (SNCF) and of the Parisian underground (RATP) who went on strike. The national leaders of the main trade union federations (CGT and FO) were obviously quick to join and to encourage the protest movement against the Juppé Plan.

The collective mobilisation of November and December 1995 against the Juppé Plan was characterised by several remarkable social phenomena: strikes, sit-ins and protests. But perhaps the most spectacular were the public transport strikes in Paris, Marseille, Bordeaux, and other large and middle-sized cities. The strikers were able literally to bring the country to a halt. The number of protesters rose regularly from November to December.[7]

The result was that the government was forced to climb down on some of the measures. On 10 December, Juppé announced the withdrawal of plans for public-sector pension reform, though the remainder of the plan was retained and the protest movement gradually faded away. According to Pierson (1994), governments wishing to reduce social expenditures must avoid blame ('blame avoidance'). Under these conditions, why did the French Prime Minister try to impose his reform and why did he fail?

Here, the impact of institutions can be observed on three different levels. First, the strong concentration of power within the government prompted it to underestimate the reaction of the labour movement and of French society. Second, the institutional design of welfare state arrangements has produced a host of interests and patterns of mass popularity. The third effect relates to the structure of French society and particularly to the 'Jacobin' relationship between state elites and civil society.

At a political level, the Juppé government wrongly thought that it could enact these reforms without major risk. Arguably, the government did not want to engage in lengthy negotiations, that carried the risk of failure, as had happened to many of their predecessors. The divisions between the trade unions on many issues concerning social protection, the balance of power in parliament, the unity of the executive (President and Prime Minister belonging to the same party) and the fact that the next general election was some three years away probably persuaded the government that it could afford not to negotiate.

The second element that explains popular reactions is the comparatively high popularity of social security in France.[8] The attitude of the general public towards the social security system has been characterised as one of strong emotional attachment. We must also refer to the fact that social insurance in France is managed jointly by the social partners. In France the issue of who controls the system is also of paramount importance. The Juppé Plan represented a clear attack against the Confédération FO, which had been among the keenest supporters of a health insurance system managed by the social partners with little state intervention, not least because it had traditionally presided over the national health insurance fund. The Juppé Plan proposed a series of measures that contributed to undermining the traditional role of the social partners in social insurance management.

But in explaining the success of the opposition to the Juppé Plan, we must not underestimate the importance of the symbolic factors and ideologies that are often underestimated by most of the new institutionalists. Here analysis in terms of interests offers a poor explanation of the level of protest against the Juppé Plan in France. The policy of cuts concerned only some social groups (railway workers, postal workers). Some measures were expansion, not retrenchment, measures. The trade unions, experts and the socialist party were divided on the meaning of the reforms. However, the opposition to the plan mobilised enormous crowds in the streets and obtained massive support from both public opinion and prominent intellectuals (like Bourdieu, among others).

In France, political ideology still counts and the propensity to protest is still high. The public saw the Juppé Plan as a betrayal of the electoral promises made by President Jacques Chirac just a few months earlier. During the 1995 presidential campaign, in fact, Chirac denied that retrenchment measures were needed in the area of social security. The Juppé Plan was seen by many as a complete reversal of Chirac's claims. It contributed to create a unified front in the public sector: among railway workers, by attempting to control the costs of their particular system (retirement at the age of 55); in one of the unions (FO), by trying to change the way of managing the social security system; among many French citizens, by announcing a major transformation of social security without consultation and with little explanation; and finally, among influential French doctors, by trying to control health expenditure. The superposition of sectoral measures with very few links between them provoked the feeling that the government wanted to open discussions on the core of the French welfare state. Furthermore, its secretive nature and top-down decision-making gave rise to the image of a state run by technocrats. In reaction, the protesters instinctively reverted to a stock of revolutionary behaviour, inherited from the past: protests, marches, slogans against the government, and confrontation rather than negotiation.

Despite the fact that a number of measures were retained, the Juppé Plan fell short of the government's ambitions in so far as cuts in social expenditure were concerned. Moreover, when the right-of-centre government announced its intention to tackle the deficit through new austerity policies and President Chirac announced an early general election, public opinion was quick to join the socialist camp, in a clear move against welfare cuts. And the socialists returned to government in 1996.

Institutions and welfare state reforms in Switzerland and France

Perhaps the impact of institutions on policy is nowhere clearer than in the comparison of the cases of Switzerland and France. How have these different institutional features affected the relative success and failure of welfare state reforms in Switzerland and France?

International comparisons indicate that, although there are theoretical reasons to believe that unitary and parliamentary systems are more capable of implementing reforms, the cases studied here show that it is nevertheless not always the case. A strong state like France has not been able to implement its reform; a weak state like Switzerland has been more capable of transforming its welfare system incrementally. We must take into account the different and interrelated levels of institutionalisation. The political culture embedded in political regimes, the different policy styles as well as the institutionalisation of relationship patterns between the state and civil society are the main factors explaining the differing capacities of implementing major welfare state reforms.

In Switzerland, a culture of consensualism is coherent with a collegiate government, proportional representation in a multi-party system, limited auto-nomy of bureaucrats *vis-à-vis* politicians and with organised interests. Consultation, cooperation and negotiation are common. The fear of referenda encourages the search for consensual decisions (Kriesi 1995).

The reforms discussed above have been subjected to referenda, which shows a weakness of well-established consensus-building mechanisms within the government and parliament. To some extent, the Swiss political system is now characterised by the presence of two different policy-making mechanisms. The traditional consensus building approach is still alive, and takes place somewhat behind the scenes within the various commissions and between the social partners. At the same time, decisions in parliament are occasionally taken in a purely majoritarian way. In that case, dominant parties have to provide compensation if legislation is to survive the referendum challenge.

By contrast, France is characterised by a power situation of a state capable of resisting interests and proceeding with its own ends regardless of group pressures (Wilson 1987). A strong centralised state with a large majority in its parliament does not tend to enter into negotiations, compromises and mutual concessions. Civil servants and ministers tend to keep their distance from particular interests, which are seen as a threat to the general interest (Merrien 1991). The temptation of the government is to take the important decisions alone, especially if it benefits from a large majority in parliament.

One of the consequences of this top-down approach to policy-making is the inability of the government to exert some sort of control over the reactions of the people to its decisions. The strong degree of centralisation of the French state leads to the creation of counter-group mobilisations that are extremely powerful. This, coupled with the importance of ideologies in French public life, and an extraordinary capacity to mobilise 'active minorities', explains the relatively frequent occurrence of protest movements, which on occasion have been rather effective in modifying government policy. On many occasions before 1995, the French government was obliged to yield in the face of pressure from the most active groups. The successive retreats of the state contribute to strengthening a culture of dissensus. Concerning social policy, the French system has to deal with serious problems of governance. The issue concerns both the ability to find solutions and the capacity to implement them. Both cases confirm the path dependency phenomenon. It does not mean that no change is possible, but rather that institutions shape the cognitive and normative preferences of decision-makers and those concerned by their policies as well as the possibility of implementing certain types of solutions rather than others.

Notes

1   Which requires the collection of 50,000 signatures.
2   During the recession of the 1970s, the unemployment rates remained very low (less than 0.5 per cent), even though employment rates decreased considerably (over 7 per cent). The reason is that more than 360,000 foreign workers were compelled to leave. This accounts for more than three-quarters of the employment decline in Switzerland.
3   In France, social security means public health insurance, public pensions insurance and family benefits system. Unemployment is not part of the social security scheme, but based on the same features.
4   However, if one includes social and family benefits, France moves nearer to the universalist, social democratic model (Merrien 1997).
5   Some of these measures had to undergo a referendum process in 1993 but more than 70 per cent of the voters approved the Federal Urgent Decrees.
6   Source: France, Direction de la sécurité sociale.
7   It rose to 382,000 on 10 October, to 390,000 on 24 November, to 520,000 on 5 December, to 700,000 on 7 December, to 985,000 on 12 December, then down to 586,000 on 16 December (Le Goff and Caillé 1996).
8   Defence of social security was the number one priority of the French in all opinion polls over last few years.

References

Badie, B. and Birnbaum, P. (1983) *The Sociology of the State*, Chicago: Chicago University Press.

Birnbaum, P. (1982) *La logique de l'Etat*, Paris: Fayard.

Bonoli, G. (1997) 'Social Insurance in Switzerland', in J. Claasen (ed.) *Social Insurance in Europe*, Bristol: The Policy Press.

Bonoli, G. and Palier, B. (1997) 'Reclaiming Welfare: The Politics of French Social Protection Reform', in M. Rhodes (ed.) *Southern European Welfare States between Crisis and Reform*, London: Frank Cass.

Bonvin, J-M. (1996) 'Les réponses suisses aux phénomènes migratoires', *L'Année sociologique*, 46: 442–73.

Bouget, D. (1998) 'The Juppé Plan and the Future of the French Welfare System', *Journal of European Social Policy*, 8, 2, 155–72.

Bourdelais, P., Gaullier, X., Imbault-Huart, M., Olivennes, D. and Poursin, J. (1996) *Etat-providence. Arguments pour une Réforme,* Paris: Le débat, Gallimard.

Bourdieu, P. (1991) *La noblesse d'Etat,* Paris: Minuit.

Catrice-Lorey, A. (1982) *Dynamique interne de la sécurité sociale,* Paris: Economica.

Cohen, E. and Bauer, M. (1989) *L'Etat brancardier: politiques du déclin industriel (1974–1984),* Paris: Calmann-Lévy.

Dehove M. and Théret, B. (1996) 'La parole de l'Etat', *Québec, Politiques et Sociétés,* no. 30: 53–90.

Droit Social (1995) special issue, 'La protection sociale demain', nos 9/10 (September–October), Paris.

—— (1996) special issues on *le plan Juppé*: no. 3 (March), nos 9/10 (September–October), Paris.

Esping-Andersen, G. (1990) *The Three Worlds of Welfare Capitalism,* Cambridge: Polity Press.

—— (ed.) (1996) *Welfare States in Transition,* London: Sage.

Evans, P., Skocpol, Th. and Rueschemeyer, D. (eds) (1985) *Bringing the State Back In,* New York: Cambridge University Press.

Fragnière, J-P. and Greber, Y. (eds) (1997) *La sécurité sociale en Europe et en Suisse,* Lausanne: Réalités sociales.

George, V. and Taylor-Gooby, P. (eds) (1996) *European Welfare Policy. Squaring the Welfare Circle,* London: Macmillan.

Gilliand, P. (1988) *Politiques sociale en Suisse,* Lausanne: Réalités sociales.

—— (ed.) (1990) *Assurance-maladie. Quelle révision? Suisse: 1889–1989,* Lausanne: Réalités sociales.

Gilliand, P. and Rossini, S. (1995) *La protection sociale en Suisse,* Lausanne: Réalités sociales.

Immergut, E. (1992) *Health Politics. Interests and Institutions in Western Europe,* New York: Cambridge University Press.

Jobert, B. (ed.) (1995) *Le tournant néo-libéral en Europe,* Paris: L'Harmattan.

Katzenstein, P. (1984) *Corporatism and Change. Austria, Switzerland, and the Politics of Industry,* Ithaca: Cornell University Press.

Kervasdoué, J. (1996) *La santé intouchable. Enquête sur une crise et ses remèdes,* Paris: Lattès.

Kriesi, H. (1995) *Le système politique suisse,* Paris: Economica.

Le Goff, J.-P. and Caillé, A. (eds) (1996) *Le tournant de décembre,* Paris: La Découverte.

Lijphart, A. (1984) *Democracies. Pattern of Majoritarian and Consensus Government in Twenty-One Countries.* New Haven and London: Yale University Press.

March, J. and Olsen, J. P. (1989) *Rediscovering Institutions,* New York: The Free Press.

Merrien, F.-X. (1990) 'Etats et politiques sociales: contribution une theorie neo-institutionaliste', *Sociologie du travail,* 3: 267–94.

—— (1991) 'L'Etat par defaut', in J.-P. Durand and F.-X. Merrien (eds) *Sortie de siècle. La France en mutation,* Paris: Vigot.

—— (1997) *L'Etat-providence,* Paris: Presses Universitaires de France.

—— (1998) 'Governance and Modern Welfare-states', *International Social Sciences Journal,* March: 57–67.

Mourriaux, A. (1992) *Le syndicalisme en France,* Paris: Presses Universitaires de France.

Neidhart, L. (1970) *Plebiszit und pluralitäre Demokratie. Eine Analyse der Funktionen des Schweizerischen Gesetzreferendums,* Berne: Francke.

OFCE (Office français de conjoncture économique) (1995) Lettre: no. 145, décembre.

Papadopoulos, Y. (1997) *Les processus de décision fédéraux en Suisse,* Paris: L'Harmattan.

Pierson, P. (1994) *Dismantling the Welfare State? Reagan, Thatcher and The Politics of Retrenchment,* Cambridge: Cambridge University Press.

—— (1996) 'The New Politics of theWelfare State', *World Politics*, 48, 2: 143–79.

Rosanvallon, P. (1988) *La question syndicale en France*, Paris: Calmann-Lévy.

—— (1995) *La nouvelle question sociale*, Paris: Seuil.

Skocpol, Th. (1993) *Protecting Soldiers and Mothers*, Cambridge, MA: Harvard University Press.

Suleiman, E. (1976) *Les hauts fonctionnaires et la politique*, Paris: Seuil.

VanWaarden, F. (1992) 'The Historical Institutionalization of Typical National Patterns in Policy Networks between State and Industry. A Comparison of the USA and the Netherlands', *European Journal of Political Research*, 21, 1–2, 131–62.

Weaver, K. and Rockman, B. (eds) (1993) *Do Institutions Matter? Government Capacities in the US and Abroad*, Washington DC: The Brookings Institution.

Wilson, F. L. (1987) *Interest-Group Politics in France*, Cambridge: Cambridge University Press.

9 The Spanish development of Southern European welfare

Luis Moreno

Introduction

The development of the welfare state in Spain has attracted little attention from academics and experts in the area of social policy. Such lack of interest is most probably related to the fact that Spain was under General Franco's rule over a period of nearly 40 years (1939–75). In their sophisticated statistical exercises and typology formulations, none of the cross-national research into social policy of the 1980s included the case of Spain – or Southern welfare as whole – (Ferrera 1996). This lack of academic interest has traditionally been rooted in a cliché idea, which tends to disregard the South of Europe as a backward and underdeveloped area with respect to the core of the Old Continent (this being somewhere in Central and Northern Europe). In other words, 'everything is different in the South.'[1]

In Spain, welfare has historically incorporated some of the most characteristic features of the continental 'conservative corporatist' model of social policy (Esping-Andersen 1990). In the last two decades, an incrementalist pattern has developed with regard to welfare services and income policies alongside some inherited corporatist practices – despotic and democratic – from both late Francoism and the transitional period to democracy (1976–79), respectively.

Spain has reconstructed a medium-sized system of social protection as compared to the countries of the European Union. At present the Spanish welfare state represents a fundamental structure for both social reproduction and political legitimisation.[2] Since its integration in the European Community (1986), Spain has followed a pattern of welfare convergence of a three-fold nature: first, a universalisation of social entitlements (education, health, pensions); second, a confluence in the pattern of welfare expenditure to the median of its European partners; third, a diversification in the provision of social services by private and subsidised organisations.

Thus, the Spanish welfare state can be labelled as a *via media* with respect to other existing welfare systems (Moreno and Sarasa 1992, 1993). Indeed, the welfare system in Spain incorporates elements of both Bismarckian and Beveridgean traditions, or rather between breadwinner 'continental' and citizenship-centred 'liberal' models. It also represents a middle way in terms of decommodification and gender considerations, and of universal and means-tested access to services and benefits.

In Spain, liberalisation in the provision of welfare services is observable in a certain extension of free-market practices and, thus, in the proliferation of 'non-profit' – but characteristically subsidised – NGOs, and the reinforcement of the process of welfare privatisation. However, a trend away from 'residualism' and a parallel growth of institutional 'stateness', or state penetration of the welfare sphere (Flora 1986/87; Kuhnle 1997), can also be detected. In fact, some reforms of universalisation (education, health pensions) have been put into effect in recent years encompassing some basic entitlements with traditional income-related programmes.

The Southern European model of welfare

In recent times, a distinct model of Southern European welfare (Greece, Italy, Portugal and Spain) has been contended (Ferrera 1996, 1997; Moreno 1996, 1997c; Rhodes 1996; MIRE 1997). The discussion revolves around the contention whether the Mediterranean type of welfare constitutes a regime of its own or is simply made up of a 'family of nations' (Castles 1993) lagging behind those of the 'continental' model of social insurance to which they belong (Katrougalos 1996). Other views regard it as a mere 'Latin rim' characterised by a rudimentary level of social provision and institutional development (Leibfried 1992; Gough 1996).

Further comparative research is needed in order to substantiate those claims for a distinct Mediterranean welfare regime. Unlike the Continental, Scandinavian or Anglo-Saxon typologies, cross-national studies including Greece, Italy, Portugal and Spain are lacking. A good few issues deserve closer examination, which could help us to define the overall picture of a Latin type of welfare. However, there is an analytical common ground to be explored.

The four Southern European countries share analogies regarding historical backgrounds, value-systems and institutional peculiarities. They all had past experiences of authoritarian and dictatorial rule (for longer periods in the case of Portugal and Spain), and have suffered from economic and industrial 'delays' in the processes of modernisation (except for early-industrialised areas in Italy and Spain) (Giner 1986). The religious factor has had a structuring role in all four countries, but the role of the church as the main organiser of social protection has diminished.[3] This feature seems to correspond with a higher degree of secularisation in the social practices of Southern Europe. The impact of Europeanisation and globalisation have brought about, respectively, increasing incentives to economic convergence with Northern and Central Europe (Economic and Monetary Union), and world-trade pressures to restrict social programmes (social dumping from less-developed countries). In broad terms, similar social-demographic trends and macroeconomic constraints can be observed in all four Southern European countries.

As concerns the cultural-axiological dimension of welfare development, there is a self-perception of differentiated needs and lifestyles (intra-familial pooling of resources, home ownership and heterogeneity of social reproduction). Also noticeable is a compelling household solidarity and a pre-eminence of values of family inclusion and life-cycle redistribution (gift mechanisms, processes of age emancipation, proliferation of family companies and jobs). Moreover, cultural choices and practices have structured their civil societies in a characteristic mode (social networking, patronage, clientelism and group predation).

On analysing politico-institutional development the pivotal role of the family in social protection cannot be overemphasised. In Southern Europe the welfare state is to a large extent the Mediterranean welfare family. Intra-familial transfers are both material and immaterial. Concerning the latter, the involvement of women in both care of the elderly and children is crucial. However, the increasing participation of female workers in the labour force, coupled with new burdens for family formation and expansion, raise big questions as to whether Mediterranean welfare, as we know it at present, can survive.

Also characteristic of Southern European labour markets is an apparent cleavage between 'insiders' (hyper-protected core workforce), 'peripheral' (in-between gainfully employed) and 'outsiders' (precarious, 'left-outs' and 'junk' labourers). There are fragmented systems of income guarantees and wide inter-generation disparities in cash benefits (e.g. overprotection of the elderly in Greece and Italy). The informal 'tax-free' economies in Southern Europe are large (estimates of the 'hidden' sector range from 15 to 25 per cent of GDP). This translates into an uneven distribution of financial burdens across the various occupational groups.

Both Mediterranean welfare mix and the gender/family/work nexus are adaptable and complementary. These practices often translate into institutional particularism and low efficiency in service provision. Publicly subsidised organisations rather than subsidiary private and/or voluntary associations carry out a greater part of the production/provision of social services. In all four Southern European countries there are limitations to comprehensive reforms (e.g. implementation of a central scheme of minimum income guarantees). Nevertheless, new functional and territorial approaches to welfare reconstruction are gradually replacing traditional voluntaristic and paternalistic attitudes deployed mainly by both main political formations of the Left (Social Democrats) and the Right (Christian Democrats).

In the case of Spain, the most relevant factor conditioning its welfare development is the current process of decentralisation both at the level of planning and policy implementation. The institutional outcome of the interplay between central, regional and local governments will respond to the very nature of a contractually open process of power accommodation. Institutional uncertainty goes hand in hand with a gradual federalisation of politics in Spain (Moreno 1997a).

Social expenditure trends

Throughout the 1970s and 1980s, the growth of public expenditure in Spain was similar to that of the OECD countries during the 1960s and 1970s. Furthermore, in none of the OECD countries has public spending increased as much as in Spain since 1975. Public spending grew from 26 per cent of GDP in 1975 to over 47 per cent in 1995. In this period, all Southern European countries more than doubled the percentage growth for the EU-12. Increases in Greece, Italy, Portugal and Spain reached 15.1 percentage points, 11.3, 10.2 and 13.1 respectively. These rates compare to the mean 5.3 percentage points for all EU countries. By the second half of the 1980s, Spanish public expenditure per capita, measured in relative purchasing units, was similar to equivalent mean figures in Germany, Italy, France and the United Kingdom.

During the period of the Socialist governments (1982–96), Spain confronted a period of constant increases in public expenditure at a higher level – in relative terms – than most European countries. This was the result of providing the means to cover new and costly social programmes (universalisation of education, public health and pensions). But, above all, it was aimed at accomplishing the objective of bringing economic rationalisation in line with the rest of the EEC/EU countries. Public finances were greatly conditioned by the substantial governmental intervention in the economy through subsidies for purposes of industrial restructuring and for the development of a comprehensive programme of public works and infrastructure (highways, railway and telecommunications).

In broad terms, the policies of modernisation implemented by the PSOE (Partido Socialista Obrero Español (Spanish Socialist Workers' Party)) governments reflected the desire for Europeanisation expressed by the Spanish population at large. Since the accession of Spain to the EEC (1986) the general feeling in the country has invariably been one of convergence with the rest of its European partners. This social consensus[4] has remained a factor of paramount importance in Spanish politics and greatly explains the legitimacy of the often-harsh economic measures carried out by the government in recent years.

The annual rate of growth of the GDP between 1970–75 was 5.2 per cent while the social expenditure increased 9.7 per cent. In the period 1975–80 social expenses grew annually at 8.9 per cent whereas the GDP did so at a rate of 1.8 per cent. During 1980–94, all Southern European countries increased their social expenditure at a higher rate than the mean figure of 4.3 per cent for EU-12: 6.3 per cent, Greece; 5.9 per cent, Italy; 6.7 per cent, Portugal; and 5.5 per cent, Spain (Eurostat 1995).

According to Eurostat, in 1994 social spending had already reached 23.6 per cent of the Spanish GDP. However, and due to a different structure of expenditure allocation, the coverage of those expenses related to social policy programmes (education, housing and pensions) was smaller than in the countries referred to above. Both bureaucracy and financial transfers granted mainly to mining and agricultural sectors were higher compared to equivalent figures in core European countries.

As has happened in other advanced industrial countries, bureaucratic 'muddling through' in Spain has to a considerable degree been for the incrementalist of public expenditure growth. Nevertheless, the various political inputs carried out by successive democratic governments since the

Table 9.1 Distribution of main categories of social protection in Spain, 1980–92 (by categories and as percentage of both GDP and SE – social expenditure)

	1980		1992		% (1980–92)	
	%GDP	%SE	%GDP	%SE	%GDP	%SE
Sickness	4.7	25.6	5.6	24.6	+0.9	−1.0
Disability	1.4	7.5	1.8	8.1	+0.4	+0.6
Work accidents	0.4	2.4	0.5	2.3	+0.1	−0.1
Old age	5.4	29.6	6.7	29.6	+1.3	0.0
Survivors	1.8	9.8	2.3	10.0	+0.5	+0.2
Maternity	0.3	1.4	0.2	0.9	−0.1	−0.5
Family	0.5	2.8	0.2	0.9	−0.3	−1.9
Employment promotion	0.1	0.6	0.2	0.9	+0.1	+0.3
Unemployment	2.7	14.9	3.8	17.0	+1.1	+2.1
Housing	0.0	0.0	0.2	0.7	+0.2	+0.7
Administration	0.7	3.7	0.9	3.8	+0.2	+0.1
Miscellaneous	0.3	1.7	0.3	1.2	0.0	−0.5
Total	18.3	100.0	22.7	100.0	+4.4	0

Source: Rodríguez-Cabrero (1994), and author's elaboration.

demise of Francoism have greatly determined the changing allocation of funds within the budgetary structure of Spanish public expenditure.

In the period 1980–92, social spending increased its share of the Spanish GDP by 4.37 per cent. Table 9.1 reproduces data regarding the functional breakdown of social expenditure composition in percentages of GDP. The increases referring to 'Old age' and 'Unemployment' add up to more than half of the growth of social spending as a percentage of GDP for the period 1980–92. These two categories plus that of 'Sickness' comprised almost three-quarters of the total social expenditure. Maternity and family expenses decreased notably.

As in most of Continental Europe, social benefits in Spain have been traditionally designed to secure 'income maintenance' for those citizens who have made contributions to the social security system during their working life. Employers' (53 per cent) and employees' (17 per cent) contributions meet the greater part of the financing of social protection spending (Eurostat 1995). However, a significant shift has taken place in recent years with a gradual transferring of public moneys from the national budget to the social security accounts.[5] This is particularly relevant as regards reforms on pensions (non-contributory) and health care, which will be outlined below.

Reforms and future scenarios

The impact that education reforms have had on the aggregate of social welfare should be emphasised. Fifteen years after the first changes in the educational public system were introduced their redistributive effects are evident. To a degree still to be assessed, such an impact has considerably affected the mechanisms of social reproduction ingrained in a liberal-meritocratic ideology. The extension of

Table 9.2 Main categories of social expenditure in Southern Europe, 1993 (as percentage of GDP)

	Old age and survivors	Sickness	Unemployment benefits	Disability	Family
Greece	10.2	2.3	0.5	1.5	0.1
Italy	15.4	5.4	0.5	2.2	0.8
Portugal	7.0	5.3	0.8	2.4	0.8
Spain	9.4	5.9	4.8	2.3	0.2
EU-12, average	11.9	6.5	1.9	2.4	1.8

Source: European Commission (1996), and author's elaboration.

means-tested schemes of educational grants has also reinforced social redistribution.

The universalisation of the educational system has meant that 100 per cent of the population in the 4–15-year age group has access to nursery, primary and secondary schooling.[6] In 1992, relatively and absolutely, more women than men were under education among groups ranging from 16 to 29 years. It is particularly worth noting that, among the 16–19 year olds, 63 per cent of women were receiving formal education as compared to 53 per cent of men. Furthermore, there was a difference of over 8 percentage points concerning the 20–24 year olds (EPA 1993).

The four areas of our subsequent analyses carry the main bulk of social expenditure: 'Pensions', 'Health care', 'Unemployment and employment promotion' and 'Social assistance'. In Table 9.2 a selection of five categories related to social protection spending in the Southern European countries are presented, plus the EU average. A look at these data reveals two main deviations: social expenses under 'Old-age and survivors' in Italy (15.4 per cent) and under 'Unemployment benefits' in Spain (4.8 per cent) are disproportionately higher than the EU-12 mean figures. In fact those percentages are the highest of all the EU-12 countries considered. These findings tell us a great deal about the most pressing challenges facing both Italy and Spain with relation to welfare financing.

Pensions

With the implementation of the 'Non-contributory Pensions Act', in 1990, coverage for both old age (over 65 years) and disability pensions (over 65 per cent for citizens between 18 and 65 years) became universal.[7] Note that in the period 1980–92, the number of pensioners rose by 2.5 million (2.1 contributory, and 0.4 non-contributory), from 4.7 to 7.2 million. The total expenditure increased from 5.9 per cent (5.8 per cent contributory, and 0.1 per cent non-contributory) to 8.6 per cent (8.1 per cent contributory, and 0.5 non-contributory) as a percentage of GDP. Average social security pension benefits increased from 66.5 per cent of the minimum salary in 1980 to 93.3 per cent in 1992. Non-contributory (social assistance) pensions were 53.3 per cent of the minimum salary in 1992 (Cruz Roche 1994).[8]

Spain has gone through significant demographic changes in recent times. Its population is nearly 40 million with a mere annual growth rate of 0.2 per cent since the beginning of the 1980s. The main reason for such a sluggish increase in population is the decline in fertility rates since the 1970s. It decreased from 3.0 per cent in 1965 to 2.8 per cent in 1970, and from 2.1 per cent in 1980 (a percentage lower than that required to ensure generation replacement) to 1.16 in 1997 (the lowest in Europe). In parallel, the proportion of the population aged 65 or over grew from 10.9 per cent of the total in 1980 to 12.7 per cent by 1990 (Council of Europe 1989). Projections for the year 2020 estimate that around 19 per cent of the total population of Spain will be over 65 years of age (European Commission 1998).

Italy and Greece are well above the EU mean percentage of 62.0 per cent for the *per capita* average old-age pension (77.6 per cent and 78.8 per cent in 1993, respectively). As seen from Table 9.3, this is not the case for Spain and Portugal (47.3 per cent and 42.1 per cent, respectively) with a more balanced inter-generation distribution of resources.[9] However, a general concern about the 'uncontrolled' increase of pensions relative to GDP growth was behind the modification in 1985 of the criteria in the annual revaluing of benefits (forecast rate instead of past inflation rate),[10] and a tightening of requirements for contributory pensions.

More restrictive criteria in the definition of disability, together with a closer overall administrative control, considerably reduced the acute increase in this type of pension up until 1985. The process in Spain has been somewhat different from that of the Italian case. In the latter both *clientelismo* and the connivance to defraud between employers and prospective claimants are among the causes for the highest public spending in the European Union for the categories of 'Disability' and 'Old-age and survivors' put together (Ferrera 1995).

Table 9.3 Intensity of old-age protection in Southern Europe, 1980–93 (average pension as percentage of GDP per head)

	1980	*1993*	*% change (1980–93)*
Greece	48.5	78.0	+29.5
Italy	62.1	77.6	+15.5
Portugal	41.3	42.1	+0.8
Spain	49.6	47.3	−2.3
EU-12	56.2	62.0	+5.8

Source: European Commission (1996), and author's elaboration.

Health care

The 1986 General Health Act was committed to the development of a National Health Service, which guaranteed access to health care for all Spaniards and all foreign citizens resident in Spain. Coverage, which was already very high in 1980 (83.1 per cent of all citizens and residents), was almost total by 1991 (99.8 per cent) (Almeda and Sarasa 1996; Guillén and Cabiedes 1997). Two thirds of the financing of Spanish health is public. Of the remaining one-third, 90 per cent are direct payments by individuals (mostly for private care and medicines). These figures have remained stable during the 1980–93 period. But the most significant variation of this period is reflected in the shift of the financing of public expenditure from contributions to taxation. In 1980, as much as 82 per cent of the spending on health was met by social contributions, whereas in 1993 the corresponding figure was 20 per cent. This dramatic change is in line with the assumption that universalisation of the public health service should be related to a system of general financing by taxation on the basis of a more equitable philosophy.

Regarding the provision of health services, the public system has continued to purchase many of its hospital services from both private and charitable sectors. The expansion of the public coverage has not been matched with equivalent increases in resources. Let us not forget that the increase of public expenditure on health during the period 1980–93 was merely 0.5 per cent. This figure seems to confirm the view that a universalisation of coverage has not been matched with an equivalent intensity in standards of care. Note that around 8 per cent of the population is covered by private health insurance (Freire 1993). Some occupational schemes remain for groups of the hyper-protected core of the workforce.

Complaints about the public health systems mostly relate to the bureaucratic-administrative impediments that hinder the functioning of hospitals rather than the quality of the services being provided by them.[11] Furthermore, levels of efficiency vary according to the powers on health provision, which have been decentralised to the 17 Autonomous Communities.[12] Some of these have implemented policies for the provision of services of a 'quasi-market' nature (Catalonia, Valencia), and have since then faced problems in the financing of their respective public health systems.[13] A rationalisation of health consumption – primarily, medicines – has come to the fore on the discussion of adapting levels of expenditure to socio-demographic changes (particularly in reference to citizens of 65 years and over). Longer time-series are needed in order to evaluate with a degree of plausibility the effects of these reforms of hospital management, financial restraining and improvement of both efficiency and equality of health care.

Unemployment and employment promotion

The unemployment rate in Spain is the highest in the European Union. According to the macro-survey on the active population carried out every term in Spanish households (*Encuesta de Población Activa*), at the end of 1997 the number of unemployed amounted to 20.5 per cent. Despite the fact that the EPA survey is methodologically sophisticated and technically accurate in its mechanisms of data collection and processing, a long-standing controversy has developed on whether its results are representative of the actual situation of the labour market in Spain. The persistence of a large 'hidden' tax-free economy in Spain largely distorts the reliability of the EPA data. Unquestionably, there is a sizeable portion of survey respondents who either hide their labour status or 'disguise' it (e.g. working within the informal sector). Some authors are of the opinion that the registered unemployed at the governmental job agencies of INEM[14] reflects more approximately the 'real' number of unemployed in Spain (12.8 per cent of the total active working population at the end of 1997). Nevertheless, on comparing the diverging EPA and INEM figures, the number of those citizens who simply do not bother to file a job application at the INEM agencies is also to be taken into account.

Given the high rate of unemployment in Spain, some observers are puzzled by the relatively stable social situation in the country, particularly concerning sections like the young (among whom unemployment rates reach percentages of around 40 per cent and 45 per cent, respectively, for males and females aged 20–24 years). Explanations for this less-traumatic phenomenon associated with unemployment in Spain rest upon two considerations: (a) the considerable public expenditure related to unemployment benefits: 4.8 per cent of GDP was allocated to this social expense, the highest percentage in all EU-12 countries in 1993; and (b) support to the unemployed by family and household networks of micro-solidarity.

A widespread perception of the need to establish a new legal framework aimed at job creation, especially for the young, and limiting the burden of labour costs to improve competitiveness had been perceived by the social partners. However, it is to be noted that the impact of deregulation on the growth of employment in Spain has been very limited. In fact, the legal framework did not seem to constitute in itself a compelling variable for the creation or destruction of employment in Spain. With the same labour legislation, half a million jobs were created in Spain in 1987 and 400,000 were destroyed in 1993 (Missé 1997).

Flexibility and deregulation were the main themes behind active labour market measures in the first half of the 1990s. But the immediate effect brought about by deregulatory policies was an exponential rise in the number of temporary and part-time occupations (nearly 40 per cent of the total labour force). In 1996 only 4 per cent of all new jobs were established on a permanent basis. New contracts benefited from fiscal subventions and some consolidated the spurious practice of formalising *de jure* temporary contracts replacing *de facto* permanent working positions.

In order to alleviate a social perception of labour precariousness and to avoid the perverse effects of the so-called 'junk' jobs, both employers' confederation (CEOE) and trade unions (CCOO and UGT) engaged in negotiations and agreements, which later became laws on the initiative of the PP (Partido Popular

(Popular Party)) government in May–June 1997. To be underlined are the labour regulations for new contracts on permanent bases. CCOO and UGT have given consent to legislation allowing a substantial reduction to be paid to newly hired employees by the employers if they are made redundant in the future.[15]

Corporate welfare measures and fiscal incentives are to be met by Spanish public expenses favouring those companies hiring employees on a full-time and permanent basis. All these provisions are aimed at counteracting the effects of what seemed an unstoppable process of job precariousness since 1994. These policies are expected to have a greater impact on family-type companies and micro-enterprises. Rebate for employers' contributions to the social security system range from between 40 per cent to 60 per cent. For those small businesses under the system of income tax modules – instead of the corporation tax regime – welfare credits will affect new employment with no payments in the first two years.[16]

The single most significant feature in the composition of the Spanish labour force is the increasing participation of women. This trend seems to correlate with the growing incorporation of women in formal education. In the last two periods of general growth of employment in Spain (1964–74 and 1985–90), women's participation in the labour market increased *vis-à-vis* male workers. In 1969 there were 32 female workers for every 100 male employees. This ratio increased to 39/100 in 1974, to 41/100 in 1985, and to 46/100 in 1990 (Garrido 1994). In relative terms, women's participation is larger in the public sector than the private. Note that in 1964 there were 17 women for every 100 male public employees.[17] The ratio jumped to 70/100 in 1991. Even more representative of this changing pattern is the fact that, within the 25–29 age group, the proportion of female public employees was 105 for every 100 male workers in 1990. Job security and stability appear to be paramount for women in this age group. In contrast with the situation in Germany and the United Kingdom, employment interruptions in Spain – and Southern Europe, as a whole – are motivated more by professional reasons and less by maternity concerns. This pattern translates into high continuity rates and fewer part-time jobs (Jurado and Naldini 1996).

A change in the priorities of greater numbers of women with respect to their traditional subordinate position within the labour market and their commitment to raising children has taken place during the last two decades. This changing role of women within both the labour market and households will have important repercussions for the future of the Spanish welfare state. The generation born between 1950 and 1970 is characterised in the main by well-educated women committed to professional activities. This pattern is coupled with a postponement in giving birth to their first child. Furthermore, marriage rates have diminished as a result of unemployment, problems of matching expectations of 'good' jobs according to higher levels of qualifications, and rising costs of living, particularly in urban areas. Transformations in family patterns are similar in other Southern European countries, which are reflected in attitudes of ambivalent familialism by women (Flaquer 1995; Saraceno 1995).

Social assistance

The process of political and administrative decentralisation, according to the 1978 Constitution, is the most compelling force behind the shaping of welfare development in Spain. De-concentration of social services has had a much larger impact than privatisation (Almeda and Sarasa 1996).

Spain has gone through a substantial social, economic and political transformation since the inception of the 1978 Constitution. The *Estado de las Autonomías* ('state of autonomies') has transcended to a large extent the traditional cultural patterns of ethnoterritorial confrontation in Spain (Moreno 1997a). In budgetary terms, variations were substantial in the period 1978–97: central government expenditure decreased from 90 to 61 per cent; regional government rose from zero to 26 per cent; and local government, from 10 to 13 per cent.[18]

According to the 1978 Spanish Constitution, social assistance is a power of the 'exclusive competence' of the 17 Autonomous Communities who have made use of this power extensively for purposes mainly of institutional legitimisation. Of great relevance for our analysis have been the programmes of *rentas mínimas* (minimum income benefits) or, in other words, *salario social* (social salary).

In order to combat poverty and situations of social exclusion, the 'Minimum Family Income' was introduced in the Basque Country in March 1989. This constituted a precedent and provoked a 'demonstration effect' in the subsequent programmes of minimum income benefits implemented in all 17 *Comunidades Autónomas*. Although showing a degree of diversity in policy design and coverage, programmes of 'minimum income' developed by the Spanish meso-governments aim at combining cash benefits with activation policies and programmes of social insertion (employment promotion and vocational training courses, primarily).

The impact of these *ab novo* programmes of 'minimum income' has had a dramatic effect in the debate about the completion of a 'safety net' in Spain. There are quasi-universalistic entitlements sharing some common features which can be identified as follows: (a) families are the units of reference even though individuals can be beneficiaries; (b) means-tested criteria are related to a threshold of household income under which cash benefits are awarded (around two-thirds of minimum wage); (c) residence status of applicants is required (ranging from 1 to 10 years); (d) periods of extension are available provided that beneficiaries have complied with programmes of social insertion activities, and their needs remain the same (Aguilar *et al.* 1995). Table 9.4 offers basic data on minimum income programmes.

These meso-governmental initiatives have certainly instigated welfare development in Spain. However, and due to their increasing financial difficulties, it remains to be seen whether these programmes will continue to be a priority for the regions. They may face a situation of either requesting cofunding from the central government or containing the scope of their coverage benefits.

In all future scenarios, the action by the regional and local government will be of decisive importance for welfare development in Spain. Indeed, the centre–periphery institutional interplay is a structuring variable, which predetermines to a great extent the diverse nature of welfare outcomes in contemporary Spain.

Table 9.4 Evolution of minimum income programmes in Spain, 1990–95

	1990	1992	1995
Andalusia	—	6,777	6,999
Aragon	—	—	990
Asturias	—	784	1,617
Balearic Islands	—	—	—
Basque Country	7,663	9,295	15,550
Canary Islands	—	61	4,510
Cantabria	400	217	203
Castille-La Mancha	—	539	2,006
Castille and Leon	—	1,794	3,092
Catalonia	370	2,870	7,522
Extremadura	515	1,782	1,955
Galicia	—	554	3,437
La Rioja	28	167	249
Madrid	1,034	7,102	6,918
Murcia	—	575	521
Navarre	417	1,018	2,117
Valencia	429	2,614	2,315
Total	10,856	36,149	60,001

Source: Ayala (1997).

Note
According to the Spanish Ministry of Labour and Social Affairs, in 1996 there were 211,221 beneficiaries in the whole of Spain including dependent family members.

Since 1988 the concerted action of the three levels of government to establish a comprehensive network of community centres has been instrumental in the extension of social services to the population at large.[19] The *Plan Concertado de Prestaciones Básicas de Servicios Sociales* (Concerted Plan for Basic Provision of Social Services) in municipalities was established in 1988.[20] It aims at providing services at the municipal level for the following purposes: (a) information and counselling; (b) social and day care services[21] for the disabled and elderly; (c) refuge for abused women, single mothers, orphans or mistreated minors, and the homeless; and (d) prevention and social insertion.

This network of community centres has taken over much of the social system developed by the Catholic Church during the 1960s. In the period 1989–96, the PSOE governments have not been opposed to lending support to private assistance and charities of a religious nature. Nevertheless, they have often tended to favour NGOs of a secular nature, as well as the Red Cross and the powerful National Organisation for the Blind (ONCE). Since 1996 the PP government has encouraged private assistance and concerted action with RC church institutions.

Targeting and selectivity

As in other Southern European countries the 'problem' with targeting is that social services and benefits do not always reach the needy or the citizens entitled to them. The mixed and fragmented nature of Southern welfare – both income-related and universalistic – makes the evaluation of welfare provision a complex task.

Debates on universality and selectivity have traditionally related to issues of equity and redistribution of welfare services and transfers. During the last decades a controversy has developed on the question whether targeting is not only more redistributive and egalitarian, but also more effective in dealing with poverty and social exclusion. One view maintains that, in general terms, public expenditure on health care, education, housing and transport systematically favours the better off to the detriment of those citizens 'targeted' to have access to those services on an equal opportunities basis (Le Grand 1982). Consequently, criteria on selectivity should be established in dealing with the least favoured groups in society. Another view acknowledges that middle classes are favoured by policies targeted on the worse off in universal welfare states. However, in the long run this 'unwanted' effect stimulates the virtuous circle of encouraging coalition formation between the working class and the middle class in support for continued welfare state policies: 'The poor need not stand alone' (Korpi 1980: 305).[22] In the case of a universal welfare state like Sweden, there is evidence that the middle classes are favoured by state institutions. However, once fiscal transfers have been taken into account, 60 per cent of the households pay more and receive much less from the social insurance system.[23] In recent times the idea of 'encompassing' welfare arrangements, whereby universal coverage and basic security form the base upon which income related benefits are erected have been put forward with relation to Scandinavian countries. This approach is partially in line with the 'Bismarckian' principle of social insurance and aims at providing income related benefits to all economically active individuals (Korpi and Palme 1994).

The situation in Southern Europe runs opposite to the direction taken by some Scandinavian reforms. In fact, from a contributory social security system, where selectivity has been the guiding principle of welfare development, a recent trend towards universalisation of benefits and services has been consolidating. As in the case of Britain, the last reforms are putting an emphasis on workfare and trying to avoid universal 'dependent' welfare. There seems to be a clear direction where most of the reforms implemented in the various systems of social protection in Europe are aiming. As it has never happened before, convergence is a noticeable development in the EU welfare states at the turn of the millennium.

At the heart of the above discussion lies the controversy related to the so-called 'Matthew effect',[24] which has far-reaching consequences in the case of Southern European welfare. This 'effect' is perceived as providing disproportionate advantages for those with information resources over those who are entitled to benefits but lack know-how and/or patronage network. However, and in contrast with the situation in other European systems, policies carried out according to targeting criteria in Southern Europe have had a 'ripple effect' upon worse-off categories expanding the 'grey zones' between both social insurance and social assistance realms. The main reasons for such phenomena can be explained by the following hypotheses:

(a) *The role played by the informal economy.* There are widespread practices involving fiscal transfers between those citizens fulfilling their fiscal obligations (mostly 'insiders' with gainful jobs and clientelist networks of social predation), and those evading taxes (in many cases 'peripheral' or 'outsider' workers with no information resources and/or excluded from contributory entitlements provided by the social security system). The strategies of the tax-free 'informal' labourers aim at maximising mainly from non-contributory selectivity programmes based on means testing. Some of them, however, refrain from doing so because of stigmatisation, a cultural behaviour widely extended in Southern Europe.

(b) *The role played by the Mediterranean family.* The increasing participation of female workers in the labour force, coupled with new burdens for family formation and expansion, raise big questions as to whether Southern welfare can maintain its internal *modus operandi* as has been the case up until now. A trend departing from the traditional functionality of the family as an indispensable complement to the action of the welfare state towards a more 'universal' system of social services and entitlements is observable, although it cannot be generalised.

These factors, among others, are responsible for an apparent paradox: Southern European countries show a 'visible' precariousness but severe poverty and social exclusion are limited and well below EU mean indicators.[25] In Spain, among the unemployed both poor and excluded take a sizeable share. However, in 1988 Spain was among the five EU countries with the lowest proportion of households where the head was unemployed and living below the poverty line.[26] All South European countries were below the EU average of 38 per cent, except Portugal, which, together with the United Kingdom, had the highest proportion of those households living below the poverty line (Goul Andersen 1997). This illustration seems to confirm the aforementioned paradox. In Spain, the means-tested sector of social protection, together with the effect of the 'informal' sector of the economy and in the context of family solidarity, has significantly limited the effects of unemployment.

Future scenarios for Europe

Spanish welfare, as well as that of the Latin countries, is closely tied to the process of European integration. Reforms of social protection in Southern Europe are to take into account the economic challenges of the increasing competition within the Single Market, and with respect to the emerging industrialised countries in other regions of the world. These challenges have led authors to label the general situation in the Old Continent as a 'frozen welfare landscape' (Esping-Andersen 1994). 'Eurosclerosis' is also regarded as a major obstacle to economic progress as global competition intensifies (Taylor-Gooby 1997). Implicit in these remarks is the quest for the achievement of a new model of development and growth within the international economic order.

There is also an alternative prescription, which proclaims the idea of a 'fortress Europe'. According to this view, the secession from the international world arena would preserve the maintenance of the European welfare regimes. An economic 'wall' around EU member states would guarantee social rights achieved by generations of Europeans. It would also stimulate a balanced growth, which, in turn, would create new employment coupled with job-sharing and the reduction of working time. Immigration would be tightly regulated. Undoubtedly this option would mean a U-turn in the cosmopolitan approach of European culture and a dramatic change in its value-system (Moreno 1997b).

The lingering 'demise' of the nation-state as the main source of economic planning seems more than plausible. Financial globalisation maximises speculation by a handful of monetary strategists in banks, investment funds, financial trusts and the like. A concerted effort within the European Union is required if goals for the preservation of social solidarity institutions are to be accomplished. The possibility of consolidating a new 'social contract' is at stake (Rodríguez-Cabrero 1997). This very much depends on the internalisation of values of compassion and solidarity by citizens at large and, in particular, by the bulk of the middle classes. Opting for the principles of social justice would be dependent on each citizen being able to place him or herself in the social position of any other person, and particularly the marginalised (Rawls 1971). The realisation of this point is essential if welfare systems of solidarity characteristic of European societies are to be revitalised.

Notes

1   This is Law 2 according to Esping-Andersen's ironic reference to the 'Four Laws of Sociology' (1993: 123–36). The other three are: (1) some do, some don't, (3) nothing ever works in India, and (4) there are no laws in Sociology.

2   According to a 1996 national survey, 46.3 per cent of Spaniards agreed that 'The state is responsible for each and every one of its citizens, and has the duty to help them to solve their problems'; 35.7 also agreed that 'The state is only responsible for the well-being of least-favoured citizens', and 13.0 per cent were of the opinion that 'Citizens are responsible themselves for their own well-being and have the duty to sort out their own problems' (Don't knows: 5.1 per cent) (CIS 1996)

3   In Greece the ubiquitous Orthodox Church of Greece continues to be the most important form of private action for the family and the poor (Symeonidou 1996). The same applies to the Roman Catholic Church – and its organisation Caritas – in Italy, Portugal and Spain. However, state welfare has widely increased in the last decades relegating the charitable action of the church to a complementary role. In Spain, for example, Caritas programmed 8,353 million pesetas to its 1988 social programme, an amount which was just above 9 per cent of the newly created Ministry of Social Affairs' budget (Rodríguez-Cabrero 1990).

4   With an increasing critical voice from the Spanish Communist party integrated in the electoral coalition United Left (*Izquierda Unida*).

5   The 'Pact of Toledo' was supported by the most representative social partners and political parties in Spain, and was ratified by the Spanish Parliament on 6 April 1996. Among its provisions a clear division for the financing of social protection in

Spain was agreed. By the year 2000 expenses incurred by the contributory Social Security system should be met by both employers' and employees' contributions. General taxation should be responsible for the cost of the universal non-contributory benefits and services.

6   Note that around 12 per cent of the public expenditure on education is paid to concerted private schools. Together with non-concerted private education, they both covered 31 per cent of the total student population in 1990 (38.6, pre-school; 34.5 per cent, elementary; 28.7 per cent, middle; and 8.1 per cent, university).

7   General requirements are (a) residence in Spain over five years, with the last two prior to the entitlement to the pension; and (b) lack of resources (means tested).

8   However the minimum salary decreased from 77.5 per cent of per capita GDP in 1980 to 52.4 per cent in 1992.

9   In Italy it may be improper to speak of a 'selfish' old-age generation but, according to F. Castles and M. Ferrera, 'clearly there is a set of life-cycle distributions which strongly favour the interests of the old' (1996: 175).

10   This was established by *Ley 26/1885* ('Act of Urgent Measures for the Rational-isation of the Structure and Protecting Action of the Social Security'). On March 1989, an additional Decree-Law regulated that compensation sums were to be added to pension payments only if the cost of living was to be higher at the end of each fiscal year.

11   There has been a traditional emphasis on hospital rather than primary care. This hospital-centred pattern of health care is ingrained in some public perception, which tends to disregard services at the primary level. Such a popular feeling has 'perverse' bureaucratic effects as regards the overcrowding of public hospitals.

12   By 1991 over half of health expenditure was managed at the meso-governmental level by both 'historical nationalities' (Basque Country, Catalonia and Galicia) and regions (Andalusia, Aragon, Asturias, Balearic Islands, Canary Islands, Cantabria, Castille and Leon, Castille-La Mancha, Extremadura, La Rioja, Madrid, Murcia, Navarre and Valencia).

13   This issue became a priority for the nationalist Catalan coalition, *Convergència i Unió*, in order to lend legislative support to the minority PP government after 1996.

14   The Spanish INEM (National Institute for Employment) classifies as registered unemployed all those citizens who have filed a job application in any of its agencies and who legally qualify as unemployed. Thus, those who have a 'visible' job – the disabled or students under the age of 25 are excluded. In order to be eligible for unemployment and social assistance benefits, citizens must comply with the requisite of being registered at the INEM agencies.

15   Redundancies should be based on objective criteria. In such an event, employers are to pay redundancy compensation to the employee up to the amount equivalent to 33 days of the worker's salary for each of the years employed by the company. The maximum sum is not to be higher than 24 monthly payments in total. These figures compare with the previous one of 45 days per year, and a maximum compensation of up to 42 monthly payments in total.

16   In implementing this new legislation, the political input of the Catalan nationalists (CiU), who have supported the minority PP government in the Spanish Parliament since the 1996 General Election, is to be underlined. Shopkeepers and owners of small businesses in Catalonia have traditionally been strong and faithful supporters of the Catalan electoral coalition.

17   In 1975 there were nearly 1 million public employees in Spain. At the beginning of 1996 the corresponding figure was nearly 1,800,000.

18   Governmental estimates for the allocation of public expenditure in the near future are 54 per cent (central), 33 per cent (regional), and 13 per cent (local): 'This hypothesis would place Spain among the most decentralised countries in the world' (MAP 1997: 4).

19   The same year the PSOE government first created the Ministry of Social Affairs. In 1996 the PP government integrated it within the Ministry of Labour and Social Affairs.

20   Central, regional and local authorities have contributed respectively 42 per cent, 33 per cent and 25 per cent to the Plan. It has covered all the Autonomous Communities except the Basque Country and Navarre. The latter maintains a regime of fiscal quasi-independence with respect to the central Treasury (by means of collecting all taxes and handing over to the central administration an agreed amount as *cupo*, or quota, in payment for the general services of the state). This arrangement has enabled the Basque Country and Navarre to enjoy a higher level of social spending.

21   These can be defined as a domain within which organised services are provided to strengthen the personal autonomy of both carers and often care receivers. Note that residential provision for the elderly reached around 2 per cent of citizens over 65 years of age. However, residences privately run for the elderly have greatly expanded in recent years.

22   According to Pzeworski (1985), the social democratic parties need to be supported by cross-class coalitions due to the shrinking numbers of the industrial working classes.

23   When judging the net impact of all economic transactions, Rothstein (1996) underlines the fact that both incomes and expenditures must be counted: the Italian bookkeeping establishes that where there is a credit entry there must also be a debit entry. Accordingly, different income groups part with different absolute terms, even if their tax rate is the same in percentage terms.

24   This 'halo effect' refers to the assertion in the Gospel according to Matthew: 'For whomsoever hath, to him shall be given, and he shall have more abundance; but whomsoever hath not, from him shall be taken away even that he hath' (13:12).

25   With the partial exception of Portugal. Although poverty has been reduced in the country as a whole, its severity has increased for rural households (Pereirinha 1996).

26   The European Commission defines (relative) poverty as having less than one-half of the consumption possibilities of the median household (corrected for household size and composition).

References

Aguilar, M., Gaviria, M. and Laparra, M. (1995) *La caña y el pez. El salario social en las Comunidades Autónomas 1989–1994*, Madrid: Fundación FOESSA.

Almeda, E. and Sarasa, S. (1996) 'Growth to Diversity', in V. George and P. Taylor-Gooby (eds) *European Welfare Policy. Squaring the Welfare Circle*, London: Macmillan.

Ayala, L. (1997) *Análisis económico de los sistemas de rentas mínimas en España desde una perspectiva comparada*. Ph.D. thesis, Universidad Complutense de Madrid, Facultad de Ciencias Económicas y Empresariales.

Castles, F. (1993) *Family of Nations. Patterns of Public Policy*, New York: Oxford University Press.

Castles, F. and Ferrera, M. (1996) 'Home Ownership and the Welfare State: Is Southern Europe Different?', *South European Society & Politics* 1, 2: 163–85.

CIS (1996) *Estudio 2.213*, Madrid: Centro de Investigaciones Sociológicas.

Council of Europe (1989) *Recent Demographic Developments in the Member States of the Council of Europe*. Strasbourg.

Cruz Roche, I. (1994) 'La dinámica y estructura de la universalización de las pensiones', *V Informe Sociológico sobre la Situación Social en España*, Madrid: Fundación FOESSA.

EPA (1993) *Encuesta de Población Activa*, Madrid: Instituto Nacional de Estadística.

Esping-Andersen, G. (1990) *Three Worlds of Welfare Capitalism*, Cambridge: Polity Press.

—— (1993) 'The Comparative Macro-sociology of Welfare States', in L. Moreno (ed.) *Social Exchange and Welfare Development*, Madrid: CSIC.

—— (1994) 'After the Golden Age', UN World Summit for Social Development, Occasional Paper no. 7. Geneva: UNRISD.

European Commission (1996) Social Protection in the Member States of the Union: Situation on 1 July 1995, Luxembourg: MISSOC.

—— (1998) *Social Protection in Europe 1997*, Luxembourg: MISSOC.

Eurostat (1995) *Eurostat Yearbook 1995: A Statistical Eye on Europe, 1983–93*, Luxembourg: OOPEC.

Ferrera, M. (1995) 'Los Estados del Bienestar del Sur en la Europa social', in S. Sarasa and L. Moreno (eds) *El Estado del Bienestar en la Europea del Sur*, Madrid: CSIC.

—— (1996) 'The "Southern Model" of Welfare in Social Europe', *Journal of European Social Policy* 6, 1: 17–37.

—— (1997) 'The Four Social Europe's: between Universalism and Selectivity', in Y. Mény and M. Rhodes (eds) *A New Social Contract? Charting the Future of European Welfare*, London: Macmillan.

Flaquer, Ll. (1995) 'El modelo de familia española en el contexto europeo', in S. Sarasa and L. Moreno (eds) *El Estado del Bienestar en la Europa del Sur*, Madrid: CSIC.

Flora, P. (1986/87) *Growth to Limits. The European Welfare States Since World War II*, Berlin: De Gruyter.

Freire, J. M. (1993) 'Cobertura sanitaria y equidad en España', *I Simposio sobre igualdad y distribución de la renta y la riqueza*, Madrid: Fundación Argentaria.

Garrido, L. (1994) 'La evolución de la situación de la mujer', *V Informe Sociológico sobre la Situación Social en España*, Madrid: Fundación FOESSA.

Giner, S. (1986) 'Political Economy, Legitimation and the State in Southern Europe', in G. O'Donnell and P. Schmitter (eds) *Transitions from Authoritarian Rule: Prospects for Democracy*, Baltimore: Johns Hopkins University Press.

Gough, I. (1996) 'Social Assistance in Southern Europe', *South European Society & Politics* 1, 1: 1–23.

Goul Andersen, J. (1997) 'The Scandinavian Welfare Model in Crisis? Achievements and Problems of the Danish Welfare State in an Age of Unemployment and Low Growth', *Scandinavian Political Studies*, 20, 1: 1–31.

Guillén, A. M. and Cabiedes, L. (1997) 'Towards a National Health Service in Spain. The Search for Equity and Efficiency', *Journal of European Social Policy*, 7, 4: 319–36.

Jurado Guerrero, T. and Naldini, M. (1996) 'Is the South so Different? Italian and Spanish Families in Comparative Perspective', working paper I/12, Mannheim Centre for European Social Research.

Katrougalos, G. (1996) 'The South European Welfare Model: The Greek Welfare State, in Search of an Identity', *Journal of European Social Policy* 6, 1: 40–60.

Korpi, W. (1980) 'Social Policy and Distributional Conflict in the Capitalist Democracies: A Preliminary Comparative Framework', *European Politics* 3, 3: 296–316.

Korpi, W. and Palme, J. (1994) 'The Strategy of Equality and the Paradox of Redistribution', paper prepared for the sessions of RC 19 (Poverty, Social Welfare, and Social Policy) at the World Congress of Sociology (Bielefeld) 18–24 July 1994.

Kuhnle, S. (1997) 'La reconstrucción política de los Estados del Bienestar europeos', in L. Moreno (ed.) *Unión Europea y Estado del Bienestar*, Madrid: CSIC.

Le Grand, J. (1982) *The Strategy of Equality. Redistribution and the Social Services.* London: George Allen & Unwin.

Leibfried, S. (1992) 'Towards a European Welfare State? On Integrating Poverty Regimes into the European Community', in Z. Ferge and J. Kolberg (eds) *Social Policy in a Changing Europe*, Boulder, CO: Westview.

MAP (1997) *Estudio sobre reparto del gasto publico en 1997 entre los distintos niveles de administración*, Madrid: Ministerio de Administraciones Públicas.

MIRE (1997) *Comparing social welfare systems in Southern Europe*, vol. 3, Florence Conference. Paris: Mission Recherche et Expérimentation (MIRE).

Missé, A. (1997) 'El espejismo de la reforma laboral', *El País* (10 February 1997).

Moreno, L. (1996) 'Southern Welfare States in Transition: Crisis, What Crisis? Issues for Discussion', paper presented at the Conference on Social Research and Social Policy in Southern Europe, 13–14 September, University of Athens.

—— (1997a) *La federalización de España. Poder político y territorio*, Madrid: Siglo XXI.

—— (1997b) 'Prefacio', in L. Moreno (ed.) *Unión Europea y Estado del Bienestar*, Madrid: CSIC.

—— (1997c) 'The Spanish Development of Southern Welfare', working paper 97-04, Madrid: IESA-CSIC. Online. Available HTTP: http://www.csic.es/iesa.

Moreno L. and Sarasa, S. (1992) 'The Spanish "Via Media" to the Development of the Welfare State', working paper 92–13, Madrid: IESA-CSIC.

—— (1993) 'Génesis y desarrollo del Estado del Bienestar en España', *Revista Internacional de Sociología* 6: 27–69.

Pereirinha, J.A. (1996) 'Welfare States and Anti-Poverty Regimes: The Case of Portugal', *South European Society & Politics* 1, 3: 198–218.

Pzeworski, A. (1985) *Capitalism and Social Democracy.* Cambridge: Cambridge University Press.

Rawls, J. (1971) *A Theory of Justice.* Cambridge, MA: Harvard University Press.

Rhodes, M. (ed.) (1996) 'Southern European Welfare States', *South European Society & Politics* 1, 3.

Rodríguez-Cabrero, G. (1990) *El gasto público en servicios sociales en España (1972–1988)*, Madrid: Ministerio de Asuntos Sociales.

—— (1994) 'La política social en España: 1980–92', *V Informe Sociológico sobre la Situación Social en España*, Madrid: Fundación FOESSA.

—— (1997) 'Por un nuevo contrato social: El desarrollo de la reforma social en el ámbito de la Unión Europea', in L. Moreno (ed.) *Unión Europea y Estado del Bienestar*, Madrid: CSIC.

Rothstein, B. (1996) 'The Moral Logic of the Universal Welfare State', in E. O. Eriksen and J. Loftager (eds) *The Rationality of the Welfare State*, Oslo: Scandinavian University Press.

Saraceno, C. (1995) 'Familismo ambivalente y clientelismo categórico en el Estado del Bienestar italiano', in S. Sarasa and L. Moreno (eds) *El Estado del Bienestar en la Europa del Sur*, Madrid: CSIC.

Symeonidou, H. (1996) 'Social Protection in Contemporary Greece', *South European Society & Politics* 1, 3: 67–86.

Taylor-Gooby, P. (1997) 'Transformaciones y tendencias en la provisión del bienestar europeo: Euroesclerosis, teorías de los regímenes y la dinámica del cambio', in L. Moreno (ed.) *Unión Europea y Estado del Bienestar*. Madrid: CSIC.

10 Reconstructing the welfare state in Southern Europe

Maurizio Ferrera

Introduction

The images of French *routiers*, German miners or Belgian automobile-workers striking to preserve their jobs and social guarantees are likely to be remembered as the most visible symbols of that struggle around welfare reform which has been dominating Europe's political landscape in the course of the last decade. Unfortunately the international media have been paying much less attention to other, less vocal protagonists of the same scene, somewhat crowded in its background: Neapolitan streetchildren living in conditions of extreme poverty; legions of Spanish youngsters with little prospect of finding a job; forgotten neighbourhoods in the peripheries of Athens, Lisbon or Palermo where the state (let alone a welfare state) is only a vague and distant presence. Yet these images are extremely relevant for a full understanding of the stakes surrounding welfare reform in Europe today. And Southern Europe is perhaps the area where these stakes are greater. Here reforming and modernising the welfare state is not just a matter of responding to demographic challenges or globalisation and meeting the new constraints of EMU, but a crucial step towards improving the life chances of millions of 'outsiders', who still remain to a large extent beyond the social reach of the state.

The structural crisis afflicting the Southern European welfare states is partly different from that of other Continental systems. The reasons are basically geo-evolutionary. In Spain, Portugal, Greece and (to a lesser extent) Italy the welfare state developed with a later timing and had to cope with more difficult socioeconomic environments – including the deep backwardness of the South's Souths. In these four countries social protection thus entered the age of 'permanent austerity' in a state of institutional and financial underdevelopment and laden with internal imbalances, of both categorical and territorial character. Their social transfer systems display at the same time peaks of generosity (at least in terms of legal formulas) for certain occupational groups and macroscopic gaps of protection for certain others. 'Insiders' and 'outsiders' are separated by a sharp divide in terms of guarantees and opportunities – in some cases with a middling group of semi-peripheral workers bouncing between the inside and the outside. Public services are still unevenly distributed and in some cases insufficient and/or inefficient. The most natural and politically simple way out of this syndrome would have been to complete the developmental parabola, gradually ironing out the internal imbalances with more (institutional and quantitative) growth. But this option has been ruled out, at least for the time being, by exogenous constraints. Southern European countries have thus been forced to tread on the politically perilous grounds of internal restructurings: less generous benefits for insiders in order to cut down deficits and debts and – to the extent that budgetary constraints allow it – to finance new benefits and services for the outsiders. The inherent difficulty of this path is aggravated not only by EMU's new constraints and by the winds of 'globalisation' but also by a particularly adverse demography. Southern European populations (especially those of Italy and Spain) are among the most rapidly ageing societies in the world. The intensity of the crisis and the turbulence of its politics of course vary in the four countries. Greece's predicament seems definitely the most serious: considering not only objective indicators, but also the degree of awareness of the main political actors, which still seems quite low. The Iberian countries, on the other hand, find themselves in relatively better shape – especially in terms of financial indicators. Italy's problems are more serious than those of Portugal and Spain – and her welfare politics is more unruly. With respect to Greece, however, there seems to be a much higher awareness of what ought to be done: some significant steps have been taken recently, moreover, on the road to welfare reform.

This chapter aims at sketching a general overview of the main problems and reform challenges of social protection in Southern Europe. The first section will discuss some common features of the Italian, Spanish, Portuguese and Greek welfare states which allow us to speak of a relatively distinct type of social policy in these four countries.[1] The second section will identify in its turn some perverse consequences arising from the interplay of these features and calling for incisive institutional changes. The third section will finally illustrate in more depth the specific predicament of Italy's welfare system, briefly discussing the reform debate currently ongoing in this country and the actual chances of overcoming the predicament in the foreseeable future. In the conclusion, an overall assessment will be drawn and future prospects for Southern European welfare will be briefly discussed.

A brief sketch of the Southern type of welfare

Is Southern Europe distinct with respect to other macro-areas of the continent? As is well known, there already exists a rich historical and social science literature which has answered positively to this question.[2] The nations of Southern Europe have followed a specific path to modernisation (in the broad sense of the concept) and still share a number of common traits in their contemporary political economies. There are, of course, significant differences between the countries of this region: the intra-area variation is certainly much greater than that of other families of nations, e.g. Scandinavia. Yet it would be difficult to deny that the notion of 'Southern Europe' has not only a geographical, but also a substantive, politico-economic connotation.

The idea that this area is distinct also as regards social policy has already started, in its turn, to be an object of debate. The question cannot be easily answered based on the literature of the 1970s and 1980s. Past research on the political economy of Southern European countries has largely neglected the social dimension, while the mainstream of comparative welfare research has not traditionally included the Southern European countries (with the partial exception of Italy) within its samples of observation. The first comparative investigations of the 1990s do confirm, however, the existence of some systematic regional similarities, such as: the relative underdevelopment of the welfare state and the gap between promised (sometimes even legislated) and *actual* achievements (Leibfried 1992; Gough 1996); the importance and resilience of the family as a sort of clearing house for the welfare of its members – with significant implications in terms of gender (Castles 1995; Moreno 1996, 1997 and Moreno, chapter 9 in this volume; Saraceno 1994; Trifiletti 1999); a social culture imbued with a specific brand of solidarism, highly influenced by the social doctrine of the church (Castles 1994; van Kersbergen 1995). Building on this literature, I suggest that a comprehensive characterisation of the Southern welfare state should include at least seven major distinctive traits.[3]

The first of these traits is the high relevance of transfer payments and especially the internal polarisation of Southern European income maintenance systems. Cash benefits play a prominent role in the countries of this area: indeed the Southern European welfare states constitute an extreme version of the transfer-centred model typical of Continental Europe (Kohl 1981; Esping-Andersen 1990; Kosonen 1994). As in the other Bismarckian countries, Southern European income maintenance is based on occupational status, with a marked degree of institutional fragmentation. The most distinctive peculiarity of these systems is, however, the dualistic, almost polarised character of the protection which is offered. On the one hand the schemes of these countries provide generous protection to the core sectors of the labour force, located within the regular or institutional labour market; on the other hand they only provide weak subsidisation to those located in the so-called irregular or non-institutional market. Spain, Portugal, Italy and Greece are also characterised by modest safety nets. In the first three countries local schemes guaranteeing a minimum income have been introduced only recently, while Greece still virtually lacks this type of scheme (Guibentif and Bouget 1997; Matsaganis 1999).

The second distinctive trait is an unbalanced distribution of protection across the standard risks, and more generally the various functions of social policy. This imbalance is especially revealed by three indicators:

1   The overprotection of the risk of old age and of the aged as a social group. This is attested by the larger share of pension expenditure, with respect to other types of expenditures (especially in Italy and Greece) and by expenditure data which break down total social expenditure by type of

beneficiary: the aged and the non-aged. According to calculations made by the OECD (1994), for instance, in 1989 the ratio between social protection expenditure on the aged and expenditure for the non-aged was above the EC average in all four countries, remarkably so in Italy and Greece (EC average: 1.27; Portugal: 1.40; Spain: 1.30; Italy: 4.14; Greece: 3.2). According to the latest Eurostat figures, in 1996 old-age pensions absorbed 54.2 per cent of total social protection expenditure in Italy, 41.2 per cent in Greece, 41 per cent in Spain (up from 36.2 in 1993) and 36 per cent in Portugal, compared to an average of 33.6 per cent in the remaining 11 member states (Eurostat 1999).

2   The underdevelopment of family benefits and services. According to Eurostat data, in 1995 family expenditures in cash and in kind averaged 2.1 per cent of GDP in the EU, but amounted to a modest 1.1 per cent in Portugal, 0.4 in Spain, 0.8 in Italy and 0.1 per cent in Greece (the four lowest figures of the 12 member states) (Commission of the European Communities 1998).[4]

3   The underdevelopment of public housing and of housing subsidies, coupled in some cases with an especially tight regulation of the private rental market. Partly as a consequence of this element, Southern European countries (especially Spain, Italy and Greece) display the highest rates of home owner-ship in Europe. They are also virtually the only countries in the advanced world in which the elderly (at least those who retire after a full career as employees) have institutionalised opportunities of both enjoying generous pensions and owning their homes, thus defying the logic of the 'home ownership/age pension' trade off, which seems to hold almost everywhere in the OECD (Castles and Ferrera 1996).[5]

These three interrelated elements work to activate a demographic bias in the Southern European welfare systems which – as will be argued in the next section – has very serious consequences for their overall functioning.

The third distinctive trait has to do with health care. While displaying high institutional fragmentation along occupational lines in their income main-tenance systems, the Southern European welfare states are characterised by a universalistic approach in their health care systems. All four countries have legislated into existence a National Health Service inspired by the British model – though only Italy has implemented a fully fledged universal service, with no occupational distinctions. The mix between income maintenance occupationalism and health care universalism is a quite peculiar trait of the welfare states of this area of Europe. Enshrined in specific and detailed provisions of the Italian, Spanish, Portuguese and Greek constitutions, this dual approach sets the Southern European *via media* of welfare (Moreno and Sarasa 1992) programmatically apart from both the pan-universalistic, citizenship-centred Beveridgean model of Northern Europe and the pan-professional, insurance-centred Bismarckian model of Germanic countries. The idea that cash benefits ought to be tied to work positions (and financed by contributions); but that health care ought to be, on the contrary, tied to citizenship alone and provided on a universal basis and in decentralised forms is a relatively distinct and original welfare project of Southern European countries.[6]

The fourth trait is constituted by a highly articulated (but occasionally collusive) mix between public and non-public actors and institutions. This trait is particularly evident in the field of health care and social services. In Britain and Scandinavia the establishment of a NHS has not only implied a universalisation of coverage and a standardisation of norms and structures, but also a crowding out of private providers from the health sector. The public/private mix has evolved differently in Southern Europe. Here the establishment of an NHS (Italian or Iberian and especially Greek style) has not promoted a strengthening of the public sphere and the crowding out of private provision, but rather a peculiar collusion of public and private, often with great advantages for the latter (Mozzicafreddo 1992; Paci 1987; Pereirinha 1992).

The fifth important trait has less to do with the formal or tangible architecture of the welfare state and has more to do instead with its concrete mode of functioning. I refer here to the persistence of 'institutional particularism', if not outright clientelism and in some cases the formation of fairly elaborated 'patronage' machines for the distribution of cash subsidies. This is especially true of Italy and Greece (Petmesidou 1991), but according to some authors also in the Iberian countries examples of partisan manipulations of certain sectors of the welfare state can be found, at least during the 1980s and early 1990s (Cazorla 1992, 1994; CEMOTI 1989; Perez Diaz 1990). It is certainly true that some degree of institutional particularism characterises all developed systems of social protection. But when particularistic ties or networks play a prominent and in some cases determinant role in granting access to important benefits or services, when they even display some sort of formal institutionalisation (as was the case in Italy in the sector of invalidity benefits or in Spain in the sector of unemployment benefits for the agricultural unemployed during the 1980s), then particularistic norms and clientelistic circuits start to make a difference in systemic terms (Ferrera 1996).

The last two traits have essentially to do with the financing of welfare. Here the problem is constituted by (a) the highly uneven distribution of burdens across the various occupational groups due to legal disparities, and (b) the high incidence of the 'black economy' and therefore of tax evasion. The black economy is estimated to produce between 15 per cent and 30 per cent of total GDP in the countries of this area and its presence has serious implications for the welfare state – not only its financial stability, but also its overall effectiveness and legitimacy. The size and persistence of the black economy in Southern Europe represents a variant of that 'inactivity trap' which operates in other Continental systems as an effect of high payroll contributions and guaranteed social minima (Scharpf 1997). The role of the latter is played in Southern Europe more by the extended family (in which various income 'crumbs' from work or from the welfare system are pooled and redistributed) than by social assistance subsidies *per se*; and subsidised inactivity should rather be thought of as 'underground activism'. But the two syndromes do display structural analogies, and have equally perverse implications. As Scharpf has shown, in Germany the high incidence of social security contributions tends to inhibit especially the expansion of the sector of personal services. The Italian variant of this syndrome is the peculiarly high incidence of black work precisely in this sector (ISTAT 1999).

These seven traits do not exhaust the list of social policy peculiarities of Southern Europe. Taken together, however, they do add up to a rather coherent set of elements which can be treated as a single institutional configuration, with a somewhat autonomous internal logic: a logic which to a large extent presupposes (and thus reinforces) that 'familialism' that is so often emphasised – as mentioned above – in debates about Southern European society and social policy. I have elsewhere discussed some possible historical causes of this configuration (Ferrera 1996). I will therefore devote the next section to highlighting some of its structural consequences.

The institutional predicament of social policy in the South

In the course of the 1990s the configuration which has just been illustrated has started to raise a number of problems, which risk entangling Southern welfare in a sort of vicious circle. The main root of such problems lies, arguably, with the polarised and demographically biased character of social protection. This state of affairs has in fact become largely incongruent with respect to the external socioeconomic context, while at the same time its internal logic works to make adaptive changes more difficult. This argument can be best spelled out in an evolutionary perspective.

In its early phases of development a polarised and demographically skewed pattern of social distribution did not pose particular problems to other institutional spheres (especially the family and the labour market) and it was indeed perfectly compatible with (a) the traditional 'Southern family', with its extended network of solidarities and its intense flow of intergenerational transfers, and (b) with the traditional 'Fordist' labour market, capable of offering a growing number of stable jobs providing a family wage to the younger generations. As is known, despite their late industrialisation and the persistence of a large informal sector, the Southern European economies have created in the past highly rigid labour markets, offering tenured jobs and relatively good wages to all regular employees. There is a systematic link between the existence of strong family ties, a rigid institutional labour market and an emphasis on pensions. Only the availability of secure jobs during active life and of high intra-familial transfers (material and immaterial) in the crucial phases of the life cycle can in fact sustain a concentration of benefits on the aged which in turns crowds out resources for welfare benefits and services to the young and/or to active workers and their families. In other words, in the past decades the Southern European con-figuration was based on the following 'circle' (maybe not a virtuous circle, but at least a relatively coherent one):

- Active workers in the regular labour market would finance – via social contributions – the benefits accruing to their parents (more generous benefits than in other Continental countries, at least for standard workers).
- Relatively high pension contributions would crowd out the possibility of other welfare benefits such as family allowances and services or public housing.
- The family and housing needs of active workers could be catered for both through the relatively generous wages drawn from tenured jobs in the regular labour market or through intra-familial transfers at the time of marriage or childrearing, etc.

The persistence of the informal economy also contributed to absorbing the adverse effect of a demographically skewed social distribution to the extent that it allowed working families to earn additional incomes through marginal activities or to avoid taxes on the second income.

Things still work this way to some extent. But the transformation of the external socioeconomic context, on the one hand, and the very maturation of generous pension systems, on the other, absorbing an increasing share of resources, has turned this relatively coherent institutional mechanism into a vicious circle, which is gradually eroding its very material foundations.

Let us, in fact, consider the effects of the configuration on the family. The lack of external supports and opportunities as regards housing, transfers and services has started to restrict the range of choices for young people and to act as a clear obstacle for family formation (marriages) and family expansion (children). There is evidence of a gradual delay in the age of first marriage and childbearing throughout Southern Europe, which partly explains the remarkable decline of fertility witnessed by the countries of this area (Jurado and Naldini 1996). Housing and welfare are not the only factors which influence marriage and reproductive decisions, but the current distributive status quo certainly works to aggravate the bleak demographic prospects of the Southern European populations, which seriously undermine the financial stability of this area's pension systems. Recent debates have started to revalue the familistic orientation of Southern European welfare systems, in both functional and normative terms (Perez Diaz *et al*. 1998). Even these debates have to recognise, however, that some sort of problematic syndrome is emerging in this area: an institutional configuration originally built to serve the family is now working to erode its own foundations by discouraging, precisely, family reproduction.

The consequences of the demographic bias and distributive distortions of the Southern European welfare states are equally serious in respect of the labour market. In the new globalising context, insisting on contribution-heavy and highly rigid regular jobs means only one thing: accelerating their decline. The low availability of public services for working parents and of flexible rental markets hinders in its turn that mobility which is increasingly becoming a prerequisite for processes of post-industrial or neo-industrial economic restructuring. Despite their long historical record of foreign migrations, Southern

European workers are today among the least mobile of Europe. Though cultural dynamics are undoubtedly at work here, one fundamental reason for this low degree of geographical mobility of the Southern Europeans is also the cost of relocation or its sheer impossibility – for instance for lack of affordable housing. It may well be true that powerful political and institutional incentives are at work to preserve the distributive status quo (i.e. a contribution-heavy social protection mainly addressed to labour market insiders). But, again, the resulting circle is vicious, as it gradually erodes its own socioeconomic preconditions, that is, a constant supply of insider jobs.[7]

Even if the predicament of the Southern European welfare state has primarily internal origins, external challenges have been working to aggravate it. These external challenges mainly stem from the process of European integration and the strong pressure to meet the Maastricht convergence criteria by 1998. This was a virtually implausible scenario for Greece, but Portugal, Spain and Italy made it in the end. Joining the EMU has markedly intensified the pressures for budgetary discipline, bureaucratic rationalisation and the containment of non-wage labour costs to maintain competitiveness. At the same time, though, the process of European integration has acted as a spur to create a more balanced system of social protection – more in line with European standards. Throughout the 1990s, the external constraint has become a major catalyst of institutional change, triggering off a much needed process of re-calibration of the welfare state. One the one hand, pensions have been the object of restrictive reforms in all four countries: in 1992 and then again in 1998 in Greece; in 1995–1997 in Spain; in 1992 in Portugal and on three subsequent occasions (1992, 1995 and 1997) in Italy. On the other hand, new benefits and services have been introduced to fill the gaps in coverage and strengthen minimum protection. European convergence has thus had both a negative and a positive side for the Southern countries and their politicians have been often able to exploit the latter in order to legitimise the former.

The difficult path to reform: the Italian experience

Italy's welfare system definitely epitomises the main Southern European's 'geo-evolutionary' contradictions – with a few extras. In comparative perspective, social expenditure is not high (25.3 per cent in 1994): above that of the other three countries, but well below that of other European countries with similar GDP per capita. The problems lie with the internal distribution of expenditure as well as with its pattern of financing (Ferrera 1997). Expenditure is markedly skewed in favour of regular employees as regards social groups and in favour of old-age pensions as regards social risks: the latter benefits alone absorb as much as 50 per cent of total social expenditure. This creates a highly polarised social distribution which, given the geography of Italy's labour markets, has also a strong territorial component. The main winners are retired civil servants and 'Fordist' workers retired from the strong sectors, while the ultimate losers are large families with unemployed spouses in the South – a social unit with virtually no access, *de facto*, to public transfers. This polarised welfare status quo rests on a highly inequitable system of financing – an element aggravated by the high levels of tax and contribution evasion. The other serious problem on the financial side is the chronic deficit between receipts and outlays of the social security sector: this deficit (which made its appearance already in the late 1960s) bears enormous responsibility for the formation of Italy's huge public debt (c. 123 per cent of GDP in 1995).

Triggered by the growing exogenous pressures connected with the 'Maastricht process', a sequence of reforms started in the early 1990s, aimed at rebalancing (in both financial and institutional terms) the Italian *stato sociale*. Not surprisingly, pensions have been the main target of retrenchment – especially the extremely generous benefit called *pensione di anzianità*, claimable after 35 years of contributions (20 for civil servants) with no age threshold. A first restrictive reform was passed in 1992 by the Amato government. In 1994 Berlusconi tried to introduce new severe cuts, but had to pull back after a harsh confrontation with the trade unions. After the fall of Berlusconi, the unions agreed, however, to negotiate with the new government a broad reform, which was eventually passed in August 1995, under the Dini government.

The main points of the Dini reform are: the shift from the old earnings-related formula to a new contribution related formula, to be phased in by 2013; the introduction of a flexible retirement age (57–65); the introduction of an age threshold for seniority pensions (57 years) for all workers, to be phased in by 2008; the gradual standardisation of rules for public and private employees; the graduation of survivor benefits according to income; finally, stricter rules on the cumulability of disability benefits and incomes from work, as well as tighter controls on the actual compliance with eligibility rules. It must be noted that opposition to patronage practices, partisan manipulations and fraudulent behaviour on the part of both administrators and beneficiaries of welfare benefits and services became an increasingly salient policy objective during the 1990s. Besides budgetary pressures, other important incentives for a move in this direction came from the judicial investigations on corruption and bribe practices launched by the Milan magistrates at the beginning of the decade and the ensuing breakdown of the traditional 'partitocratic' establishment.

The autumn of 1992 marked an important turning point also as regards health care: an incisive reform of the NHS was passed, aimed at streamlining financial flows, introducing quasi-market incentives and increasing administrative professionalism, with a view to countering the perverse effects of the existing public–private mix in provision.

The 1992–95 reforms represented major breakthroughs with respect to the institutional legacies of the past. They were also, however, the result of social and political compromises in which the government had to make a number of concessions (e.g. on the phasing in of the reforms) with respect to its own original plans. The most emblematic example of such concessions came in 1995, when Dini had to exempt all workers who had matured 18 years of insurance from the application of the new, less generously defined contribution pension formula.

The approximation of the EMU deadlines was keeping Italian authorities under acute budgetary pressures, so, soon after each one of these compromises, the government relaunched its reformist efforts, even widening the scope of its ambitions. In this vein, the new centre-left 'Olive-Tree' coalition led by Romano Prodi and voted into office in the spring of 1996 made a comprehensive reform of the *stato sociale* one of its highest priority. The objective of rebalancing the Italian model of welfare became explicit and was publicly emphasised with the motto *'più ai figli, meno ai padri'* ('more to children, less to fathers').[8] In January 1997 Mr Prodi appointed a commission of experts to draft a broad plan for reform. An articulated report was submitted by this commission (known as the Onofri Commission, after the name of its chairperson, a Bologna economist) and was centred on the idea of re-equilibrating and containing (though not reducing in the aggregate) social expenditure. The main proposals of the Onofri Commission were:

1   The introduction of additional measures of restriction and rationalisation of public pensions.[9]
2   A thorough reform of unemployment benefits and employment promotion schemes.
3   A further rationalisation of the incentive structure within the NHS.
4   A clear separation between social insurance and social assistance benefits (especially on the financing side).
5   A rationalisation of social assistance through the establishment of a guaranteed minimum income scheme.
6   The introduction of new, more effective 'selectivity' rules and procedures.

The Onofri Report was the object of a rather heated debate in the summer and autumn of 1997. In the budget law for 1997 the Prodi government tried to adopt many of the Commission's recommendations. The fierce opposition of the Refounded Communists (whose votes were crucial for reaching a majority in parliament) and difficult negotiations with social partners forced, however, the government substantially to scale down its ambitions. In the field of pensions, Prodi was able to introduce some cuts in seniority pensions, especially for public employees: their contributory requirement for claiming a seniority pension was aligned with that applying to private employees. Contributions for the self-employed were raised, a temporary freeze on the indexation of higher pensions was introduced and some steps were made on the 'harmonisation' front. However modest (with respect to the government's original ambitions), these cuts had the advantage of being immediately effective and thus made a small contribution (0.2 per cent of GDP) towards reaching the budgetary targets for 1998. The most important recommendation of the Onofri plan, i.e. a much faster phasing in of the new pension formula introduced in 1995, could not be adopted and by creating a cabinet crisis the Refounded Communists were able to obtain the exemption of blue-collar workers from the cuts in seniority pensions.[10] Nothing was achieved in the field of unemployment insurance either. But the government was able to push through some important innovations on the social assistance and selectivity fronts. More transparent rules for the financing of social assistance were introduced and the budget law for 1998 – which was approved in December 1997 – delegated the executive to take measures in two important directions: (1) the introduction of a new 'indicator of socioeconomic conditions' (ISE), based on both income and asset criteria, to be used as a yardstick for all means-tested benefits; (2) the introduction of a new (experimental) scheme of 'minimum insertion income' (RMI), i.e. a last resort guaranteed safety net administered by local governments. Both the ISE and the experimental RMI were actually introduced in the course of 1998.[11]

Since the mid-1990s significant steps have been made also on the financing side of welfare and on the black economy front. The legal disparities in contribution rates across occupational categories have been ironed out, the financing of the NHS has been completely fiscalised (i.e. based on taxes and user charges rather than on contributions) and specific incentives have been introduced for the emergence of underground activities.[12]

This sequence of reforms has not fully eradicated the distributive and allocative distortions of the Italian welfare state which have been mentioned above. They have, however, made significant steps in this direction. More importantly, they have planted promising institutional seeds that may trigger off a sort of spontaneous and self-sustaining dynamic of internal re-equilibration. On the one hand, the setting of more transparent and clear-cut boundaries between social insurance and social assistance as well as the consolidation of new instruments such as the ISE and the RMI will work to strengthen that safety net of means-tested and need-based benefits and services which have been historically lacking (or very weak) in Italy. In this vein, the D'Alema government formed in October 1998 decided to raise social and minimum pensions and to introduce two new means-tested benefits: an allowance for families with three or more children and a maternity allowance for women not covered by compulsory insurance. On the other hand, the new architecture of the pension system will work to gradually downsize (or at least contain the further expansion of) a sector which has been historically hypertrophic. It is true that, in spite of the reforms, at the end of the 1990s, Italy still displays one of the highest ratios of pension expenditure/GDP in the whole OECD area and that the situation is going to worsen. But if one looks at the internal composition of total social expenditures, some positive signs seem to be emerging. In 1996 for the first time in several decades the share of old-age pensions started to decline (from 54.5 per cent to 54.2 per cent) with a parallel (if tiny) increase of the relative share of family benefits and services (from 3.5 per cent to 3.6 per cent). Moreover, the significance of the 1992/1995/1997 pension reforms must be appreciated when contrasted with the status quo and the 'no change' trends. As Figure 10.1 shows, in the absence of reforms, pension expenditure would have reached the impressive peak of 23.2 per cent of GDP in the year 2040, before starting to decline. After the reforms, the peak is expected to reach 'only' 15.8 per cent of GDP in the year 2032. The virtual stabilisation of pension expenditure may not have been enough to cure fully the long-standing

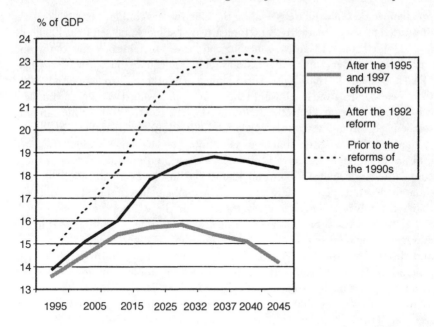

Figure 10.1 Pension expenditure projections for Italy, 1995–2045. Source: Ministero del Tesoro (1998).

disease of Italy's imbalanced welfare state. But it has certainly contained its fatal aggravation.

Conclusion

During the 1990s Italy and the other three Southern European countries have undertaken a process of gradual adjustment, in response to the institutional predicament outlined above. The specific ingredients and timing of this adjustment have obviously varied. But some basic similarities can be discerned in the reformist trends across this area: the ironing out of benefit formulas for privileged occupational groups and for standard 'Fordist' workers while at the same time upgrading minimum benefits; the introduction and consolidation of safety net programmes; steps towards remedying the conspicuous deficiency of social services to families; rationalising and, in some cases, decentralising, the organisational framework and financial incentives of the 'national' health services; and various moralising measures to combat corruption, clientelism and tax evasion. A new, accurate check on the 'state of the art' in respect of the seven traits identified above as characteristic of the Southern European welfare scene may well reveal, some time from now, that the syndrome has withered away,[13] and that the Italian, Spanish, Portuguese and Greek welfare states will have become national variants of the familiar Continental configuration – though with an unusual healthcare system. But even if this scenario should materialise, one big problem would unfortunately remain: the Continental configuration as such. As illustrated by a vast literature (and typically by Esping-Andersen 1996, 1999), the mix of labour market rigidity, generous and passive social protection and strong 'familialism' renders this configuration highly inadequate to respond to the new social and economic challenges. An alignment of Southern European standards to Continental norms and levels would thus only mean a walk down a dead end. And if it is true – as argued by some analysts – that the Continental regime can only rescue itself through a strategy of 'de-familialisation', then Southern European systems would have little chance of salvation. The challenge is indeed serious, and not adequately perceived by the key social and political actors of these countries. The decline of Italian and Spanish fertility, for example, should be more squarely debated and explicitly addressed by public policy in these two countries than it actually is. It is most unlikely, though, that the appropriate answer to such a challenge can be a Scandinavian style collectivisation of family needs in the hands of the state: because of financial, organisational and (not least) cultural and 'discursive' obstacles. A more viable strategy in the South would be the promotion of a novel *family-serving welfare mix*, whose profile seems to be emerging in some regions of this area, such as Catalunia, or Emilia-Romagna: a mix of intelligent public regulations and incentives, corporate arrangements, third sector activism and private entrepreneurship to respond to family (and especially women's) needs. In parallel with labour market reforms introduced via social and territorial pacts, gradually establishing conditions of 'flexible security' in the labour market, easing mobility and re-absorbing the outsiders, the new family-serving mix may be a crucial ingredient for effectively reforming the Southern type of welfare: and even for turning it, perhaps, into a proper 'model'.

Notes

1   The international debate often uses the term 'model' to denote a set of attributes which are common to a given number of national experiences: e.g. the Scandinavian model or the Continental model. I have myself used this term in an earlier article on Southern Europe (Ferrera 1996). In this chapter I prefer, however, to use the term 'type', which has no normative overtones while still conveying the idea of some systemic interdependence among the attributes under discussion.

2   The state of the art of this literature is discussed in Gunther *et al.* (1995).

3   The following discussion re-elaborates what is already said in Ferrera (1996, 1998a). As all typological efforts, my characterisation is – in Weberian terms – a 'unilateral accentuation' of a much richer and heterogeneous reality. It is not intended to unveil the 'true' nature of Southern European welfare, but more simply to highlight some features that are relevant for analysing the social policies of Portugal, Spain, Italy and Greece that to some extent are interconnected. Besides these features, there remain, of course, a number of significant differences across these four countries, which are well worth exploring, as typically recommended by the *'per genus et differentiam'* approach (for a more specific discussion of such methodological issues, cf. Ferrera (1998b)). For interesting

observations on the intra-area variations within Southern Europe, cf. Petmesidou (1996). A collection of contributions on Southern European social policies is contained in Rhodes (1998).

4 The figure for Greece refers to 1993. The EU average refers to 14 member states, excluding Greece.

5 Housing policies are not normally regarded as a central component of the welfare state (though Eurostat does include 'housing' as a function of social protection). This is a pity, as the distribution of housing resources – as shaped by specific governmental policies – does play an important role in determining the outcomes of the welfare state as a whole.

6 A project which – at least in Italy – has local ideal roots (in the latter country it made its first appearance as early as in 1918, after Bismarck, but long before Beveridge) connected not only with social Christianism, but also with a specific workerist and Marxist tradition (Ferrera 1993). For a survey of recent trends in Southern European health care, cf. Guillén (1999a).

7 For an analysis of the politico-institutional determinants of high unemployment in Spain and of the insider/outsider divide, cf. Maravall and Fraile (1998).

8 This was the title of a short book by Nicola Rossi, a Rome professor advising the government, which became very popular in 1997 (Rossi 1997).

9 Including: the complete harmonisation of rules across occupational funds; a more rapid phasing in of the Dini formula; more stringent rules on seniority pensions; higher contributions for the self-employed; an increase in the minimum age for retirement.

10 For a full review of the 1997 pension reform and its financial impact, cf. Mira d'Ercole and Terribile (1998).

11 A more detailed discussion of these new developments is contained in Ferrera (2000) (forthcoming).

12 The most important measure in this field has been the estabishment of 'emersion contracts' whereby underground employers can negotiate with the social security administration an amnesty on past evasion and a gradual alignment to legal rates of contribution if they commit themselves to becoming legal.

13 This is at least what some optimistic observers believe (e.g. Guillén 1999b).

References

Castles, F. (1994) 'On Religion and Public Policy', *European Journal of Political Research*, 25, 1: 19–39.
—— (1995) 'Welfare State Development in Southern Europe', *West European Politics*, 18, 1: 291–313.
Castles, F. and Ferrera, M. (1996) 'Home Ownership and the Welfare State: Is Southern Europe Different?', *Southern European Society and Politics*, no. 2: 163–85.
Cazorla, J. (1992) 'Del clientelismo tradicional al clientelismo de partido: evolucion y caracteristicas', Barcelona, Institut de Ciencies Politiques i Socials, WP 92/55.
—— (1994) 'El clientelismo de partido en España ante la opinion publica', Barcelona, Institut de Ciencies Politiques i Socials, WP 94/86.
CEMOTI (Cahiers d'études sur la Mediterranée orientale et le monde turco-iranien) (1989) 'Etats des travaux sur le clientèlisme de parti en Europe du Sud', cahier no 7, Paris: CNRS.

Commission of the European Communities (1995, 1998), *Social Protection in Europe*, Luxembourg.

Esping-Andersen, G. (1990) *The Three Worlds of Welfare Capitalism*, New York: Polity Press.

—— (1996) 'After the Golden Age? Welfare State Dilemmas in a Global Economy', in G. Esping-Andersen (ed.) *Welfare States in Transition. National Adaptations to Global Economies*, London: Sage.

—— (1999) *The Social Foundations of Post-Industrial Economies*, Oxford: Oxford University Press.

Eurostat (1999) *Dépenses et recettes de protection sociale. Données 1980–1996*, Luxembourg.

Ferrera, M. (1993) *Modelli di solidarietà*, Bologna: Il Mulino.

—— (1996) 'The Southern Model of Welfare in Social Europe', *Journal of European Social Policy*, 6, 1: 17–37.

—— (1997) 'The Uncertain Future of the Italian Welfare State', *West European Politics*, no. 2: 231–49.

—— (1998a) 'Welfare Reform in Southern Europe: Institutional Constraints and Opportunities', in H. Cavanna (ed.) *Challenges to the Welfare State*, Aldershot: Edward Elgar.

—— (1998b) 'General Introduction', in MIRE, *Comparing Social Protection Systems in Southern Europe*, Paris: Mire.

—— (2000) 'Targeting Welfare in a Soft State', in N. Gilbert (ed.) *Targeted Social Benefits*, New Brunswick: Transaction (forthcoming).

Gough, I. (1996) 'Social Assistance in Southern Europe', *South European Society and Politics*, 1, 1: 1–23.

Guibentif, P. and Bouget, D. (1997) *Minimum Income Policies in the European Union*, Lisbon: Uniao das Mutualidades Portuguesas.

Guillén, A. M. (1999a) 'Improving Efficiency and Constraining Costs: Health Care Reform in Southern Europe', Conference Paper WS/31, Florence: European Forum, EUI.

—— (1999b) 'Pension Reform in Spain (1975–1997): the Role of Organized Labour', seminar paper WS/22, Florence: European Forum, EUI.

Gunther, R., Diamanduros, P. N. and Puhle, H. J. (eds) (1995) *The Politics of Democratic Consolidation: Southern Europe in Comparative Perspective*, Baltimore: The Johns Hopkins University Press.

ISTAT (1999) *Rapporto annuale*, Series no. 8. Stat, Roma.

Jurado Guerrero, T. and Naldini, M. (1996) 'Is the South So Different? Italian and Spanish Families in Comparative Perspective', Working paper of the MZES, Mannheim, January.

Kohl, J. (1981) 'Trends and Problems in Postwar Public Expenditure Development', in P. Flora and A. J. Heidenheimer (eds) *The Development of Welfare States in Europe and America*, New Brunswick: Transaction Books.

Kosonen, P. (1994) *European Integration: a Welfare State Perspective*, Helsinki: University of Helsinki, Sociology of Law.

Leibfried, S. (1992) 'Towards a European Welfare State', in S. Ferge and J. Kolberg (eds) *Social Policy in a Changing Europe*, Boulder, CO: Westview Press.

Maravall, J. M. and Fraile, M. (1998) 'The Politics of Unemployment. The Spanish Experience in Comparative Perspective', WP 1998/124, Madrid: Instituto Juan March.

Matsaganis, M. (1999) 'Social Assistance in Greece Revisited', unpublished paper, University of Crete.

Ministero del Tesoro (1998) *Convergenze dell'Italia verso l'Uem*, Rome.

Mira d'Ercole, M. and Terribile, F. (1998) 'Pension Spending: Developments in 1996 and in 1997', in L. Bardi and M. Rhodes (eds), *Italian Politics. Mapping the Future*, Boulder, CO: Westview Press.

Moreno, L. (1996) 'Southern Welfare States in Transition', paper presented at the conference on South European Politics, Univerisy of Athens, 13–14 September.

—— (1997) 'The Spanish Development of Southern Welfare', Madrid: IESA (dt 97-04) (*http://www.csic.es/iesa*).

Moreno, L. and Sarasa, S. (1992) 'The Spanish Via Media to the Development of the Welfare State', Madrid: IESA (dt 92-13) (*http://www.csic.es/iesa*).

Mozzicafreddo, J. (1992) 'The Portuguese Welfare State: Dimensions and Specific Features', paper presented at the RC19 annual conference on 'Comparative Studies of Welfare State Development', University of Bremen, 4–6 September.

Negri, N. and Saraceno, C. (1996) *La lotta contro la povertà*, Bologna: Il Mulino.

OECD (1994) *New Orientations in Social Policy*, Paris: OECD.

Paci, M. (1987) 'Pubblico e privato nel sistema italiano di welfare', in P. Lange and M. Regini (eds) *Stato e regolazione sociale in Italia*, Bologna: Il Mulino.

Pereirinha, J. (1992) 'Portugal', consolidated report prepared for the Observatory on National Policies to Combat Social Exclusion, Brussels: DGV-European Commission.

Perez Diaz, V. (1990) 'El espectro del neo-clientelismo', *El Pais*, 5 June.

Perez Diaz, V., Chulià, E. and Alvarez-Miranda, B. (1998) *Family and Welfare Systems: the Spanish Experience*, Madrid: ASP-Gabinete de Estudios.

Petmesidou, M. (1991) 'Statism, Social Policy and the Middle Classes in Greece', *Journal of European Social Policy*, 1, 1: 31–48.

—— (1996) 'Social Protection in Southern Europe: Trends and Problems', *Journal of Area Studies*, vol. 9: 95–125.

Rhodes, M. (ed.) (1998) *The Southern European Welfare States*, London, Frank Cass.

Rossi, N. (1997) *Più ai figli, meno ai padri*, Bologna: Il Mulino.

Saraceno, C. (1994) 'The Ambivalent Familism of the Italian Welfare State', *Social Politics*, 1: 60–82.

Scharpf, F. (1997) 'Combating Unemployment in Continental Europe. Policy Options under Internationalization', WP 3/97, Florence: Robert Schuman Centre, EUI.

Trifiletti, R. (1999) 'Southern European Welfare Regimes and the Worsening Position of Women', *Journal of European Social Policy*, 9, 1: 49–64.

Van Kersbergen, K. (1995) *Social Capitalism*, London: Routledge.

Part III

Towards consolidated European welfare states?

11 The treaty on European Union and its revision

Sea change or empty shell for European social policies?

Gerda Falkner

Introduction

This chapter argues that since the outset of European integration, two 'advocacy coalitions' (cf. Sabatier and Jenkins-Smith 1993) oppose each other with a view to social policy harmonisation. Each coalition consists of actors from various EC and national institutions as well as from private organisations at either level (mainly pressure groups). While persons have changed over time (notably the representatives of national governments), the positions as such were only adapted to the changing circumstances. The 'pro-regulation' camp argues that increased market integration should go hand in hand with common social regulation in order to prevent distortions of competition. This line of argument was first applied to the Common Market, then to the Internal Market, and is now used with regard to European Economic and Monetary Union (EMU). The opposing advocacy coalition continues to hold that social costs (in the widest sense) constitute just another element of market competition which should not be tampered with at the supranational level. In recent years, the principle of subsidiarity is usually being mentioned in this context by the 'con-regulation' advocates (cf. Art. 3b ECT).

Over time, the pro-regulation coalition (supported by the grand majority of the European Parliament, frequently by the majority of the European Commission, and the European Trade Union Confederation, ETUC) gained in ground, and a significant number of EC social regulations (mainly on labour law issues but also social security co-ordination) were adopted despite the meagre treaty basis. While this was happening, however, economic integration continued to deepen – so that the social dimension still lags behind. The 1992 Maastricht Treaty was a prime example of this pattern: while it extended social policy competences and allowed for more qualified majority voting it set up EMU without a proper 'social dimension'. The 1997 Amsterdam Treaty, once again, did not allow social policy to really catch up with economic integration. It extended the Maastricht Social Agreement to all member states (what may be seen as a sort of sea change) without, however, outlining significant policy innovation. Therefore, one might also dub the Amsterdam Treaty an empty shell for European social policies.

This chapter will first outline the basic division of social policy competences between the EC and its member states, in both the original Rome Treaty (EEC) and the Single European Act (SEA). It will then analyse the incremental development of EC social policy, both on the levels of EC secondary law and of the perception of central actors, notably the Commission and the governments. The Maastricht Treaty's innovative social policy regime is outlined as a basis for the study of the changes in the Amsterdam Treaty and the latter's evaluation with a view to the future of social affairs in the wider sense, i.e. the question of the survival of the welfare state in Europe.

Social policy and European integration from Rome to Maastricht: the distribution of competences between the EC and its member states

Even during the negotiations preceding the EEC Treaty, different schools of thought on social policy were present. While some member states pleaded for the neo-liberal concept of market-making only and wanted to set the market forces free even in the realm of labour and social security costs (in the first place Germany), others opted for at least a limited degree of harmonisation with a view to social and labour costs (Beutler *et al.* 1987: 437). Notably the French delegation argued that its comparatively high social charges and the constitutional principle of equal pay for men and women might constitute a competitive disadvantage. Italy argued that the opening of market frontiers might be costly for the already disadvantaged south of the country. In the end, a compromise was found which did not provide for active social policy harmonisation at the European level. The dominant philosophy of the Treaty was that welfare would be provided by the economic growth stemming from the economics of a liberalised market and not from the regulatory and distributive capacity of public policy (Kohler-Koch 1997: 76).

Nevertheless, the Treaty contained a small number of concessions for the more 'interventionist' delegations. These are mainly the provisions on equal pay for both sexes (Art. 119 EEC Treaty), on maintaining 'the existing equivalence between paid holiday schemes' (Art. 120 EEC Treaty), and the establishment of a 'European Social Fund' (Art. 123–28 EEC Treaty). Two of the three above-mentioned concessions (i.e. equal pay and the Social Fund) should gain significant importance during the process of European integration, while the statement regarding the equivalence of paid holiday schemes saw no follow-up. The other provisions of the EC Treaty's Title III 'social policy' bear witness of the will to include some solemn social policy provisions, yet without empowering the EEC to act. 'Underwriting this arrangement was the relative feasibility of nation-state strategies for economic development in the first decades after the Second World War. The common market, as it was constructed, was designed to aid and abet such national strategies, not transcend them' (Ross 1995: 360). Where necessary or functional for market integration, intervention in the social policy field was – implicitly – allowed via the subsidiary competence provisions (Art.

100 and 235 EEC Treaty). The latter provided, from the 1970s onwards, a 'back-door' for social policy harmonisation at the EU level. The necessary unanimous Council votes, however, constituted high thresholds for joint action.

The sole explicit Community competence for social policy regulation under the original EEC Treaty was outside the title on social policy, i.e. in Part II (Foundations of the Community) which contains the free movement of goods, labour, services and capital. Articles 48–51 EEC Treaty thus provide for the establishment of the freedom of movement for workers as part of the Treaty's market-making activities. This entails the abolition of any discrimination based on nationality between workers of the member states as regards employment, remuneration and other conditions of work and employment (Art. 48 EEC Treaty).[1] In order to 'adopt such measures in the field of social security as are necessary to provide freedom of movement for workers' (Art. 51 EEC Treaty), the Council was mandated to secure for migrant workers and their dependants the aggregation of all periods taken into account under the laws of the several EEC countries for the purpose of acquiring and retaining the rights to benefit and of calculating the amount of benefit.

In 1987, the Single European Act came into force as the first major EEC Treaty revision. As in the 1950s, an economic enterprise was at the heart of a fresh impetus for European integration. But along with the Internal Market Programme being solemnly put on track, social policy again constituted a controversial issue: how much social state building should go along with even more far-reaching market integration? In various so-called 'flanking' policy areas, notably environmental and research policy, EEC competence was formally extended (see Art. 130r-t and 130f-q EEC Treaty). Not so for social policy: the delegations were not willing to give the EEC a greater role in this field. Only two exceptions were made to this general rule. One of them was (at least in the short run) rather minor: Art. 118b EEC Treaty provided that '(t)he Commission shall endeavour to develop the dialogue between management and labour at European level which could, if the two sides consider it desirable, lead to relations based on agreement'. But the second concession, i.e. Art. 118a EEC Treaty on minimum harmonisation related to health and safety of workers, should soon provide an escape route out of the unanimity requirement:[2] it allowed, for the first time in European social policy, for Directives based on a *qualified majority* of the Council members only. The provisions adopted pursuant to this article are minimum regulations, i.e. they do not prevent any member state from maintaining or introducing more stringent measures for the protection of working conditions otherwise compatible with the Treaty. Nevertheless, reluctant member states can under this provision be forced to align with the majority of the EU member states, even against their will. This was agreeable to all delegations because occupational health and safety is closely connected to the Internal Market.[3] Neither the Thatcher government nor any other did, however, expect this perceivedly 'technical' issue to significantly facilitate social policy integration in the decade to come. In general, the persisting unanimity requirements in EC social policy posed a major problem for the development of a 'social dimension of the Internal

Market' as advocated by the Commission, the European Parliament, the ETUC, and an over time increasing number of governments in the Council.

The delay of the EC's social dimension

As outlined above, social affairs was a 'last order' policy at the European level, both in the original EEC Treaty (1957) and in the Single European Act (1986), fully subordinated to the economic policy focus of the EC. If slowly but surely, social regulation was nevertheless developed, this was mainly as a corollary of the EC's market-making activities. A persisting pro-social-regulation advocacy coalition and functional pressures resulted in spillovers[4] from market integration to social policy (which can only be summarised crudely here; for more detail see e.g. Falkner 1997).

Almost immediately after the EEC Treaty came into force, a coordination of national social security systems was put in place with a view to protecting the social security rights of migrants.[5] Coordination does not harmonise the social security systems as such, but it imposes the equal treatment of EU citizens and of nationals within them. The central features of this coordination are the aggregation of insurance claims collected anywhere within the Community, and the export of benefits to the member state where the person actually lives. The various member states where a person lived will pay on a *pro-rata-temporis* basis. Manifold problems and dissimilarities in the application of the free movement of workers and their equal treatment in social security have brought about a wealth (not to say: a jungle) of European Court of Justice jurisprudence. Although the substance of the various national social insurance systems is not directly touched by the EC coordination, there are indirect effects which indeed restrict the national welfare states' room for manoeuvre, notably via financial pressure.[6]

In addition, manifold issues under the heading of *worker health and safety* were regulated on the basis of various action programmes, notably in the 1980s and 1990s. They include protection of workers exposed to emissions and loads, protection against risks of chemical, physical and biological agents at work (e.g. lead or asbestos; Schnorr and Egger 1990: 82). The EEC Treaty included no explicit competence to harmonise national provisions in the area of *labour law*, either. Nevertheless, a number of Directives was adopted already during the 1970s: on collective redundancies, on the transfer of undertakings, and on securing workers rights in cases of employer insolvency. A major development brought about by the European Court of Justice is in the area of *gender equality*, where matters such as equal pay and equal treatment of men and women at the work place were regulated (see e.g. Hoskyns 1995).

Although this list of EC social regulation may – against the background of an absent social policy agenda in the Treaties – appear impressive at first glance, its completely eclectic character if compared to national provisions is obvious. In the absence of a commonly accepted theory on which parts of the enterprises' 'social costs' actually constitute a distortion of competition, the Community has pragmatically followed a step-by-step approach of suggesting selective harmonisation of the disparate conditions which both enterprises and citizens find in the various member states of the Common Market. In addition, spillover in the social policy area has proved to be selective rather than automatic.[7] Frequently, proposed EC social regulation would be blocked in the Council, or be adopted only after many years.

When the Internal Market programme was designed and later implemented, the weakness on social policy (more specifically, labour law) integration became a controversial issue. As early as 1985, the Commission stated in its annual working programme that the realisation of an enlarged market should go hand in hand with a European social area, if social dumping with a negative effect on overall employment was to be prevented (EC Bulletin supplement 4/1985). Nevertheless, the Commission White Paper on the Internal Market Programme did not include a social policy chapter. Reportedly, the unanimous approval of all governments was only achieved under this condition (Salisch 1989: 10). As outlined above, the sole relevant social policy innovation of the SEA was in the market-related area of health and safety of workers. But several actors (the pro-harmonisation advocacy coalition) would not stop urging that the European market should be accompanied by social and labour law measures: national and European trade unions, the (majority of the) EP, the Commission as a collegiate body,[8] (a majority of the) ECOSOC – to name just a few. In its working programme of 1986, the Commission formulated that only minimal harmonisation of certain working conditions could prevent distortions of competition which might otherwise harm the functioning of the enlarged market (EC Bulletin 1/1986: 10f). But no significant progress was reached until the very end of the 1980s, when a weakened version of the Commission proposal on a *Social Charter* was adopted by the EC governments except the UK. In a political (although not in a legal) sense, the Social Charter marks a turning point in European social policy. The eleven heads of state and government explicitly declared that the Internal Market in their view necessitated active labour law intervention at the EC level:

> The completion of the internal market must lead to an improvement in the living and working conditions of workers in the European Community. This process must result from an approximation of these conditions while the improvement is being maintained, as regards in particular the duration and organisation of working time and forms of employment other than open-ended contracts, such as fixed-term contracts, part-time working, temporary work and seasonal work. Every worker in the European Community shall have a right to a weekly rest period and to annual paid leave, the duration of which must be progressively harmonised in accordance with national practices.

This indicates that 11 out of 12 governments did indeed change their minds with a view to the need for European labour law in the Internal Market between 1986 (when the SEA was signed) and the European Council of Strasbourg in December 1989. One could say that they partially and temporally aligned with the 'pro-regulation camp' in the face of the Internal Market.

In parallel with the Charter, the Commission presented an *action programme* on the implementation of the Social Charter (COM[89] 568 final) which the Strasbourg summit took note of. The central goals of the action programme (Ross 1995: 376) were several binding EC Directives in the area of labour law (formally proposed by the Commission between June 1990 and August 1991). These measures fall into two groups. The first concerns developments which are in direct relation to the Internal Market. The best example is the question which labour law should apply in cases of posted workers under the free movement of services: should Portuguese construction workers on German sites be paid according to Portuguese rules only? If so, the German system suffers from significant competitive disadvantages, and workers at the same site might be treated unequally because of their nationality – which seems not 'European', indeed. Another example for a direct effect of the Internal Market on social policy in the wider sense is that with increased Europeanisation, the national laws on worker information and consultation become *de facto* void of substance: all transnational enterprises escape from their scope because their important decisions are taken outside the national realm. Therefore, only *European* works councils can guarantee that the status quo ante of worker participation is being upheld in the enlarged European market.

The second group of measures under the 1989 Commission social action programme, by contrast, relates only indirectly to the Internal Market. They are labour law standards such as applicable for young or pregnant workers; rules on written employment contracts for all employees; or rules relating to working time which, in principle, concern only state-wide active enterprises as much as transnationals. Nevertheless, they are not left untouched by economic integration either, because the competitive pressures increase and national differences gain in weight when capital is free to exit. For these more general grounds, one may thus opt for Europe-wide minimum standards in order to create a more level playing field for economic operators. Neo-liberal market purists do, however, clearly reject such an option.

The Commission (with strong backing by the EP and some governments) decided that both groups of measures should be part of the 'social dimension' of European integration. By the time of writing, basically all measures proposed under the 1989 social action programme have indeed been adopted. This was, however, not possible without a major change in the EC's social policy rules and practice.[9] By the end of the Intergovernmental Conference on political union in December 1991, only two minor proposals of the 1989 social action programme's innovative proposals had been adopted in the Council.[10] All other draft law was blocked in the Council, mostly by the UK. The same was true for several measures which had already been presented before the 1989 action programme (e.g. on parental leave, on the burden of proof in sex discrimination cases, on more far-reaching equal treatment of the sexes in social security). Therefore, a Treaty reform seemed indispensable to the overwhelming majority of Council delegations by the early 1990s.

The Maastricht innovations

The Intergovernmental Conference preceding the Maastricht Treaty negotiated a reform of the social policy provisions under the EEC Treaty. However, under the requirement of unanimous approval by all twelve member states the social provisions could not be significantly altered because of the strong opposition from Great Britain. At the end of most difficult negotiations which even threatened the rest of the Intergovernmental Conference's compromises, the UK was granted an opt-out from the social policy measures agreed by the rest of the member states. In the *Protocol on Social Policy* annexed to the EC Treaty,[11] the eleven (after 1995: 14) member states except the UK were authorised to have recourse to the institutions, procedures and mechanisms of the Treaty for the purposes of implementing their 'Agreement on Social Policy'.

Because of the UK opt-out, the European Union possessed two legal bases for the adoption of social policy measures after the Maastricht Treaty came into force by 1 November 1993.[12] The EC Treaty's social provisions remained valid for all EU member states. As introduced by the 1986 Single Act, it allowed for minimum harmonisation as well as for qualified majority voting in the area of worker health and safety provisions only. By contrast, the innovative social policy provisions of the Social Agreement – applicable only to the EC members except Great Britain – comprised what had been perceived during the Inter-governmental Conference as amendments to the social provisions of the EEC Treaty. They brought an extension of the Community competence into a wide range of social policy problems. These include working conditions, the information and consultation of workers, equality between men and women with regard to labour market opportunities and treatment at work (as opposed to only equal pay before), and the integration of persons excluded from the labour market (Art. 2.1 Social Agreement). Some issues were, however, explicitly excluded from the scope of minimum harmonisation under the Maastricht social policy provisions: pay, the right of association, the right to strike and the right to impose lock-outs (Art. 2.6).[13]

The probability of an active use of the new social competences under the Social Agreement was crucially enhanced by the extension of *majority voting* to many more issues than before, including the information and consultation of workers. Unanimous decisions were restricted to social security and social protection of workers; protection of workers where their employment contract is terminated; representation and collective defence of interests of workers and employers, including codetermination; conditions of employment for third-country nationals legally residing in Community territory; and financial contributions for promotion of employment and job creation (see Art. 3 Social Agreement). That the burden of unanimous decision-making in the Council was lifted for most aspects of social policy strengthened supranational dynamics at the dispense of intergovernmentalism. To sum up, the Maastricht Treaty included some relevant reforms of the previous social provisions, with a view to both competences and procedures[14] – but they applied to the members except the UK only.

For a fundamental assessment of the Maastricht Treaty's impact in the social policy realm, it is, however, crucial to look beyond the 'social provisions'. Above all, the Maastricht Treaty provided for an *economic and monetary union* with irrevocably fixed exchange rates among the participants. Effects on national labour law and social standards are multiple, although mostly indirect (see e.g. Busch 1994). Nevertheless, the fight against unemployment was not included in the convergence criteria, and neither were other flanking social policy measures imposed. Once again, it seems that European economic integration touches national social policies much more profoundly than 'EC social policy'. The Maastricht convergence criteria play a major role in reshaping the member states' budgets and welfare systems. Although this was no legal necessity, the adaptation processes with a view to qualifying for EMU have, together with demographic pressures, *de facto* led basically all EC governments to a reform path which focused on cuts in social security. Although further research is needed on the 'reform packages' which were endorsed in the various member states, the political debate around the Summit of Amsterdam in June 1997 shows that even in the perception of some political leaders, the pre-EMU process has resulted in a sort of 'downward spiral' of public spending which has finally resulted in less aggregate demand and therefore less growth and less employment than Europe might have had (in addition to the direct cuts in public sector employment).[15] In the academic literature, the important role of 'real economic convergence' (especially of employment and wages which were neglected in the Maastricht Treaty) as opposed to only monetary convergence (which is the central focus of the convergence criteria) was much debated while the Amsterdam EC Treaty reforms were being prepared (cf. e.g. Busch 1994; Foden 1996).

Although by the late 1990s, the contentious Commission proposals on the 'social dimension to the Internal Market' have almost all been adopted (see below), a 'social dimension of the Economic and Monetary Union' is still only wishful thinking by the pro-regulation camp.

Social policy in the Treaty of Amsterdam

In fact, material social policy reform (as opposed to employment policy) was not a major issue of the negotiations of the 1996–97 Intergovernmental Conference. This was also expressed in the single governments' official starting positions for the negotiations, which hardly ever referred to any specific social policy goals for the Intergovernmental Conference, apart from the end of the opt-out. The latter aspect was indeed raised by almost all governments (cf. Griller *et al.* 1996: 42). Also the EP, the Commission, the Economic and Social Committee, and the ETUC, explicitly stated in their inputs to the Intergovernmental Conference that they opted for an integration of the Social Agreement into the to-be-revised Treaty. For the EP, 'Social policy should be a core area of EU competence (with incorporation of the Social Charter, and an ending of the United Kingdom opt-out) and should be better integrated with economic policy as a whole' (Resolution on the functioning of the Treaty on

European Union with a view to the 1996 Intergovernmental Conference, A4-0102/95, 17 May 1995, point 10 ii).

Because of the fierce reluctance towards social policy reforms of the UK Tory government (in office until May 1997), the Intergovernmental Conference indeed decided to postpone the topic until the very end. The interim report drawn up by the Irish Presidency in December 1996 only briefly mentioned that reforms would probably result in the inclusion of the Social Agreement into the Treaty, making necessary some technical and institutional adaptations. In addition, the Irish Presidency suggested checking if some material improvements should be made in order to enhance the efficiency of EC social policy (Document SN 401/96, A/II/5: 46). During 1997, the EP presented a detailed and far-reaching proposal for social policy reform to the Intergovernmental Conference, including the generalisation of qualified majority voting, the end of excluded issues, and basic social rights (goals which were basically shared by the ETUC).

Nevertheless, the Amsterdam Treaty in the end fell short of the hopes of the pro-regulation coalition. Although the minimum requirement formulated by this group was fulfilled (i.e. the inclusion of the UK under the innovative post-Maastricht social policy regime), the more far-reaching reform proposals were reportedly not even seriously discussed in the Intergovernmental Conference (interview with Commission officials, July 1997). This is even true for the more controversial and problematic aspects of the Social Agreement, i.e. the explicit exclusion from Community action under the social provisions of some major social policy issues,[16] the absence of a delineation from other topics[17] of those issues where labour and industry should indeed negotiate, and the *de facto* exclusion of the EP when the social partners shape EC social policy.

The only crucial innovation of the Amsterdam Treaty (if compared to the Social Agreement) in the realm of social affairs in the wider sense is the *new employment chapter* which was introduced in the ECT (cf. Art. 109n-s ECT i.e. Art. 125–30 after renumbering) and provides for the coordination of national policies.[18] These new provisions have to be seen against the background of the debate on an additional convergence criterion on unemployment, which had occasionally been advocated by (parts of) the EP and the ETUC. Because the success of EMU as such was of crucial importance to both organisations, however, they did not want to endanger the anyhow fragile compromise which had been embedded in the Maastricht Treaty. After many controversial debates within both the EP and the ETUC (and despite some adverse public statements), it was clear that both in fact[19] accepted that the Amsterdam Treaty would not once again 'depackage' the EMU provisions of the Maastricht Treaty. That the EMU chapter remained untouched had always been a central issue for the Commission.

With a view to the EP's target to give a counterweight to the monetary policy provisions, it is crucial to compare the new employment chapter with the economic policy coordination provisions which were already set up in the Maastricht Treaty and at Amsterdam reinforced with the much debated Council pact on 'stability and growth' (cf. Presidency conclusions to the Amsterdam European Council, SN 150/97, Annex). In this declaration, the fight against excessive deficits in stage three of EMU is underlined. The European Council invited the EC Council 'always to impose sanctions if a participating Member State fails to take the necessary steps to bring the excessive deficit situation to an end'. In addition, two Council regulations laid down further details on the strengthening of the surveillance of budgetary positions; and on speeding up and clarifying the implementation of the excessive deficit procedure.

The new employment policy coordination, by contrast, is much more 'soft law' than binding provision. There will be no Community competence for employment policy, and not even a 'common employment policy'. Rather, the 'coordination' of national employment policies is aimed at: 'Member States, . . . shall regard promoting employment as a matter of common concern and shall coordinate their action in this respect within the Council' (Art. 109o par. 2 ECT, i.e. Art. 126 after renumbering). On the basis of a report by the Council and the Commission, the European Council will each year adopt conclusions on the employment situation in the Community. The Council shall, on this basis, draw up guidelines which the member states shall take into account in their employment policies.[20] The Council shall annually examine the implementation of the employment policy guidelines and may, acting by a qualified majority on a recommendation from the Commission, make recommendations to member states (cf. Art. 109q, i.e. Art. 128 ECT after renumbering). As opposed to the economic policy guidelines pursuant to Art. 103 ECT, there are *no sanctions* provided for in the new employment chapter (some governments, notably the Swedish and the Austrian, had promoted this in vain). Neither is the possibility to publish such recommendations to member states being mentioned, which could have created public pressure.

The impact of the Amsterdam Treaty's employment chapter will crucially depend on how the new provisions shall be put into practice. Although the new employment provisions are less far-reaching than some had hoped for, one should certainly not underestimate the power of coordination processes and report duties being set up. Nevertheless, it is undeniable that there is still an imbalance between more far-reaching and binding EC economic policy integration (which impinges on social standards and employment in the member states), and social and employment policies under the Amsterdam Treaty.

Conclusion: Amsterdam is both sea change and empty shell

The sea change: the end of the UK opt-out

As outlined above, the Maastricht Treaty had been preceded by years of intense debate on the need to enlarge EC social policy competence and to employ qualified majority voting. By the time of the Intergovernmental Conference 1991–92, the central policy projects of the 1989 social action programme had been blocked in the Council. Therefore, it seemed plausible that the material and procedural innovation enshrined in the Maastricht Social Agreement would readily be brought to fruition. The Agreement's practice nevertheless shows that the governments were reticent to have recourse to the Social Protocol even after it became a viable route towards common social policy by 1 November 1993 (Falkner 1998: 146ff).

This seems to be related to the fact that as an emergency solution, the UK had been granted an opt-out. Thus, a two-class Europe had been created: any acts adopted under the Social Agreement and any financial consequences other than administrative costs entailed for the institutions were not applicable to the UK. This had made John Major rejoice: 'Europe can have the social chapter. We shall have employment ... Let Jacques Delors accuse us of creating a paradise for foreign investors: I am happy to plead guilty' (quoted in *Agence Europe* 3 March 1993: 13). Under these conditions, the other member state governments turned out to be hesitant to proceed at a comparatively faster social policy pace in a time where social and labour standards are ever more susceptible to arguments of competitiveness.

The Commission had tried to push things when it put the draft European works councils directive under the Social Agreement only a few days after the TEU entered into force (1 November 1993). This seemed a good subject to test the new corporatist procedures because the problem of competitive disadvantage was less salient due to the comparatively low costs involved. However, no collective agreement between labour and industry was reached, but a Council Directive was finally adopted (Blanpain and Windey 1994; Streeck 1997; Falkner 1998: 97–113). Only by autumn 1994 were both the Council and the Commission ready to use the Social Agreement again. The second case under the Social Agreement, on parental leave, indeed saw a social partner agreement implemented by a Council Directive (Falkner 1998: 114–28). The third issue, atypical work, was also settled by a social partner agreement and later Council Directive on part-time work, in 1997 (Falkner 1998: 129–45).

The practice of the Maastricht Social Agreement to date proves that both qualified majority voting and the corporatist policy-making procedures[21] are indeed workable. The real breakthrough in the use of the Social Agreement happened only in 1995, however. It seems no coincidence that the result of all issues negotiated since then could only enter into force after the British elections of May 1997 (when everybody expected Labour to win), and after the end of the Intergovernmental Conference 1996–97. Therefore, the chances that the UK would be bound by the new rules were very high from the outset. In this light, the recently increased use of the Maastricht Social Agreement supports rather than contradicts the argument that the full employment of the Social Agreement's potentials for policy development was hampered by the opt-out of one member state.

It seems therefore justified to conclude that the UK's adherence to the innovative post-Maastricht social policy rules *represents a sea change* which might activate EC social policy-making. In any case, the end of the opt-out shows a renewed conviction that all beneficiaries of a common market should share some joint social standards.

The empty shell: no forward-looking strategy for EC social policy

Against the background of originally lacking competences and unanimity requirements, it is certainly a success for the pro-social policy coalition that under the innovative post-Maastricht rules which are now extended to all EC member states, the 1989 social action programme was meanwhile basically completed. However, it had from the outset only contained limited and punctual action which was in addition concentrated in the sub-field of labour law. Effects of European economic integration on national social policy, by contrast, are much wider than this. At least in the opinion of the 'pro-regulation' camp, the following topics seem to need much more attention than hitherto, under the 'EC social dimension':

(a) Social security   Even after the Amsterdam Treaty, 'social security and social protection of workers' still need unanimous decision-taking in the Council of Ministers. This clearly impinges on the EC's action capacity. While there is no binding EC law[22] in the area except accompanying measures to the free movement of labour, EMU seems to bring about a convergence of reform paths (towards lower contributions from the public budgets to the national social security institutions) while institutional and material diversity of the systems continues. However, different levels of employers' social security contributions may be seen to constitute distortions of competition, just as differing indirect labour costs which arise from labour law provisions (such as, for example, parental leave or working time). In a way, it seems inconsistent not to have some sort of harmonisation in this area and potentially to allow for 'social dumping' via competitive decreases of social security contributions. This is why some authors have suggested the development of innovative approaches, e.g. to bind the aggregate minimum level of social expenses to the development of the gross national product and to agree on a minimum ratio of employer contributions (cf. Busch 1988; Dispersyn and Van der Vorst 1990).

(b) Pay and taxation   Under the conditions of EMU which impede national devaluations, pay will be the major available adaptation mechanism to answer regional economic crises (cf. Busch 1994). This could bring the workers and their unions under considerable pressure to agree to comparatively lower wages as a lesser evil to unemployment, and another competitive devaluation effect might result. The EC continues not to achieve tax harmonisation with a view to capital gains while the single states have difficulties coping with this on their own, in times of open economic borders (e.g. Scharpf 1997). Consequently, a general redistribution towards financial capital is expected which will also impinge on the *de facto* capacity to finance the welfare state (e.g. Altvater and Mahnkopf 1993). This suggests that pay coordination as well as tax harmonisation might be crucial topics within EC social policy (in the wider sense) in the years to come. However, pay is still excluded from Community competence in the social chapter of the Treaty,[23] and tax harmonisation is hampered by unanimity requirements in the Council.

Summing up, crucial issues must be tackled in the years to come: should EC social policy stay as labour-law oriented and as eclectic as it stands today? Or should the Union have a larger role to play in the recasting of the social security systems and in matters of pay and taxation? The Amsterdam Treaty offers no answer to the question how to adapt the European welfare states to the ever increasing competitive pressures at the end of the twentieth century, while not subordinating and, in the longer run, dismissing them. In fact, the Intergovernmental Conference 1996–97 did not even pose this question.

If EC social policy remains as eclectic and restricted to minimum labour law standards as it has been, however, the burden of adaptation stays with the member states, whose unilateral steering capacity in an internationalised economy is at least doubtful. While EC social policy as it stands does not actively dismantle the welfare state in Europe, there are good arguments that the prospects for a survival of this model could be improved if there was more backing from the EU, in the fight against pressures for social devaluation. Since the much-quoted globalisation is in fact rather a 'triadisation' and the large majority of European trade is actually within the Internal Market, the EU's capacity in defending social standards despite global competition is not only much larger than the single member states' but in general greater than often assumed.

Exploiting the hypothetical problem solving *potentials* of European integration with a view to the protection and improvement of the welfare state still seems a rather distant goal, but the recent social democratic majority in the Council of Ministers might at least improve the chances for placing it on the official agenda.

Notes

1 Excluded is employment in the public service (Art. 48 EEC Treaty).
2 An extensive use of this provision was possible mainly because the wording and the definition of key terms of Article 118a were all but unequivocal.
3 If all goods should circulate freely, there has to be some common policy with a view to the security of those goods which are later used in factories (e.g. machines) and constitute an important factor of human security. The elimination of 'technical barriers to trade' made Community action attractive in the perception of relevant policy-makers (cf. Schulz 1996: 18f).
4 In a simple formulation by Ernst Haas, the 'founding father' of neofunctionalism, spillover refers to a situation where 'policies made in carrying out an initial task and grant of power can be made real only if the task itself is expanded' (Haas 1964: 111).
5 Regulations 3/58 and 4/58 were replaced by Regulations 1408/71 and 574/72, which were frequently amended since, and constitute a most complex body of legal provisions. For details see Schulte (1990).
6 For an excellent overview on how labour mobility requirements have via the ECJ impinged on national social security systems, see Leibfried and Pierson (1995, 1996).
7 See also Rhodes (1995: 3): 'social integration has proven to be anything but spontaneous'.

8   Clearly, there are diverse views as to the desirability of social policy harmonisation within the Commission, and interest diverges from Directorate General to Directorate General.

9   The change in practice consisted in a 'Treaty-Base-Game' (Rhodes 1995: 99), i.e. an extensive interpretation of Article 118a EECT on health and safety (see above). The pro-harmonisation coalition claimed that the SEA had not introduced the more far-reaching social policy competences and majority votes urged the Commission to extensively use Art. 118a, i.e. to go beyond the 'working environment' and include working conditions. While the governments were initially reluctant to accept this, the Maastricht Treaty made a change because even if the ECJ had afterwards declared illegal the outvoting of the UK under Article 118a, the Social Agreement was available to secure that the provision itself would be upheld.

10   A not disputed part of the proposed atypical work package (i.e. on health and safety for part-time workers), and the Directive on workers' right to an explicit employment contract.

11   At Maastricht it was decided to change the name of the 'European Economic Community' to 'European Community'. The EEC Treaty (whose contents were at the same time reformed) is since called EC Treaty (Treaty establishing the European Community).

12   A single legal basis for EC social policy will only be re-established after the implementation of the 1997 Amsterdam Treaty, most likely by 1999.

13   These matters can nevertheless be the subject of an autonomous social partner agreement; from a legal viewpoint, they may even be the subject of EC law under different legal bases (e.g. Art. 100, 100a or 235 ECT).

14   It might in the long run be as significant a procedural innovation as qualified majority voting that the Maastricht Social Agreement made labour and industry formal co-actors within the social policy process. Without their consultation, no action may be taken by the EC institutions. They may themselves implement European social policy. Most importantly: even when it comes actually to formulating specific social standards which subsequently become binding for economic actors within the EU, the legislative institutions (i.e. mainly the EC Council, supported by the EP and acting on initiative of the Commission) have lost their monopoly. In fact, the 'social partners' may decide independently on matters which may later on be adopted as formal EC social law by the Council (cf. Article 4 Social Agreement; cf. Falkner 1998).

15   A study by the rather pro-European Austrian Institute for Economic Research (WIFO) revealed that the austerity programmes might cost 2 per cent of the Union's purchasing power and actually increase unemployment by 1.5% (*Der Standard* 25 February 1996).

16   i.e. pay, the right of association, the right to strike and the right to impose lock-outs (cf. Art. 118 par. 6 ECT, i.e. Art. 137 after renumbering).

17   Such as e.g. non-binding Council declarations, action programmes, or issues such as social insurance which are even in corporatist member states often not directly tackled by the social partners.

18   In addition, pilot projects may be initiated by the EC.

19   In the EP's official input to the Intergovernmental Conference (Resolution of 17 May 1995: pt. 5), it asked for a 'more balanced EMU' but stated that 'the timetable should be maintained and the convergence criteria should not be modified but

the monetary policy provisions should have their counterweight in reinforced economic policy coordination (i.e. in the field of multilateral surveillance and in establishing broad economic policy guidelines at EU level)'. The ETUC, in turn, had first called for 'EMU now' (December 1995), but then called for an additional convergence criteria when it could not really impact any longer on the eve of the Amsterdam Council.

20 That these guidelines 'shall be consistent with the broad guidelines adopted pursuant to Article 103(2)' ECT (i.e. the economic policy guidelines) points at the persisting priority of other economic policy goals. At least, the Amsterdam European Council has in its 'Resolution on Growth and Employment' (SN 150/97, Annex) called upon the EC Council 'to take the multi-annual employment programmes ... into account when formulating the broad guidelines (of the economic policies), in order to strengthen their employment focus.'

21 By the late 1990s, it is no longer true that 'centralized collective bargaining between capital and labor ... is entirely missing at the European level, and nothing is in sight that would indicate its impending appearance' (Streeck and Schmitter 1991).

22 Two non-binding Council Recommendations were adopted in 1992 with a view to safeguarding social security in times of the Internal Market, on 'the convergence of social protection objectives and policies' and on 'common criteria concerning sufficient resources and social assistance in social protection systems' (OJ 1992/L 245/49 and 1992/L 245/46). In 1995, the Commission presented a 'Framework for a European Debate on the Future of Social Protection' (COM(95) 466), and in 1997 the debate was continued with a Commission Communication on 'Modernising and improving social protection in the European Union' (COM(97) 102). Therein, the Commission underlines that the Union is only competent as far as social security concerns trans-border workers. Beyond this, only an exchange of experiences is aimed at. However, making social protection more employment-friendly is seen as a part of employment policy where potential for Euro-level action is acknowledged (point 3).

23 Under other provisions, pay could from a legal perspective be made subject of EC law.

References

Altvater, E. and Mahnkopf, B. (1993) *Gewerkschaften vor der europäischen Herausforderung. Tarifpolitik nach Mauer und Maastricht*, Münster: Westfälisches Dampfboot.

Beutler, B., Bieber, R., Pipkorn, J. and Streil, J. (1987) *Die Europäische Gemeinschaft – Rechtsordnung und Politik*, 3rd edn, Baden-Baden: Nomos.

Blanpain, R. and Windey, P. (1994) *European Works Councils. Information and Consultation of Employees in Multinational Enterprises in Europe*, Leuven: Uitgervij Peeters.

Busch, K. (1988) *The Corridor Model – a Concept for Further Development of an EU Social Policy*, Discussion and Working Paper, European Trade Union Institute, Brussels.

—— (1994) *Europäische Integration und Tarifpolitik. Lohnpolitische Konsequenzen der Wirtschafts- und Währungsunion*, Köln: Bund Verlag.

Dispersyn, M. and Van der Vorst u.a., P. (1990) 'La construction d'un serpent social européen', *Revue Belge de Sécurité Sociale*, 12.

Falkner, G. (1997) 'European Integration and Social Policy: Between Stalemate and

Spillover', in J. Hesse and T. Toonen (eds) *The European Yearbook of Comparative Government and Public Administration,* Baden-Baden: Nomos.

—— (1998) *Social Europe in the 1990s: Towards a Corporatist Policy Community,* London: Routledge.

Foden, D. (1996) 'EMU, Employment and Social Cohesion', *Transfer: European Review of Labour and Research,* 2: 273–86.

Griller, S., Droutsas, D., Falkner, G., Forgó, K., Klatzer, E., Mayer, G. and Nentwich, M. (1996) 'Regierungskonferenz 1996: Ausgangspositionen', working papers des Forschungsinstituts für Europafragen der Wirtschaftsuniversität Wien (IEF Working Paper 20), Wien.

Haas, E. B. (1964) *Beyond the Nation-State. Functionalism and Internatinal Organization,* California: Stanford University Press.

Hoskyns, C. (1995) *Integrating Gender:* London: Verso.

Jacobs, A. (1990) 'Das Prinzip der Freizügigkeit in seiner Bedeutung für das Sozialrecht', in F. Maydell (ed.) *Soziale Rechte in der EG,* Berlin: Erich Schmidt Verlag.

Kohler-Koch, B. (1997) 'Organized Interests in European Integration: The Evolution of a New Type of Governance?', in H. Wallace and A. Young (eds) *Participation and Policy-Making in the European Union,* Oxford: Oxford University Press.

Leibfried, S. and Pierson, P. (1995) 'Semisovereign Welfare States: Social Policy in a Multitiered Europe', in S. Leibfried and P. Pierson (eds) *European Social Policy: Between Fragmentation and Integration,* Washington DC: The Brookings Institution.

—— (1996) 'Social Policy', in H. Wallace and W. Wallace (eds) *Policy-Making in the European Union,* Oxford: Oxford University Press.

—— (eds) (1995) *European Social Policy: Between Fragmentation and Integration,* Washington DC: The Brookings Institution.

Pierson, P. and Leibfried, S. (1995) 'The Dynamics of Social Policy Integration', in S. Leibfried and P. Pierson (eds) *European Social Policy: Between Fragmentation and Integration,* Washington DC: The Brookings Institution.

Rhodes, M. (1995) 'A Regulatory Conundrum: Industrial Relations and the "Social Dimension"', in S. Leibfried and P. Pierson (eds) *Fragmented Social Policy: The European Union's Social Dimension in Comparative Perspective,* Washington DC: The Brookings Institution.

Ross, G. (1995) 'Assessing the Delors Era and Social Policy', in S. Leibfried and P. Pierson (eds) *European Social Policy: Between Fragmentation and Integration,* Washington DC: The Brookings Institution.

Ruland, F. (1989) 'Der Europäische Binnenmarkt und die sozialen Alterssicherungs-systeme', *Europarecht,* 4: 303–37.

Sabatier, P. A. and Jenkins-Smith, H. C. (eds) (1993) *Policy Change and Learning: an Advocacy Coalition Approach,* Boulder, CO: Westview Press.

Salisch, H. (1989) 'Zwischen Spargang und Vollgas', *Das Parlament* 13.1.1989, 3: 10.

Scharpf, F. W. (1997) 'Introduction: the Problem-solving Capacity of Multi-level Governance', *Journal of European Public Policy* 4, 4: 520–38.

Schmitter, P. C. (1981) 'Interest Intermediation and Regime Governability in Contemporary Western Europe and North America', in S. Berger (ed.) *Organising Interests in Western Europe: Pluralism, Corporatism, and the Transformation of Politics,* Cambridge: Cambridge University Press.

Schnorr, G. and Egger, J. (1990) 'European Communities', *International Encyclopaedia for Labour Law and Industrial Relations* (Suppl. 108), The Netherlands: Kluwer Law and Taxation Publishers.

Schulte, B. (1990) *Soziale Sicherheit in der EG* (Einleitung zur Textausgabe): München.

Schulz, O. (1996) *Maastricht und die Grundlagen einer Europäischen Sozialpolitik,* Köln u.a.: Heymans.

Streeck, W. (1995) 'Neo-Voluntarism: A New European Social Policy Regime?', *European Law Journal* 1, 1: 31–59.

—— (1997) 'Citizenship Under Regime Competition: The Case of the European Works Councils', European Integration online Papers (http://eiop.or.at/eiop/texte/1997-005a.htm) 1997, / 1.

Streeck, W. and Schmitter, P. C. (1991) 'From National Corporatism to Transnational Pluralism: Organized Interests in the Single European Market', *Politics and Society* 19, 2: 133–65.

12 Models for Europe?

The lessons of other institutional designs

Francis G. Castles

Introduction

The doubts that have been expressed concerning the survival characteristics of European models of social provision have led some commentators – particularly those of the political Right and those with a training in economics – to debate the possible virtues of redesigning the welfare state. Naturally enough, such commentators have shown an interest in other institutional designs for social provision elsewhere in the world, which appear to have the survival characteristics that the European welfare states supposedly lack. Since the major criticism of the European welfare state models is that they have progressively become an impediment to economic efficiency and a source of rising levels of unemployment, the main interest has been in welfare state arrangements which are seen as being exemplars to Europe in economic performance terms.

Looking at the experience of other nations is a perfectly sensible first step in the process of institutional redesign. A problem, however, is that those who most frequently use cross-national examples supposedly in order to facilitate policy learning often have an axe to grind. They choose cases not to instruct, but to warn of dangers and to offer visions of salvation. The technique, boiled down to essentials, consists of pointing to a particular welfare state design and saying isn't it awful or isn't it wonderful. Sweden, a country often self-proclaimed as a welfare exemplar to the rest of the world, has been a target of both kinds of caricature, but other countries or ideal types based on the experience of groups of countries sometimes come in for a similar treatment. Because those who use this technique tend to restrict the focus of their debate to a limited range of features of the models and countries they are discussing, and because other institutional designs are rarely compared or contrasted, it is difficult to assess the validity of the arguments being presented.

In what follows, we seek to describe the social policy arrangements, the welfare outcomes and the recent economic performance records of three non-European nations or groups of nations, which have been prominent as exemplars in the recent debate on the survival characteristics of the European welfare state. They are the Newly Industrialised Countries (NICs) of East and South-East Asia, the United States and New Zealand. In each case, the institutional designs of the welfare state in these exemplar nations have been presented as leading to superior economic outcomes to those experienced in Western Europe in recent decades, but commentators have often been more reticent in pointing to the welfare costs of such institutional arrangements. The aim of our discussion is to offer an even-handed account of these non-European examples of welfare state development, so that readers are in a better position to make an assessment of their strengths and weaknesses as models for European welfare state reform.

The Asian NICs

Until very recently, it has been fashionable amongst economic commentators to regard the Asian NICs as exemplars to other advanced nations because of an exceptional record of economic performance to which social policy arrangements were supposed to contribute. In simplistic accounts, the imputed causal relationship was between sustained high levels of economic growth and low levels of government intervention and, most particularly, low levels of government expenditure. In more sophisticated accounts, the focus was on high savings ratios as the ultimate determinant of growth, with the finger of suspicion pointed at the welfare state as a deterrent to personal savings.

The validity of such arguments clearly has a potential relevance to the situation presently confronted by many European nations, but with the dramatic decline of economic performance in the industrialised and industrialising countries of Asia in the latter part of the 1990s, the status of these countries as exemplars has been undermined. Even before that, however, there were legitimate questions that should have been asked. A major difficulty with the analysis presented by admirers of the Asian miracle was its focus on the statics of the Asian experience rather than on likely developmental tendencies. It is true that these countries have experienced exceptional rates of economic growth in recent decades. It is also true that they have had extremely high levels of gross savings as a percentage of GDP (in 1992, the figure for Taiwan was 28.0 per cent and for South Korea it was 37.2 per cent; see Goodman and Peng 1996: table 2). Finally, it is true that, in general, Asian expenditure levels on social security have been relatively low, coverage has often been incomplete and only a limited number of risks have been covered. However, even as commentators lauded the virtues of these economic and social arrangements, things were already changing.

Japan (the first Asian NIC?), illustrates the process. Although, in the early post-war decades, Japan shared all the characteristics which supposedly made the NICs worthy exemplars for other nations, from the 1970s onwards that country experienced a major expansion of social expenditure as it became more affluent and as its population aged. Today, Japan's population aged 65 years and over at 13.1 per cent is only about one percentage point below the OECD average and its expenditures on the aged have increased very markedly in recent decades (see OECD 1994b). There are signs of a similar dynamic elsewhere. Taiwanese and Korean expenditures remain far lower than those of Japan, but the affluence of these nations is more recent and their aged populations far smaller. Nevertheless, over the past decade, both countries have experienced a major growth in welfare expenditure (Goodman and Peng 1996). In other words, the story may well be quite the reverse of that implied by the simplistic story: namely, a version of one of the standard accounts of the origins of the welfare state, that economic development and its demographic correlates lead to increased social policy intervention (Wilensky 1975).

Indeed, the real story may be one of a dual convergence, with the East Asian countries experiencing a simultaneous slow down in economic growth and an expansion of the welfare state as they catch up with the West in levels of affluence. Garnaut (1989) points out that economic convergence is the single most important force determining differences between the growth rates of advanced nations and the emerging industrial nations of Asia. The same factor almost certainly accounts for differences in the developmental trajectories of welfare state expenditure. But if what explains the economic success of the NICs accounts for the subsequent trajectory of welfare state expansion along European lines, there may be little if anything in the institutional design of these countries' economies or social policy systems for Europe to emulate.

These issues aside, there are other difficulties in drawing lessons from the experience of the Asian NICs. One relates to a major inconsistency in the concepts routinely used to describe the economic and social experience of Asian as compared to Western nations, which in some part accounts for the seemingly vast discrepancies in savings behaviour in the two types of nations. In the West, when a government intervenes to provide income maintenance in old age and sickness, we categorise its activities in terms of taxation and public expenditure. Very frequently, these interventions are seen by economists as involving major distortions of the operation of the market economy. On the other hand, government interventions in many NICs have often been designed to offer unusually high returns to personal savings or to compel such savings. However, these latter kinds of intervention are generally regarded in a quite different light, with Garnaut being only one of many economic policy analysts commenting approvingly on the devices used by Asian policy-makers to secure high levels of saving, seen as the *sine qua non* of investment growth (Garnaut 1989). However, the substance of the distinction drawn between government welfare expenditure in the West and induced savings behaviour in the East is very far from obvious, given that both distort economic signals and that both derive their primary rationale in terms of human motivation from the wish to secure a horizontal redistribution of income across the life-cycle, with benefits/savings being used to meet income deficiencies at a later date.

The confusions that can arise from such a conceptual inconsistency are clearly demonstrated by a recent account of the welfare state in Singapore. The account begins by pointing out that social protection is 'minimal', and quotes the then Singaporean Prime Minister as urging his people to 'steer clear of welfare mentality' and the *Straits Times* as suggesting that taxation for welfare 'sucks dry personal and corporate initiatives', while welfare 'destroys family and community networks' (Ramesh 1993: 111–16). The account then goes on to describe Singapore's

Central Provident Fund (CPF), which was established in 1953 and is presently funded by an employer's contribution of 22 per cent of wages and an employee's contribution of 18 per cent. Accumulated deposits can be withdrawn when a contributor reaches age 55, Singapore's normal age of retirement, and interim withdrawals can be used to fund home purchase. Since 1984, a sub-scheme of the CPF called Medisave has covered hospital expenses (Ramesh 1993: 11–13). Given the uses to which the CPF is put, the description of protection as 'minimal' seems anomalous, and the domestic statement of anxieties about the corrosive effects of a 'welfare mentality' appear either misplaced or perhaps designed to allay the anxieties of international capital. All this is not, of course, to say that the CPF offers a comprehensive system of social security on the European model (see below). Its major deficiency lies in the weakness of its coverage of those with intermittent labour force participation, but to argue that is to point to a design fault inherent in most contributory schemes – especially in their early years of operation before democratic pressures are brought to bear to fill in coverage (see Overbye 1995) – rather than to demonstrate the virtual absence of social protection in the normal sense.

A further difficulty in using the Asian NICs as exemplar is the very considerable difference in traditional social mores between these countries and the West. The incompleteness of risk coverage in the NICs has sometimes been attributed to the strength of the Confucian family ethic, which sees reciprocal obligations within the extended family (and particularly the obligations of children to their parents) as the foremost instrument of social protection (see Rose and Shiratori 1986). Moreover, in recent times, Asian governments have called upon notions of family self-sufficiency and self-help as a means of justifying calls for welfare retrenchment (Goodman and Peng 1996). Clearly, these are forces for welfare containment – and, also, incidentally, attitudes more than somewhat propitious to high levels of personal savings – for which there is no analogy in contemporary Western nations.

They are, however, forces and attitudes which may well not persist forever. In thinking about the relevance of the example offered by the NICs to the Western welfare states, it is important continually to be aware of how short-lived has been the former's experience of modernisation. The rapidity of economic affluence and urbanisation has been the phenomenon of only a few decades and social structural and attitudinal change has, quite understandably, lagged behind. Arguably, social policy is as much or more contingent on the latter than the former. To the extent that this is so, we might expect the convergence of social policy to follow somewhat behind the undoubted convergence in income levels.

Indeed, the major source of interest for those who compare the social policy systems of the NICs and of the West should quite possibly be the rapidity with which that convergence is occurring rather than the gulf of difference that still separates the two groups of nations. In Europe the lag between industrialisation and major state intervention for social protection was far greater than it has been in industrialising Asia. One may argue, for instance, that the great success of compulsory savings schemes as a means of fostering increasing levels of productive investment in East and South-East Asia has been a function of the relatively short time such schemes have been in existence. Just as has been true of funded superannuation schemes in the West, the initial accumulation of savings scheme capital will cease to be a factor in a reduced need for public borrowing and/or a lessened demand for overseas borrowing when the draw down by individuals on their savings entitlements balances the quantum of new savings entering the schemes. One may also point to the emergence in Japan over only half a century of a welfare state for the aged which, in terms of percentage of GDP expended by the government, is on a par with countries like Australia and Canada (OECD 1994b) and one may note that, in still fewer years, South Korea has established a National Health Service and Singapore its Central Provident Fund. Finally, we may note that reliance on the extended family as a source of support in old age is most unlikely to survive unscathed in an era in which, in all the Asian NICs, a major symptom of social modernity has been a dramatic decline in family size. A few more decades on, when fertility declines (fertility rates in Japan and South Korea are almost as low as those in Southern Europe), greater female labour force participation and rapid population ageing will inevitably increase pressures for greater provision, it may well be that the effectiveness of the Confucianist ethic as a bulwark against welfare statism will be about as great as the appeal to the tradition of 'individual self-help' or 'old-fashioned family values' currently is in Western nations.

Now of course, with the Asian meltdown, we have a final reason for doubting the relevance of the Asian example to the present dilemmas of the European welfare state. Economic growth in East and South-East Asia is now at best static and at worst in rapid economic decline. Unemployment is also rising to a degree not experienced in these countries in recent decades. But because of the weak development of social entitlements, these nations are ill prepared to cope with the human problems and inequalities that result from mass unemployment. Under these circumstances, the major lesson for Europe in the experience of the Asian NICs may well be as a reminder of the dangers that can result from a single-minded focus on economic growth without comparable attention to the need for a safety-net capable of dealing with the dramatic fluctuations to which capitalist economies are so prone.

The United States

At first sight, the American welfare state does not offer a model with any coherent and consistent institutional design principles for the welfare state. Instead of a single principle and mechanism of provision, the American system manifests an institutional design which appears strongly fragmented – contributory in parts, means tested in others – and which offers a patchwork of coverage for the major risks covered by most other modern welfare states. The grounds for seeing this system as an exemplar to Europe are not in terms of a promise of superior economic growth – for much of the post-war period, American growth rates have been much weaker than European ones – but rather because of claims that it delivers superior labour market outcomes. Those who laud the virtues of the American model of social provision do so because it supposedly results in lower levels of unemployment than are currently experienced by most European nations.

The fragmented nature of United States social provision stems from several sources. One crucial factor has been a lack of uniform national benefits resulting from a diversity of state legislation and coverage, leading to a 'fiscal competition among jurisdictions that puts downward pressure on social spending' (Myles 1996). Another impediment to uniform provision has resulted from the political leverage the American system of government gives to vested interests (see Pierson 1995). This has led to massive holes in the welfare safety net, with an historically significant example being the American Medical Association's hitherto successful veto on anything seen as 'socialised medicine'. Another was the also largely successful effort of Southern Democrats, prior to the mechanisation of the cotton industry, to exclude black agricultural labour from welfare rights that would undercut the low wage levels of the Southern 'plantation' economy (see Quadagno 1988).

In effect, America has two quite different kinds of welfare state. On the one hand, it has a social security welfare state for the aged and the disabled on lines not wholly dissimilar to those of Continental Western Europe. Most prominently, this involves a system of contributory employer and employee-funded and earnings-related age pensions and disability benefits. In addition, it involves a system of medical care for the aged called Medicare. For those with long and relatively uninterrupted records of labour market participation, contributory age care benefits are relatively generous. However, those elderly people whose participation records do not qualify them for such benefits receive means-tested Supplemental Security Income at a minimum rate – c. the mid-1980s – of 34 per cent of median household income for single recipients and 37 per cent for couples. This has produced an aged poverty rate which – at 22.4 per cent – is the highest in the West (see Smeeding *et al.* 1993).

The other main contributory benefit is unemployment insurance, which is a federal programme, but one over which the states have control of eligibility criteria and benefit levels. In consequence, unemployment benefits have very uneven coverage and vary on a state by state basis from the relatively generous to the quite vestigial. In general, it is clear that unemployment benefits for the able-bodied are a much lower priority than pensions for the aged. In 1990, at a time when unemployment in the United States was 5.4 per cent, unemployment insurance expenditure was only around 7 per cent of that devoted to the aged (Marmor *et al.* 1990: 32). At that date, only 29 per cent of the unemployed were receiving benefit (Card and Riddell 1993: 180).

America's other welfare state caters for what Michael Harrington (1964) once called *The Other America,* the poor and dispossessed, who are seen as members of what is now sometimes called an 'underclass' (see Ricketts and Sawhill 1988). This welfare state for the poor – which Americans call 'welfare' to distinguish it from the politically untouchable social security system for the aged, and which generally has very negative (and racist) connotations – has been designed around the principle of selectivity, with most cash benefits going to female headed households with dependent children. Until recently, the main vehicle of such provision has been a programme called Aid for Families with Dependent Children (AFDC). In addition, the majority of states have utilised supplementary General Assistance (GA) programmes, which have offered needy applicants who did not qualify for AFDC (i.e. males and women without dependent children), benefits very markedly below the official US poverty line.

Right-wing critics of these programmes have frequently suggested that such benefits have primarily gone to African-American families. In fact, although a higher percentage of blacks than whites received AFDC and GA benefits, most cash benefits have gone to whites, simply because most poor Americans are white. By far the greatest proportion of means tested benefits targeted to the 8 million or so Americans who are 'persistently poor' (Marmor *et al.* 1990: 114) do not take the form of cash at all, but consist of in-kind benefits, such as food stamps and some access to medical facilities. These are 'welfare handouts' in a very literal sense!

The 'welfare' component of the American income maintenance system has lacked popular legitimacy and has been under continuing political threat. Although 'welfare' benefits have always been ungenerous, their level has been much reduced since the peak period of the so-called 'War Against Poverty' initiated by Lyndon Johnson in the mid-1960s. This decline in benefit levels has not, however, resulted in increased legitimacy for expenditure on welfare families. Under the circumstances of the recession of the early 1990s, AFDC numbers increased to 14.2 million by 1994, with one in seven children being supported by the payment at an annual cost to the budget – federal and State – of US$23 billion (*The Economist*, 18 June 1994). US$23 billion is, in reality, relatively small change – a mere 1 per cent of the federal budget – but generally presented in uncontextualised, 'shock/horror' terms, such figures are frequently used to mobilise voter support for political manifestos, such as the Republicans' Contract With America, which promise further radically to reduce welfare expenditure and the taxes which pay for it.

Such figures, used as prima-facie evidence of the inadequacy of the welfare system and of the need to do something about the moral decline it has supposedly engendered, similarly provide the rationale for policy proposals, such as 'Workfare' or working for the dole, seen as a way of fighting against what many point to as signs of an emergent 'culture of dependence' and a 'welfare mentality'. Together with the assumption that most welfare recipients could easily find work if they really tried, the apparent enormity of the expenditures involved has been used to justify the abandonment of entire programmes, as was the case of the Michigan General Assistance programme in 1991 (see Kossoudji *et al.* 1993). In 1996, motivations such as these were behind even more fundamental reforms, which promised to 'end welfare as we have known it' and to limit the number of years that claimants could obtain benefit irrespective of their degree of need.

The distinction between old-age social security and 'welfare' is not just a distinction between the moderately well off and the very poor; it is also, crucially, a distinction between those who are no longer part of the labour market and those who are on its outer fringes and whose level of social compensation can be seen as defining the bottom rung of the wages pyramid. Looked at in this light, developments in the USA over recent decades may be seen as a precursor of subsequent, far more consciously articulated, moves to greater labour market flexibility and reduced social protection in countries such as New Zealand, which we consider in the next section of this chapter.

The trend towards greater wage dispersion has been a phenomenon that has affected more than half the OECD since the early 1980s, but the trend emerged earliest in North America and has gone further there than elsewhere, with workers in the bottom earnings decile in the USA circa 1990 getting only around 40 per cent of the income accruing to those in the fifth decile (see OECD 1993: 159–61). Under such circumstances – whether shaped by changes in the composition of the labour force or induced by conscious policy transformation – it is quite apparent that the only way to avoid a greater reliance on the welfare state is to keep lowering the welfare safety-net so that it remains below the market clearing wage. Leaving aside questions concerning the intrinsic desirability of such a social policy development, it seems probable that each reduction in the level of social protection will catch up increasingly larger numbers of individuals whose need for income support is more a function of incapacity to work than of welfare-dependent unwillingness to work. Certainly, research on the abandonment of Michigan's GA programme has demonstrated that a substantial percentage of the recipient population were older women whose health status made full-time employment relatively unlikely (Kossoudji *et al.* 1993).

In the North American context, the downward pressure on wages has served as an impetus to institutional innovation, with the emergence in recent decades of a variety of schemes built on negative income tax principles which may serve as mechanisms for making more precisely calibrated adjustments between wages and welfare. As John Myles, a leading commentator on these developments, has noted, negative income tax schemes change the role of the welfare state, so that, 'instead of providing income security for average workers, its task is to provide wage subsidies to a growing pool of low-wage and underemployed people' (Myles 1996).

It is the labour market conforming features of the American social policy set-up which give it exemplar status in the eyes of many economists. In effect, this argument suggests that the United States' superior unemployment performance of recent decades may be attributed to a welfare state sufficiently residual and ungenerous as not to discourage the poor from working. Since the 1970s, the US unemployment trend has tracked that of most other Western nations, but, compared with most major European nations, at a lower level and with a declining trajectory. Perhaps still more significantly, US long-term unemployment rates have been very much lower than in all OECD nations bar Sweden (see OECD 1994a: table P). The argument goes that the US success in providing jobs for those who seek them rests on the fact that, for the able-bodied (i.e. all but the aged), there is no welfare state alternative to gainful employment.

This may very well be so, but the advantages and disadvantages of policy prescriptions may be very clearly seen. The absence of all but the most vestigial of in-kind social safety net may guarantee some kind of employment for all those who are willing or who have no choice but to accept market clearing wages, but the cost is the still more rapid emergence of a highly inegalitarian 'dual labour market', in which a declining part of the working population enjoy well-paid and protected jobs and an increasing minority (perhaps eventually a majority) endure poorly paid and highly insecure employment conditions. The trade-off is starkly posed: somewhat lower unemployment and markedly lower long-term unemployment against the creation of a substantial stratum of the working poor and an underclass of the permanently poor.

New Zealand

It is, perhaps, hardly surprising that neither the Asian NICs nor the USA offer particularly good role models for the present dilemmas of the advanced welfare states of Western Europe. The countries of East and South-East Asia have experienced high levels of growth in recent decades, but neither their economies nor their welfare states are in any real sense mature. The USA has a mature economy, but many decades past adopted a path of social policy development which diverged markedly from European models. New Zealand, our final exemplar, is different. Although New Zealand's welfare state is differently structured from those of Europe, New Zealand has been a welfare pioneer for much of this century and as late as the early 1980s could still be regarded as an exemplar in terms of the generosity of its pension schemes and the innovativeness of its accident compensation legislation. Moreover, until the mid-1980s, New Zealand prided itself on a record of full employment no less impressive than that of Sweden or Switzerland. Yet, in the mid-1980s, New Zealand embarked on a massive programme of economic and welfare state restructuring in the hope of turning around a post-war trajectory of economic growth that was much the weakest in the OECD. Thus, New Zealand did what many feel Europe must do. It reshaped its economic and welfare institutions in the quest for higher economic growth. In what follows, we describe the New Zealand welfare state as it was and as it has become, seeking to provide a basis of evidence for assessing the gains and losses resulting from this 'great experiment' (see Castles *et al.* 1995) in social engineering.

Early social policy development in New Zealand, as in Australia, started out on the basis of what has been described as the 'wage-earners' welfare state' (Castles 1985). This model betrays its origins as a response to poverty in certain affluent nations in the late nineteenth and early twentieth centuries prior to the elaboration of interventionist and welfare strategies in most other advanced countries. Rather than relying on state expenditures as the agency of amelioration, the emphasis was on compulsory wage arbitration as a means of guaranteeing that most families in employment had wage levels sufficient to provide a decent standard of life. For ordinary wage earners, this minimum standard meant that reliance on state expenditure was supposedly unnecessary except in old age, and these countries were among the pioneers of means-tested old-age pensions at the turn of the century. Although pension benefits in both countries were traditionally rather low, this was to a considerable extent offset by private home ownership on a scale much greater than in most other nations, leading to extraordinarily high owner-occupation rates among the aged in all social classes (see Thorns 1984; Travers and Richardson 1993; Mitchell 1995; Castles 1997).

Given that the wages system was supposed to cope with all normal contingencies, the remainder of the social policy safety-net as it developed in the twentieth century was very strictly means-tested, leaving Australia and New Zealand with the most strongly needs-tested systems in the advanced world (see Kaim-Caudle 1973; Bolderson and Mabbett 1995). In both countries, over the course of the century, means tests changed their character. Instead of being discretionary and highly residual, they became rights-based and designed to exclude only the well off rather than include only the poor. This has been the most significant difference between the means-testing regimes of these countries and of social assistance programmes in Western Europe. The other distinguishing feature of the institutional design of these countries' traditional welfare model was that benefits were flat-rate and funded from general taxation. Together means-testing and flat-rate expenditures have led to levels of social expenditure, which are substantially lower than in most European nations.

In New Zealand, however, a needs-based conception of the welfare state was more contested than in Australia. From the mid-1930s onwards, under the auspices of its first Labour government, New Zealand adopted a rather more generous and encompassing stance in respect to welfare, being the first country in the world to adopt a national health service and much later in the post-war era becoming a pioneer of comprehensive accident coverage. In contrast to the Australian development, universalism had become a part of Labour welfare ideology at an early date and, in the Social Security Act of 1938, was entrenched as the operating principle for health provision and as the guiding aspiration for old-age coverage. In the early, post-war era, New Zealand had some real claim to being the world's most advanced welfare state (ILO 1949).

In general, replacement rates of benefits in New Zealand have until quite recently tended to be higher than in Australia. In New Zealand universalist aspirations became reality in the form of a taxed universal superannuation payment at age 65. This scheme was superseded by National Superannuation in 1977, which was like the Australian age pension in being flat-rate and paid from the General Exchequer, but utterly unlike it in being much more generous (initially replacing 48 per cent of pre-tax average wages for a single person and 80 per cent for a couple), universal and paid as a demogrant (received by all men and women over age 60 irrespective of whether they were earning or not).

National Superannuation was enacted at a time when New Zealand faced very serious economic problems. The First Oil shock of the mid-1970s exacerbated a weakness in economic growth that had been manifest throughout the post-war period and, although full employment continued to be the first priority of economic policy, success was only achieved at the cost of high and continuing levels of inflation. The electoral victory of the Labour Party in 1984 brought into power a group of politicians who saw fundamental institutional reform as the only answer to the country's economic problems. The process of institutional redesign began by Labour continued under subsequent National Party administration in the 1990s. It is the degree of success of this reform programme, on a scale matched only by similarly motivated social policy reform carried out by the Pinochet, military, regime in Chile which has been of interest to commentators in other countries.

The goal of all New Zealand's post-1984 reform efforts was to accommodate to the increasing internationalisation of the world economy by offering high incentives to capital and skilled labour, whilst reducing the wages of less skilled labour, effectively reversing the wage compression that once was the hallmark of the wage earners' welfare state. Perhaps ironically, it was a Labour government that rewarded the well-off with a flattening of the tax system as great as any that has occurred in the OECD. However, it was left to the National Party after 1990, to remove the existing protections for wages conferred by the arbitration system and by collective bargaining institutions and to undermine the social minima underpinning the wages systems. The Employment Contracts Act was the culmination of a series of Labour and National reforms which transformed industrial relations. Where once there was centralised wage fixing, a complex system of award wages and compulsory unionism, now there are only enterprise contracts and unions acting as bargaining agents for individuals. The object of the new system has been to enhance 'labour market flexibility' – for which may be read 'wage flexibility' – and the evidence of the working of the new system in its early days under depressed employment conditions has been that, in this respect, at least, it has been successful (see Walsh 1993). There is also some evidence that this greater flexibility of New Zealand's labour market has been particularly disadvantageous for women workers (see Hammond and Harbridge 1993; Sayers 1993).

At the same time, stringent means tests in all income support areas as well as in new policy arenas – most particularly the health system and higher education have radically reduced the protective functions of the state. In particular, since the National Party's accession to power in 1990 there has been a very substantial reduction in the replacement rates of benefits and a tightening of eligibility conditions for most benefits. It has been calculated that benefit cuts led to an increase in poverty of around 40 per cent in the two-year period 1989/90 to 1991/92 (Easton 1993: 11). One of the benefits to be abolished under the National Party was the formerly universal family benefit. Initial threats to this benefit had emerged under the preceding Labour administration, but had been strongly resisted by a women's lobby which saw in the universal nature of the provision an affirmation of women's dignity and independence (Curtin and Sawer 1995).

Serving to further emphasise the work incentives emphasis of the transformed social policy system, these benefit cuts have been particularly pronounced in respect of unemployment benefits, where rates – and, most conspicuously, rates for workers in the age group 20–24 – have been radically reduced, resulting in a marked decline in the baseline wage level for unskilled labour. Overall, the New Zealand experience of the past decade seems to be in line with the view that a low wage strategy of economic adjustment exerts continuing downward pressure on replacement rates for all social benefits received by labour market and potential labour market participants and that, the more adjacent to labour market status the welfare clientele, the greater the pressure on benefits.

The only area that has been partly cushioned from attack has been the National Superannuation scheme, which is somewhat surprising given the generosity of this flat-rate benefit in international comparison and its large cost to the New Zealand Treasury. This demonstrates just how difficult it is to make radical cuts in areas where the beneficiaries constitute a strategic segment of the electorate (see Pierson 1994). Admittedly the value of the benefit has been progressively reduced since its inception: from an after-tax 86 per cent of the average wage for a couple in 1978 to an after-tax 69 per cent in 1995, with further reductions in prospect for the future. For the most part, however, changes have taken the form of increased selectivity through progressively increasing taxation on better-off recipients of old-aged pensions.

Perhaps, more than anywhere else in the OECD over the past decade, New Zealand has been an exemplar of a conscious programme of institutional reform in so far as successive governments have deliberately sought to reshape institutional structures in a manner which would maximise competitive pressures for improved economic performance. Benefit cuts, tax clawbacks and tightened eligibility scarcely warrant the label of institutional innovations, but in one respect at least there has been some attempt to think of new ways of tackling real problems of social policy delivery. The global abatement regime envisaged in the National Party's programmatic statement *Welfare That Works* (Shipley 1991) was an attempt to come to grips with the perennial problem of welfare selectivity that means tests lead to poverty traps and high effective marginal rates of taxation. The solution offered was the abatement of a recipient's total benefit entitlement in a consistent manner and at a standard rate. In effect, global abatement would have amounted to a kind of negative income tax of the kind advocated by Milton Friedman and other apostles of economic rationalism. The New Zealand scheme was flawed in many ways, not least by a basic entitlement too low and a rate of abatement too high to contain poverty at even existing levels. In the end, the proposal was never implemented, leaving only 'a welfare mess' of a plethora of highly selective benefits targeted in inconsistent ways (St John and Heynes 1993). It should, however, be recognised that the scheme addressed what is a central issue for all selective systems: i.e. how to cater for need without creating disincentives to labour market participation.

The New Zealand experience of economic and institutional reform properly stands as an exemplar of the costs and benefits of a single-minded push to economic reform on the basis of an agenda of economic rationalism. Given New Zealand's economic performance record in the mid-1980s, the need for reform of some kind was undoubted. As yet, however, the evidence that would be required to establish that the policy changes that were made had led to a sustained improvement is not available (see Easton and Gerritsen 1995). The most impressive aspect of recent performance has been a decline in the level of unemployment substantially more rapid than that of many countries, but it still remains the case that New Zealand has a very long way to go in order to make up for the stagnation which accompanied the early years of economic transformation.

Commentators on the so-called New Zealand 'economic miracle' tend to concentrate their attention on recent trajectories of economic performance rather than on the levels of achievement in respect of such aggregates as output and trade. Moreover, even if economic benefits are eventually apparent, the social costs may simply be too high. For those who embrace the egalitarian and socially protective objectives served by the welfare state, it may well be that any demonstrated benefits in terms of greater competitiveness and growth would have to be very large indeed in order to outweigh a social transformation which has made a nation once justly famed for its advanced welfare state and high degree of society equality into a community where no less than one-sixth of the population were living in poverty in 1993 (Kelsey 1995).

Conclusion

An important lesson to be learnt from looking at the experience of other nations as exemplars of the kind of institutional restructuring that may be required of the European welfare states is that there are no quick fixes which are readily available. Different institutional arrangements provide quite different balances of economic and welfare outcomes and there are major costs attendant on shifting from one set of institutional arrangements to another. The recent decline in New Zealand's unemployment rate is often lauded as a victory for its reform programmes, but it is worth remembering that, before reform, that country had one of the lowest unemployment rates in the world. Another lesson is that there is not much point in adopting reforms which threaten deeply held social objectives. For the European welfare states, one such objective is the maintenance of a high level of social citizenship rights. That suggests that the best exemplars for those European welfare states which currently manifest high levels of unemployment and weak economic growth are countries which have managed to preserve such rights and still maintain a relatively sound record of economic performance. There are such countries, as earlier chapters on Denmark, the Netherlands and Norway have demonstrated, but they are in Europe, not outside it.

References

Bolderson, H. and Mabbett, D. (1995) 'Mongrels or Thoroughbreds: A Cross-National Look at Social Security Systems', *European Journal of Political Research*, 28, 1: 19–39.
Card, D. and Riddell, C. (1993) 'A Comparative Analysis of Unemployment in Canada and the United States', in D. Card and R. Freeman (eds) *Small Differences that Matter: Labor*

Markets and Income Maintenance in Canada and the United States, Chicago: University of Chicago Press.

Castles, F. G. (1985) *The Working Class and Welfare*, Sydney: Allen & Unwin.

—— (1997) 'The Institutional Design of the Australian Welfare State', *International Social Security Review*, 25–42.

Castles, F. G., Gerritsen, R. and Vowles, J. (eds) (1995) *The Great Experiment: Labour Parties and Public Policy Transformation in Australia and New Zealand*, Sydney: Allen & Unwin.

Curtin, J. and Sawer, M. (1995) 'Gender Equity in the Shrinking State: Women and the Great Experiment', in F. G. Castles, R. Gerritsen and J. Vowles (eds) *The Great Experiment: Labour Parties and Public Policy Transformation in Australia and New Zealand*, Sydney: Allen & Unwin.

Easton, B. (1993) 'Poverty and Families: Priority or Piety?', Wellington: Economic and Social Trust on New Zealand, mimeo, 1–23.

Easton, B. and Gerritsen, R. (1995) 'Economic Reform: Parallels and Divergences', in F. G. Castles, R. Gerritsen and J. Vowles (eds) *The Great Experiment: Labour Parties and Public Policy Transformation in Australia and New Zealand*, Sydney: Allen & Unwin.

Garnaut, R. (1989) *Australia and the North-East Asian Ascendancy*, Canberra: AGPS.

Goodman, R. and Peng, I. (1996) 'The East Asian Welfare States: Peripatetic Learning, Adaptive Changes, and Nation Building', in G. Esping-Andersen (ed.) *The Welfare State in Transition*, Berkeley and London: Sage.

Hammond, S. and Harbridge, R. (1993) 'The Impact of the Employment Contracts Act on Women at Work', *New Zealand Journal of Industrial Relations*, 18, 1.

Harrington, M. (1964) *The Other America: Poverty in the United States*, Baltimore: Penguin Books.

International Labour Office (ILO) (1949) *Systems of Social Security: New Zealand*, Geneva.

Kaim-Caudle, P. R. (1973) *Comparative Social Policy and Social Security*, London: Martin Robertson.

Kelsey, J. (1995) *The New Zealand Experiment: a World Model for Structural Adjustment*, Auckland: Auckland University Press.

Kossoudji, S., Danziger, S. and Lovell, R. (1993) 'Michigan's General Assistance Population: An Interim Report of The General Assistance Termination Project', Ford Foundation.

Marmor, T. R., Mashaw, J. L. and Harvey, P. L. (1990) *America's Misunderstood Welfare State*, New York: Basic Books.

Mitchell, D. (1995) 'International Comparisons of Income Inequality', in J. Nevile (ed.) *As The Rich Get Richer: Changes in Income Distribution in Australia*, Sydney: Committee for Economic Development of Australia.

Myles, J. (1996) 'Social Welfare in North America: Adapting to a Low Wage Economy', in G. Esping-Andersen (ed.) *The Welfare State in Transition*, Berkeley and London: Sage.

OECD (1993) *Employment Outlook*, Paris, July.

—— (1994a) *Employment Outlook*, Paris, July.

—— (1994b) 'New Orientations For Social Policy', *Social Policy Studies*, no. 12, Paris.

Overbye, E. (1995) 'Convergence in Policy Outcomes: Social Security Schemes in Perspective', *Journal of Public Policy*, 15, 2: 147–74.

Pierson, P. (1994) *Dismantling the Welfare State?*, Cambridge: Cambridge University Press.

—— (1995) 'Fragmented Welfare States: Federal Institutions and the Development of Social Policy', *Governance*, 8, 4: 449–78.

Quadagno, J. (1988) *The Transformation of Old Age Security*, Chicago: University of Chicago Press.

Ramesh, M. (1993) 'Social Security in Singapore: The State and Changing Social and Political Circumstances', *Commonwealth & Comparative Politics*, XXXI, 3: 111–21.

Ricketts, E. R. and Sawhill, I. (1988) 'Defining and Measuring the Underclass', *Journal of Policy Analysis and Management*, 7: 316–25.

Rose, R. and Shiratori, R. (eds) (1986) *The Welfare State East and West*, Oxford: Oxford University Press.

Rudd, C. (1992) 'Controlling and Restructuring Public Expenditure', in J. Boston and P. Dalziel (eds) *The Decent Society?* Auckland: Oxford University Press.

Sayers, J. (1993) 'Women, the Employment Contracts Act and Labour Flexibility', in R. Harbridge (ed.) *Employment Contracts: New Zealand Experiences*, Wellington: Victoria University Press.

Shipley, J. (1991) *Social Assistance: Welfare that Works*, Wellington: Government Printer.

Smeeding, T., Torrey, B. and Rainwater, L. (1993) 'Going to Extremes: an International Perspective on the Economic Status of the U.S. Aged', Working Paper no. 87, Luxembourg Income Study.

St John, S. and Heynes, A. (1993) 'The Welfare Mess', Department of Economics, Policy Discussion Papers, no. 15, University of Auckland: Department of Economics.

Thorns, D. (1984) 'Owner Occupation, the State and Class Relations in New Zealand', in C. Wilkes and I. Shirley (eds) *In The Public Interest*, Auckland: Bention Ross.

Travers, P. and Richardson, S. (1993) *Living Decently: Material Well-being in Australia*, Melbourne: Oxford University Press.

Walsh, P. (1993) 'The State and Industrial Relations in New Zealand', in B. Roper and C. Rudd (eds) *State and Economy in New Zealand*, Auckland: Oxford University Press, 172–91.

Wilensky, H. (1975) *The Welfare State and Equality*, Berkeley: University of California Press.

13 The future of the universal welfare state

An institutional approach[1]

Bo Rothstein

The puzzle of increased variation

In the comparative welfare state research, two major findings are of interest when thinking about its possible future. The first is well-known, the differences that exist in the quality and scope of welfare state programmes among the industrialised Western democracies (Esping-Andersen 1990). To take just a quantitative measure, in the mid-1990s, the Scandinavian countries spent about twice as much as a percentage of GDP on social insurance and social assistance than did the United States, with most other European countries somewhere in between. The other finding is less well-known, this huge difference in welfare state ambitions is a rather recent phenomenon. If we go back to the early 1960s, these countries spent almost the same as a percentage of GDP on welfare policies (OECD 1994). Given the internationalisation of values, increase in trade, globalisation of capital, etc. this is a rather unexpected development. After all, these are countries with basically the same type of social, economic and political structures, that is, they are all Western democratic capitalist market economies. Speculating about the future of the welfare state, it is a fair guess to say that most social scientists working in the early 1960s would probably, without our benefit of hindsight, have predicted convergence in social policy between these countries, not this rather dramatic divergence.

One way to explain the differences in welfare state programmes would be through standard political variables – the ideological orientation of dominant political parties in Scandinavia are different (read: more social democratic) from those in the United States or Canada. This is of course true, but then it should also be said that all the Scandinavian countries have had extended periods with non-socialist/conservative parties in government during this period and, moreover, these have been periods marked more by expansion than contraction of welfare state spending (Rothstein 1998). A second type of explanation would point at general norms and values, for example that Scandinavians, for whatever historical and cultural reasons, are more inclined to embrace norms such as equality and social justice. The problem, however, is that comparative studies based on survey data find very little, if any, support for this type of explanation. To the contrary, findings from such studies report a striking similarity in such basic values and norms about justice, equality, etc. between countries with very different ambitions in welfare state measures (Svallfors 1997). A third type of explanation has pointed at differences in class power and class formation, what has come to be known as the 'power-resource' approach (Korpi 1983). This has been a much more fruitful way of explaining the puzzle of increased variation, but there are two main problems which it cannot solve. While there is definitely a strong relationship between the strength of the labour movement and social spending, the causal mechanism is double-linked. The strength of the labour movement in, for example, Sweden can to a large extent be explained by the character of social policy initiatives and forms of institutionalisation which took place in the early 1930s (Rothstein 1992). The implication is that the organisational power of the working class is as much an effect of as it is a cause behind social policy. In the Scandinavian countries, support for the welfare state goes far beyond the working class or the social democratic parties. In fact, it can be argued that some of the most expansionary periods have taken place with non-socialist governments in power (Lindbeck 1997). So, we are left with a genuine puzzle – standard theories about economic development, political power or social norms seem not to be able to explain the differences in welfare state programmes.

It should be remembered that behind the macroeconomic figures describing the differences between welfare states are the lives of real people. Comparing the economic situation of single parent families in the mid-1980s, 54 per cent in the US and 46 per cent in Canada lived in severe poverty (defined as having less than half of the median income) compared to 6 per cent in the Netherlands and 7 per cent in Sweden (McFate *et al.* 1995). Another interesting figure here is the difference in prison interns. Of 100,000 persons, 580 are in prison in the United States compared to an average of 40 in the Scandinavian countries (Wacquant 1998). There are, of course, many different reasons behind crime and imprisonment, but sheer poverty would clearly count as one.

The moral and political logic of the universal welfare state

I will here put forward an explanation that this puzzle can be understood from a neo-institutionalist perspective. The argument is that the explanation of the puzzle of increased variation has to do with how the institutions of the welfare state programmes have been historically established. In order to highlight the differences, I will concentrate the analysis on one of the so-called outliers, namely Sweden, which in various studies has been shown to be the most expansive welfare state.

Speaking from an institutionalist perspective, what characterises the Swedish and the other Scandinavian (and some other North European) welfare states is that most programmes are universal, not selective. This means that social programmes such as old-age pensions, health care, child care, education, child allowances, health insurance, etc., are not targeted on 'the poor', but instead cover the whole segment of the population without consideration of their ability to pay.

Many scholars have maintained that, since benefits and services are distributed in roughly equal shares to everyone, and since the tax system is proportional on the whole, then no real redistribution between income groups takes place in universal welfare states (Barry 1990; Gutman 1990). Some economists have even claimed that a universal welfare system amounts largely to a costly bureaucratic roundabout with very little redistributive effects (Tullock 1983). Nothing could be further from the truth. Table 13.1 serves to illustrate why.[2]

The redistributive logic of the model is as follows. In the first column, income earners are divided for the sake of simplicity into five groups of equal size, according to average income. We assume the average income of the group earning most is five times that of the group earning least. This difference, which we may call the inequality quotient, is 5/1. We further assume, *nota bene*, not a progressive but rather a strictly proportional system of income taxes. We set the tax rate at 40 per cent, which corresponds roughly to that part of the Swedish public sector's presently 56.2 per cent of GNP that is spent on social, educational and other welfare policy. Finally, we assume that all public benefits and services are universal, which means that the individuals in each group receive *on average* the same sum in the form of cash benefits and/or subsidised public services. The result, as seen in the last column, is a dramatic reduction in inequality between group A and group E, from 5/1 down to 2.33/1. The level of inequality has thus been reduced by more than half in this model of how the universal welfare policy works. Note that this redistributive logic works the same if you take the group's (or person's) income over a lifetime as well as if you compare at one single point in time. It is only if you can argue that over time the persons in groups A and B will switch with the persons in groups D and E that the redistributive effect decreases.

This model has, in fact, a strong support in empirical data of how different welfare states redistribute income (McFate *et al.* 1995). It turns out that, perhaps contrary to one's intuition, it is the states that tax everyone 'the same' and give everyone 'the same', i.e. the universal systems, that end up effectively redistributing economic resources, while the ones that intend to tax the rich to give to

Table 13.1 The redistributive effect of the universal welfare state

Group	Average income	Tax (40%)	Transfers	Income after taxes and transfers
A (20%)	1,000	400	240	840
B (20%)	800	320	240	720
C (20%)	600	240	240	600
D (20%)	400	160	240	480
E (20%)	200	80	240	360
Ratio between groups A and E	5/1	(= 1,200)	(1,200/5 = 24)	2.33/1

the poor, end up with much less redistribution. The reason for this paradox of redistribution, as shown in Table 13.1, is that while taxes usually are relative (a fixed percentage of income for example) benefits or services are usually nominal. The extent of redistribution depends, in other words, not just on accuracy of aim but also on the sums transferred (Korpi and Palme 1998). To put it in other words: if you tax the rich and give to the poor, the rich will not accept high taxes.

Rationality, information and support for the universal welfare state

The question is, of course, whether such a system is politically stable, that is, can it survive? If we start from a pure self-interest utility-maximising point, the table above does show that there is, to use a game-theoretical expression, no stable equilibria. The model cannot predict what will be the likely outcome if agents act solely out of self-interest (for a somewhat different argument about this, see Moene and Wallerstein 1996). The reason is that while groups E and D will clearly be in favour of a universal system because they get more benefits than what they pay in taxes, groups A and B will be against a universal system for the opposite reason (they contribute more than they get). This means that the group which in the model determines if a universal welfare state will persist or not is group C (i.e. 'the middle class'). The reason for this is twofold. First, for this group, the system is cost neutral, that is, they pay in as much as they get out from the system. Second, in a democratic polity, and again following the standard economic theory of self-interested behaviour, group C (henceforth 'the middle class') will be what in political science is known as the 'swing voters', that is, they will decide what the majority will be. Swedish survey data confirms this picture, i.e. that support for the universal welfare state decreases with higher social class (Svallfors 1996). From an electoral perspective, it is only if the middle class opt for a political alliance with groups D and E that the universal welfare state will be stable. This means that from a standard economic utility-maximising point, we cannot predict what will happen in this model, that is, if the universal welfare state is not stable. This is, as stated above, also the empirical case. Some modern capitalist democracies have more universal welfare systems, while others have more selective arrangements, following to a large extent from the electoral behaviour of the middle class.

However, if we relax the assumption about the individual tax payer's/voter's/social insurance recipient's economic rationality in three ways, another picture comes through. First, following the work by Kahnemann and Tversky, we know from experimental data that people tend to be risk averse (Kahneman and Tversky 1996). Given the guarantees that government insurance can provide compared to a private insurance company, the middle class may be more prone to support universal public social insurance. However, this depends on whether the government is perceived as trustworthy or not.

Second, it is in this case very difficult for the (middle class) individual to get accurate information about the gains and losses when she compares taxes and benefits. This lack of information, and if we add to that uncertainty about the future, may very likely change the basis upon which people act. Following a recent argument put forward by Arthur Denzau and Douglas North as well as John Scholz, in such situations marked by uncertainty and lack of information, people do not act as if they have computers in their head solving equations about possible gains and losses. Instead, shared mental maps, heuristics, ideological persuasions and moral standards are used when agents form decisions (Denzau and North 1994; Scholz 1998). This implies that, in particular for group C in our model, the decision to support a universal system (or not) is very likely to be a *combination* of rational utility-maximising calculation (so far as it can be made) *and* ideological/normative orientations. This has recently been stated in the approach named 'evolutionary game theory' as follows:

> agents are not perfectly rational and fully informed about the world in which they live. They base their decisions on fragmentary information, they have incomplete models of the process they are engaged in, and they may not be especially forward looking. Still, they are not completely irrational: they adjust to their behavior based on what they think other agents are going to do, and these expectations are generated endogenously by information about what other agents have done in the past.
>
> (Young 1998: 6)

Third, we know from experimental studies of collective action problems that a considerable number of individuals do not follow the self-interested utility-maximising script at all. Especially if given the possibility to communicate, people do not free ride as much as standard rational choice theory predicts (Tyler 1998). To quote one recent survey of the results from this experimental research: *'hard-nosed game theory cannot explain the data'* (Ledyard 1995). The willingness to act out of norms of solidarity is simply much higher and more widespread than the standard economic theory about human behaviour predicts (Sally 1995).

If democracy is considered not only as a system for the simple aggregation of preferences, but also as a deliberative and discursive process, the results about the importance of communication from experimental studies should have implications for how agents behave (Mackie 1998). As we are dealing with electoral behaviour, it should be underlined that the negative results for the public choice theory are confirmed in survey studies about how people vote. Empirical studies about voting behaviour have refuted the economic logic of voting put forward by the public choice school in political science. Instead of voting out of pure self-interest, citizens take the overall well-being of the society into account. In electoral research, this is known as *sociotropic* voting (Lewin 1991).

Empirical results about political behaviour and behaviour in experimental collective action situations have led a couple of political scientists to suggest that we must build our analyses on a more realistic foundation of what type of utility functions people have (Levi 1998; Ostrom 1998; Rothstein 1998). From this perspective, it should be clear that most people do not act out of one single rational utility-maximising utility function, because in that case, most collective action problems would end up in pathological social traps (Platt 1973; Young 1998: 18). One way to solve this problem is to start the analysis that most people do not have one single, but have (at least) two different utility functions. Margaret Levi, who has done research under what conditions young men volunteer for war, has put this as follows,

> there are segments of the citizenry whose utility function is unitary; they are purely income maximizers or purely moral. A large proportion, however, appear to have *dual utilities*. They wish to contribute to the social good, at least as long as they believe a social good is being produced. They also want to ensure that their individualistic interests are being satisfied as far as possible.
>
> (Levi 1991: 133)

This idea of a *dual utility function* can serve as a useful tool when we try to understand how collective action problems can be solved. In line with the experimental studies mentioned above, it shows that most people do want to contribute to solve collective action problems instead of acting as free riders, what they do not want to be is 'suckers', contributing when 'the others' are not contributing.

One of the things needed to solve problems of collective action is thus trust and other such norms of reciprocity which assures the individual that enough others will behave cooperatively (Levi 1998; Putnam 1993). What complicates the problem in our case is that when it comes to social insurance, the individual citizen is clearly in *two different* collective action situations where trust is important. The first is with the government – will the state actually, when the day comes, deliver what it has promised to deliver. For the individual, many things provided for by the welfare state have a rather long time horizon (college education for one's children, old-age pensions and old-age health care). Thus, the individual does not only have to consider if the current government can be trusted, but also any government likely to hold power in the future.

The second collective action situation is with all other citizens – will they financially support the system or are they more likely to cheat and avoid paying taxes. And will they try to undermine the system by claiming benefits they are not entitled to, or will they play by the rules. In many social insurance cases, 'moral hazard' is a problem, i.e. it is difficult to know if the unemployed are really unable to find work, etc. This means that even if an individual in principle, out of some moral conviction, would favour a universal welfare state system, he or she may nevertheless withhold support because mistrust of either the government or of fellow citizens (Scholz and Lubell 1998). Thus, these two strategic situations (citizen vs. the government and citizen vs. all other citizens) can be understood as two 'nested games' (Tsebelis 1990).

Margaret Levi has conceptualised this as the problem of *contingent consent*. The idea is that citizens will consent under certain conditions to collective (in this case government-organised) action to produce *public goods*. The starting point is that citizens will try to balance their wish to act according to the norm of contributing to 'the common good' with their rational self-interest. The theory of contingent consent entails the following: we imagine a situation in which citizens attach positive moral value to the object sought by collective measures, for example some form of social insurance. In the face of problems of free riding, achieving sufficient support for such measures presupposes that three conditions be fulfilled. These are the following:

1   Citizens regard the good to be produced in itself as valuable. We will call this the question about *substantial justice*.
2   They consider the administrative process needed to implement this value to be organised in keeping with *procedural justice*, i.e. that the government will deliver what it has promised to deliver in a fair and impartial way.
3   They believe their fellow citizens also contribute to the programme on a solidaristic basis (non or insignificant 'free-riding').

Most discussions of social policy concerns only the first normative condition of substantial justice. The reason for adding the second is studies showing that in addition to substantial justice, people seem to care a lot about procedural justice (Tyler 1998). The reason for adding the second and third conditions comes out of the literature on non-cooperative game theory which stress the importance of trust in institutions and trust in other agents. Below, I will discuss the institutional implications of each of these three conditions.

Substantive justice

The first condition of contingent consent has to do with the normative question of *substantive justice*. That is, can one argue that the goals of a particular social policy measure are just? This first principle lies, we might say, at the heart of a universal welfare policy (Titmuss 1968). Indeed, the whole point of a universal welfare policy is not to discriminate between citizens, not to separate 'the needy' and 'the poor' from other citizens and to treat them differently. Social policy should look instead to a moral obligation to furnish all citizens with, in Amartya Sen's words, *basic capabilities* (Sen 1982). In contrast to the situation under a selective system, the public discourse about social policy in a universal system cannot be conducted in the terms indicated by the question: 'What shall we do about these deviant groups/individuals?' Or as former US Vice-President Dan Quayle put it in a debate: 'those people' (Katz 1989: 236). The public discussion of social policy in a selective system often becomes a question of what the well-adjusted majority should do about 'the others', i.e. the socially marginalised minority. The *substantial justice* of the system can thereby come under question by the majority, who might start asking (a) where the line between the needy and non-needy should be drawn, and (b) whether the needy ('the others') themselves are not to blame for their predicament (and so cannot legitimately claim assistance). We may refer to the first as the general and the second as the individual boundary-drawing problem. In the selective model, the discussion often comes to focus on how to separate the 'deserving' from the 'undeserving' poor (Katz 1989) which translates into a seemingly unending debate about how and where to draw these two boundary lines. Leading politicians are therefore likely to find themselves in a situation where it becomes increasingly difficult to argue that the selective programmes are normatively fair. Public consent to the system is undermined, rather, because the social policy debate comes to turn not on what is *generally fair*, but on what is *specifically necessary for 'the others'*.

Moreover, in a selective system, the moral logic of the discourse tends in itself to undermine the legitimacy of the system. The reason is that most selective types of policies that are structured to integrate a specific group with the rest of society, seem to entail a paradox of the following kind: to motivate selective measures, e.g. affirmative action, the targeted group must first be singled out as inherently *different* from ordinary citizens. But if the group is that different, how can they ever by any social policy initiative, become like 'ordinary citizens'. If the selective policy has only marginal effects, the usual strategy for those advocating it is to argue that the group is even more different (and thus have even more special needs) than what had initially been presumed, and therefore needs more selective/targeted policies.

Under a universal system – in which the state furnishes all citizens with *basic capabilities* – the moral logic is altogether different. Since the universal welfare policy embraces all citizens, the debate assumes quite another character: social policy is now thought to concern the entire community, and the question becomes what, *from a general standpoint*, is a fair manner in which to organise social policy. No discussion of the type above – concerning how and where to draw the two boundary lines for 'the others' – need ever take place, for the simple reason that no such lines need be drawn. Welfare policy does not, therefore, turn into a question of what should be done about 'the poor' and 'the maladjusted', but rather a question of what constitutes *general fairness* in respect to the relation between citizens and the state. The question becomes not 'how shall we solve *their* problem?' but rather 'how shall we solve our common problems' with social insurance.

Procedural justice

Condition number two concerns the implementation of policy. Can welfare policy be *carried out* in a fair manner? How does the choice of a universal or selective welfare policy affect the public's view of state capacity? To begin with the former: one should bear in mind that a typical universal welfare programme – like flat-rate pensions or child allowances – is a great deal simpler, cheaper and easier to implement than its selective counterpart. This is largely because there is no need, in a programme of a universal type, for an administrative apparatus charged with carrying out the two types of eligibility tests which are a necessary concomitant of a selective programme: for ascertaining (1) whether a given applicant is entitled to support, and (2) if so, to how much. Social policy can thus be given the form of specified citizen rights, and the social duties of the state can be rigorously defined in order to respect the integrity of citizens. The point is that, depending on the institutions we select for furnishing citizens with *basic capabilities*, we create different types of moral logic in the social policy discourse. In the case of a selective policy, the state separates out those citizens unable to provide such basic *capabilities* for themselves, and furnishes them with said *capabilities*. To do this, however, it must first determine whether or not they belong to the needy group, and if so, how much they need. The problem that arises is that it is very hard to do these things without violating the principle that the state should treat all citizens with, as it has been stated by Ronald Dworkin, 'equal concern and respect' (Dworkin 1977: 180ff). The very act of separating out the needy almost always stamps them as socially inferior, as 'others' with other types of social characteristics and needs, and results most often in stigmatisation (Salonen 1993: 176–80). In his important book *Spheres of Justice*, Michael Walzer argues that social policy of this sort is incompatible with the maintenance of recipients' self-respect (Walzer 1983: 227).

Selective programmes present serious problems of procedural justice because they must allow local administrators a wide field for discretionary action. The difficulty of finding usable criteria for selecting recipients can often become unmanageable. This creates a 'black hole of democracy', in which citizens find themselves faced with an administration or system of rules which no one really understands, and in which no one can be held responsible. In sum, the selective model leads, as Robert Goodin has stated, to 'unavoidable', 'insurmountable', and 'insoluble' problems in respect to the arbitrary treatment of citizens seeking assistance (Goodin 1988: 219).

The difficulty of handling the discretionary power of administrators in selective programmes has two important consequences. These consequences are often thought to be opposites, but in fact they are two sides of the same coin. They are the bureaucratic abuse of power, and fraud on the part of clients. Applicants in a selective system, if rational, will claim that their situation is worse than it actually is, and to describe their prospects for solving their problems on their own as small to nonexistent. The administrators in such a system, for their part, often have incentives from their superiors to be suspicious of clients' claims. In game theory, this is known as 'the control game', a rather sad game because it has no stable equilibria and thus no solution. Fraud by a few clients feeds into increased control which in its turn feeds into increased fraud by more clients, and so on (Hermansson 1990).

The question of procedural justice therefore looms large in selective systems. Even if cases of cheating, fraud and the abuse of power are in fact relatively rare, the sensationalistic logic of mass media means that such cases will receive great attention and thereby influence the majorities' 'cognitive maps' on what social policy is about. It is very difficult to combine means-testing with procedural justice, for means-testing itself entails a violation of citizens' integrity – either in the means-test itself, or in the verification checks which often follow.

The just distribution of burdens

Condition number three in the theory of contingent consent has to do with whether or not all citizens bear their share of the costs of a given policy, i.e. it concerns *the just distribution of burdens*. Citizens are portrayed here as players in a so-called assurance game, i.e. they are prepared to support the programme in question – even if they cannot be sure they will themselves directly gain by it – as long as they can be convinced that all (or almost all) other citizens will also contribute to carrying it out. The willingness to contribute depends, that is, not just on the fulfilment of the requirements of procedural and substantive justice; it also assumes a credible organisation of the collective efforts (so that such efforts are, in truth, *collective*). The other side of the question, of course, is how to discourage the unsolidaristic use of the benefits the welfare policy brings.

The universal model differs from the selective on this point as well. Typical for the latter is that assistance is granted only to those citizens who cannot in some other way provide for themselves or meet their 'basic needs'. This means as a rule that such citizens have no income, and therefore pay no tax. They constitute a category, then, which does not contribute economically. In a universal system, the vast majority of those who are recipients do work and thus do pay taxes.

In sum, to the extent the welfare system is designed so that even net beneficiaries can play a role as partners who contribute, according to their ability, to the defraying of costs, the legitimacy of welfare policy will increase. It becomes a question of how citizens shall undertake to solve their common problems, rather than a question of what 'we' shall do about 'them'.

We observe here, then, two wholly distinct moral logics. The difficulty of implementing selective programmes in such a way that their objectives are attained, and their processes considered fair, undermines public support for social policy in general. For example, the majority might be open to supporting social policy in principle, but constant reports of cheating, fraud, bureaucratic abuse of power, waste, inefficiency and other irregularities lead to their taking the view that the policy's implementation is so deficient as to make the whole affair a waste of time and money. It is very hard to imagine, moreover, that a population with such a negative view of welfare policy would be receptive to proposals to give it a more universal form (for this would involve *expanding* social policy). Instead, a suspicion of state measures becomes the dominant attitude. A state that fails to take care of 'the poor' cannot, of course, be entrusted with the larger task of attending to the welfare of the entire population. Citizens are more willing, on the other hand, to agree to collective undertakings of this kind if they have confidence in the state as an institution.

Attitudes towards different types of social programme

One consequence that modern social science has brought is that citizens are asked now and again about their attitudes towards various matters. So also with welfare policy. How does the empirical evidence look, then, in relation to the theory of contingent consent? Can empirical support be found for the proposition that, if the institutions of social policy are structured according to the principles of this theory, they will create norms forming a basis for the reproduction of the policy? Axel Hadenius in 1986 and Stefan Svallfors thereafter have conducted survey research which speak to this problem. They have asked identical questions of representative samples of the Swedish population about their support for different welfare state programmes. The results may be seen in Table 13.2.

At least two results of these studies are worthy of note. The first is the marked and stable difference in support for different types of programmes over time. Support for the universal programmes is unambiguously strong and stable, while the opposite is true for the two selective programmes (housing allowances and social assistance).

This seems to support our model of how people behave combining self-interest, uncertainty, risk-aversion and solidarity. First, considering self-interest, these universal programmes can be expected to have strong support because large segments of the population benefit from them. But, as shown in our model above, the crucial middle segment of the population might still opt out if acting from a strict rational self-interested perspective. Adding uncertainty, risk-aversion and solidarity may explain the figures above.

Second, the programmes with strong support are all within the model of contingent consent, while the two programmes with weak support are clearly outside this model. The most crucial difference is that both housing allowances and social assistance are means-tested programmes and thus difficult to implement with respect to procedural justice. There is also an argument that these are programmes serving citizens who either do not pay taxes at all, or pay very little.

One programme that stands out is employment policy which is, for most parts, selective. Nevertheless, it has fairly strong support, although it has declined somewhat in the latest survey. One reason may be that this is a programme which,

Table 13.2 Attitudes towards public expenditures

Answers to following question: 'Taxes are used for various purposes. Do you think the revenues spent on the purposes mentioned below should be increased, held the same, or reduced?' The figures in the table represent the percentage of those wishing to increase expenditures minus the percentage of those wishing to reduce them.

Year	1981	1986	1992	1997
Health care	+42	+44	+48	+75
Support for the elderly	+29	+33	+58	+68
Support to families with children	+19	+35	+17	+30
Housing allowances	−23	−23	−25	−20
Social assistance	−5	−5	−13	±0
Primary and secondary education	+20	+30	+49	+69
Employment policy	+63	+46	+55	+27
State and municipal administration	−54	−53	−68	−65

Sources: Hadenius (1986); Svallfors (1996, 1998).

at least in Sweden, does not only serve 'the poor', but for historical reasons has a much broader range in what is known as 'active labour market policy'. Not only unemployed workers, but also workers who in the future risk unemployment, including many white-collar workers, attend job-counselling and vocational training. Second, this is a programme in which historically the ruling Social Democratic Party has paid special attention to the problems of legitimacy in the implementation process. One example is that decisions about who is eligible for unemployment insurance are taken by union representatives (Rothstein 1996).

There is reason to compare with the US on this point. As Margaret Weir has noted, it is striking that no form of active labour market policy has been successfully established in the US, despite the fact that a strong work ethic pervades American society (Weir 1992). The attempt made beginning in the 1960s – CETA (Comprehensive Employment and Training Act) – was the social programme which the Reagan administration found easiest to dismantle upon assuming office in 1981. This was because CETA was equated, in public opinion, with waste, bureaucracy and a focus on helping just certain socially distinct minority groups; it was, in short, a programme exhibiting all the problematic features of selective policies. An American scholar puts it this way:

> The legitimacy of CETA was seriously eroded by the stream of 'bad press' it was receiving – adverse publicity on waste, nepotism, patronage and corruption. Perhaps nothing contributed more to the loss of confidence and legitimacy in CETA and, ultimately, to its demise.
>
> (Mucciaroni 1990: 176)

While part of this explanation presented here is ideological, i.e. what political leaders hold forth as substantially just, the two other parts (*procedural justice* and the *fair sharing of burdens*) has to do with how the government arranges the administrative institutions of the welfare state. The evidence from the Swedish system of welfare policies provides empirical support for the theory of contingent consent as a way to solve large collective action problems. It is precisely the universal programmes – which fulfil the institutional conditions specified in this theory – that command widespread support in the population. At the same time, it is the two programmes (social assistance and housing allowances) which appear most clearly to violate the principles of this theory that enjoy the least support. It is hard to argue on behalf of these programmes by appeal to a conception of substantive justice. Moreover, they are difficult (not to say impossible) to implement in a procedurally fair manner. They make it easy, finally (at least in the case of public assistance), to argue that those receiving benefits do not contribute according to ability to defray the costs of the programme, i.e. the benefits generally go to people who do not work and therefore do not pay income tax. In other words, citizens have reason to distrust both the government institutions and their fellow citizens. It should perhaps be added that in the Swedish case, the construction of the institutions that made it possible to solve the collective action problem in this case, by no means came into existence by chance or as unintended consequences of other political decisions. Instead, they were deliberately crafted by centrally placed political actors, very much with the problem of procedural legitimacy in mind (Olsson 1993; Rothstein 1998).

The future economic viability of the universal welfare state

Instead of summing up the argument above, I would like to end by addressing the problem of the economic viability of the universal welfare state. I have come to realise that the welfare state is understood, by most economists, as a sort of altruistic luxury established to take care of 'the poor' (Freeman 1997; Lindbeck 1997). The major flaw in this analysis is that the demand side is totally neglected. What is missing is that in a universal system, as should be clear from the argument above, the major part of the demand does not come from the 'poor minority' or from any altruistic ideals within the majority to help the disadvantaged part of the population. Instead, because the system is universal, the demand comes from the vast majority of the population. To present this argument, I have to ask the reader to follow me in a simple thought experiment. Assume that all of the welfare state programmes in the Nordic countries were abolished, and that the taxes people pay for these goods were to be reduced as well. What would the majority living in these countries do? My guess, which is substantiated by survey research (Svallfors 1997, 1998) as well as by the American example, is that they would try to buy these goods on the market. Thus, the vast majority of the population would buy health insurance, pension plans, education and day care for their children, unemployment insurance, and so on. Contrary to what the public choice approach tells us, what governments in democratic welfare states produce, for the most part, cannot be explained by budget-maximising bureaucrats or politicians seeking re-election, because the demand is there.

Second, would such a private market system be more efficient than the universal and mandatory systems that exist in the Nordic countries? This we cannot say for sure, but there are strong theoretical arguments as well as empirical indications, that show that private market systems are less cost-efficient than universal systems with regard to social insurance and social services. This occurs because social insurance systems are particularly sensitive to what are known as problems of asymmetric information between producers and consumers. To give a few examples of what this means, first, insurance companies will have to make very costly efforts to screen applicants to get rid of 'bad risks'. Second, they must engage in costly surveillance to make sure the (naturally rent-seeking) providers of health care and other such services do not engage in various kinds of fraud. This turns out to be very difficult because the provider (i.e. the doctor or the hospital) and the consumer (the patient) have ample opportunities as well as a mutual interest to shield information about treatments and costs from the insurance companies. Third, those who apply for social insurance will do whatever they can to try to hide that they may be 'bad risks' (labelled 'lemons' by economists), making it all the more necessary for insurance providers to obtain and run costly information systems. In sum, the transaction costs in private insurance systems tend to become much higher than in universal and public systems. In an overview of this argument, Nicholas Barr has stated that these information problems 'provide both a theoretical *justification of* and an *explanation for* a welfare state which is much more than a safety net. Such a welfare state is justified not simply by redistributive aims one may (or may not) have, but because it does things which private markets for technical reasons would either do inefficiently, or would not do at all' (Barr 1992).

Another question in this thought experiment is whether we would increase social utility if we let people decide to take the 'James Dean' option in life. This means letting people choose to stand the risk of getting old, unemployed or ill without relying on any public assistance (and, of course, to be able to spend the money as they wish while they are young, healthy and in demand on the labour market). Theoretically, the answer is yes. The utility for both the 'James Dean' types as well as the more cautious types, would be increased. In practice though, it turns out that there seems to be no democratic country where the public or the politicians have been able to muster the moral strength to actually say no to the 'James Dean' types when that day arrives. Thus, these persons will be taken care of, and this is the argument for making the basic forms of social insurance mandatory.

The empirical side of this argument is more problematic, but it has not been possible to show a negative relation between high public spending and economic growth (Dowrick 1996; Korpi 1996). In health care, there seems to be ample evidence that the US system with private insurance is much less cost-efficient than the Nordic model with universal insurance (Gerdtham and Löthgren 1998).

My point is, the Nordic type of welfare state is not an altruistic luxury item established to take care of 'the poor' and should thus not be evaluated by only comparing efficiency costs with gains in the form of increased equality. Since the demand for social insurance and social service exists, the costs will be there, whether or not the demand is filled by government provision or by market forces. Most of the evidence seems to show that, due to the problem of asymmetric information in this area, mandatory and universal systems are more cost-efficient than private insurance systems.

Still, one could add that the level of social insurance and social services in the Nordic welfare states is so high, a large part of the population (i.e. 'the poor') would not be able to, or choose to, afford it if provided by market forces at production costs. This is of course correct, but it may also be the case that the efficiency gains with mandatory and universal systems compared to a private market system, cover these 'costs'. This we don't know, but it is a possibility that should not be ruled out without further empirical research.

In conclusion, it seems as if the economists analysing the Nordic welfare states have forgotten the oldest of all economic lessons, namely, that if there is a credit account, there should be a debit account. They seem to take for granted that anything provided for by the government is not truly in demand. Why this is so, and why their analyses of the universal welfare states have such a marked ideological leaning to the right, I leave for others to speculate.

Notes

1   *Editor's note:* this chapter is partly based on extracts from Chapters 5, 6 and 8 in Bo Rothstein (1998) *Just Institutions Matter: The Moral and Political Logic of the Universal Welfare State*, Cambridge: Cambridge University Press. The editor kindly acknowledges the permission given by Cambridge University Press to use extracts from the book.
2   The following builds on many discussions with Peter Mayers, whose ideas and suggestions have been most valuable.

References

Barr, N. (1992) 'Economic Theory and the Welfare State: A Survey and Interpretation', *Journal of Economic Literature* 30, 2: 741–803.

Barry, B. (1990) 'The Welfare State vs. the Relief of Poverty', *Ethics*, 100, 3: 503–29.

Denzau, A. T. and North, D. C. (1994) 'Shared Mental Models: Ideologies and Institutions', *Kyklos*, 47: 3–31.

Dowrick, S. (1996) 'Swedish Economic Performance and Swedish Economic Debate: A View From Outside', *Economic Journal*, 106: 1772–79.

Dworkin, R. (1977) *Taking Rights Seriously*, London: Duckworth.

Esping-Andersen, G. (1990) *The Three Worlds of Welfare Capitalism*, Cambridge: Polity Press.

Freeman, R. B. (1997) 'Are Norway's Solidaristic and Welfare State Policies Viable in the Modern Global Economy?', in J. E. Dølvik and A. H. Steen (eds) *Making Solidarity Work?*, Oslo: Scandinavian University Press.

Gerdtham, U. G. and Löthgren, M. (1998) 'Health Care System Effects on Cost Efficiency in the OECD Countries', Working Paper Series in Economics and Finance 247, Stockholm: Stockholm School of Economics.

Goodin, R. E. (1988) *Reasons for Welfare: The Political Theory of the Welfare State*, Princeton, NJ: Princeton University Press.

Gutman, A. (1990) 'Introduction', in A. Gutman (ed.) *Democracy and the Welfare State*, Princeton, NJ: Princeton University Press.

Hadenius, A. (1986) *A Crisis of the Welfare State?*, Uppsala: Almqvist & Wiksell.

Hermansson, J. (1990) *Spelteorins nytta. Om rationalitet i politik och vetenskap*, Uppsala: Statsvetenskapliga föreningen.

Kahneman, D. and Tversky, A. (1996) 'On the Reality of Cognitive Illusions', *Psychological Review*, 103, 3: 582–91.

Katz, M. B. (1989) *The Undeserving Poor: From the War on Poverty to the War on Welfare*, New York: Pantheon Books.

Korpi, W. (1983) *The Democratic Class Struggle*, London: Routledge & Kegan Paul.

—— (1996) 'Eurosclerosis and the Sclerosis of Objectivity: On the Role of Values among Economic Policy Experts', *Economic Journal*, 106, 2: 439–56.

Korpi, W. and Palme, J. (1998) 'The Paradox of Redistribution and Strategies of Equality: Welfare State Institutions, Inequality, and Poverty in the Western Countries', *American Sociological Review*, 63, 5: 661–87.

Ledyard, J. O. (1995) 'Public Goods: A Survey of Experimental Research', in J. H. Kagel and A. E. Roth (eds) *The Handbook of Experimental Economics*, Princeton, NJ: Princeton University Press.

Levi, M. (1991) 'Are There Limits to Rationality?', *Achives Européennes de Sociologie*, 32, 1: 130–41.

—— (1998) *Consent, Dissent, and Patriotism*, New York: Cambridge University Press.

Lewin, L. (1991) *Self-Interest and Public Interest in Western Politics*, Oxford: Oxford University Press.

Lindbeck, A. (1997) *The Swedish Experiment*, Stockholm: SNS Förlag.

Mackie, G. (1998) 'All Men Are Liars: Is Democracy Meaningless?', in J. Elster (ed.) *Deliberative Democracy*, New York: Cambridge University Press.

McFate, K., Smeeding, T. and Rainwater, L. (1995) 'Markets and States: Poverty Trends and Transfer System Effectiveness in the 1980s', in K. McFate, R. Lawson and W. J. Wilson (eds) *Poverty, Inequality and the Future of Social Policy: Western States in the New World Order*, New York: Russell Sage Foundation.

Moene, K-O. and Wallerstein, M. (1996) 'Targeting and Political Support for Welfare Spending', paper presented at the Annual Meeting of the American Political Science Association, San Francisco, 28–30 August.

Mucciaroni, G. (1990) *The Political Failure of Unemployment Policy 1945–1982*, Pittsburgh: University of Pittsburgh Press.

OECD (1994) *New Orientations for Social Policy*, Paris: OECD.

Olsson, S. E. (1993) *Social Policy and Welfare State in Sweden*, Lund: Arkiv.

Ostrom, E. (1998) 'A Behavioral Approach to the Rational Choice Theory of Collective Action', *American Political Science Review* 92, 1: 1–23.

Platt, J. (1973) 'Social Traps', *American Psychologist* 28: 641–51.

Putnam, R. D. (1993) *Making Democracy Work: Civic Traditions in Modern Italy*, Princeton, NJ: Princeton University Press.

Rothstein, B. (1992) 'Labor-market Institutions and Working-class Strength', in S. Steinmo, K. Thelen and F. Longstreth (eds) *Structuring Politics: Historical Institutionalism in a Comparative Perspective*, Cambridge: Cambridge University Press.

—— (1996) *The Social Democratic State: The Swedish Model and the Bureaucratic Problem of Social Reforms*, Pittsburgh: University of Pittsburgh Press.

—— (1998) *Just Institutions Matter: The Moral and Political Logic of the Universal Welfare State*, Cambridge: Cambridge University Press.

Sally, D. (1995) 'Conversation and Cooperation in Social Dilemmas – A Metaanalysis of Experiments from 1958 to 1992', *Rationality and Society*, 7, 1: 58–92.

Salonen, T. (1993) *Margins of Welfare: A Study of Modern Functions of Social Assistance*, Lund: Hällestad Press.

Scholz, J. T. (1998) 'Trust, Taxes and Compliance', in V. Braithwaite and M. Levi (eds) *Trust & Governance*, New York: Russell Sage Foundation.

Scholz, J. and Lubell, M. (1998) 'Trust and Taxpaying: Testing the Heuristic Approach to Collective Action', *American Journal of Political Science*, 42, 2: 398–417.

Sen, A. (1982) *Choice, Welfare and Measurement*, Cambridge, MA: MIT Press.

Svallfors, S. (1996) *Välfärdsstatens moraliska ekonomi*, Umeå: Borea Förlag.

—— (1997) 'Worlds of Welfare and Attitudes to Redistribution – A Comparison of 8 Western Nations', *European Sociological Review*, 13, 3: 283–304.

—— (1998) 'Mellan risk och tilltro: Opinionsstödet för en kollektiv välfärdspolitik', working paper, Department of Sociology, Umeå University.

Titmuss, R. (1968) *Commitment to Welfare*, London: Allen & Unwin.

Tsebelis, G. (1990) *Nested Games: Rational Choice in a Comparative Perspective*, New York: Cambridge University Press.

Tullock, G. (1983) *Economics of Income Redistribution*, Boston: Kluwer and Nijhoff.

Tyler, T. R. (1998) 'Trust and Democratic Governance', in V. Braithwaite and M. Levi (eds) *Trust & Governance*, New York: Russell Sage Foundation.

Wacquant, L. (1998) 'L'emprisonnement de "classes dangereuse" aux Etats-Unis', *Le Monde Diplomatique*, 21–22 July.

Walzer, M. (1983) *Spheres of Justice. A Defense of Pluralism and Justice*, New York: Basic Books.

Weir, M. (1992) *Politics and Jobs: The Boundaries of Employment Policy in the United States*, Princeton, NJ: Princeton University Press.

Young, H. P. (1998) *Individual Strategy and Social Structure: An Evolutionary Theory of Institutions*, Princeton, NJ: Princeton University Press.

14 European welfare lessons of the 1990s

Stein Kuhnle

West European national welfare states have been built over a 100-year period. Institutions have survived world wars. The welfare state has great importance for European citizens today, who in between intermittent complaints about bureaucracy, inefficiency and other shortcomings also seem to value its achievements and ambitions (see Chapter 2, and Ferrera 1993). Large majorities of European voters – across the 'four social Europes' distinguished between in this volume – are generally far more favourable of governmental ('state') responsibility for basic income for all, for reducing income differences, and for creating jobs for all, compared with, for example, voters in the USA (Flora 1993). Among the achievements of the European welfare state(s) are on average relatively high standard of living, universal health services, rights to old-age and disability pensions, and income when sick, unemployed or poor. The welfare state has in all likelihood been conducive to a relatively high degree of social and political stability – also in periods of economic recession and high unemployment. The welfare state appears to be a significant societal 'stabiliser'. The welfare state has undoubtedly consolidated democratic development, and democratic institutions have consolidated welfare state growth and adjustments. Welfare state growth, democratic consolidation and economic growth have gone hand in hand through most of the period after the Second World War. The welfare state has not fallen apart in times of economic backlashes. In fact it may, for example, be argued that thanks to a well-developed welfare state in place Finland recuperated swiftly and without social upheavals and social misery when hit by a sudden and severe economic downturn at the beginning of the 1990s (see Chapters 3 and 4).

Differences between national welfare states in terms of expenditure levels, public service employment and institutional characteristics persist, but there are also examples of convergence between different types of European welfare states. Universal health services have been introduced in Southern Europe as in early post-war Scandinavia and the United Kingdom. In Finland and Sweden, new pension reforms aim at a stronger link between contributions and prospective pensions, bringing these welfare systems closer to the Continental European type. Cutbacks in social security and welfare programmes have on average been modest during the 1980s and 1990s. Cuts may have long-term beneficial effects on the financing of the welfare state as the proportion of old people with rights to pensions, health services and personal care will increase significantly from about 2010. Overall social expenditure in real terms and as a proportion of GDP (also when GDP has increased) has generally increased far into the 1990s, even if various types of benefits have been cut. A changing demographic composition, established entitlements, new technology in the health system, and new social problems and needs have contributed to comprehensive and to some extent expanding welfare state programmes. Frozen historical institutional relationships and 'political culture' are factors that sometimes prevent reforms even when many politicians, bureaucrats and 'experts' agree on the need for reforms (see, for example, the analysis of Germany in Chapter 7 and of France in Chapter 8). In other countries, institutional relationships and political culture are factors conducive to broad political compromises for reforms (see in particular the analysis of the Netherlands in Chapter 7, Switzerland in Chapter 8, and the Nordic countries in Chapters 3, 4 and 5).

Despite big or small reforms, European welfare states have 'survived' the 1990s, but with varying degrees of success and with a differential basis for meeting future challenges to the welfare state. From a study of the different paths chosen, and the different experiences with reform efforts, lessons can be learnt. And as pointed out in Chapter 12, European governments with little success with welfare reforms may have more to learn from European examples of success (as measured, for example, by more employment, declining unemployment, or economic growth) than from non-European welfare 'models' and institutional designs.

In spite of a number of similar challenges associated with demographic change, financial constraints, unemployment levels and common external challenges associated with European and global economic integration, European welfare states remain generally institutionally strong with solid basic support from voters and major political parties. And social protection and welfare remain basically within the sphere of responsibility of the nation-state. The importance of the institutions of governance of the European Union for social policy in Europe is so far limited, but this may change, and probably should change into more pro-active and active governance if survival of comprehensive national welfare states is a goal. Joint European or cross-national political action may be needed to guard against unintended social and political consequences of increased European and global economic integration. The present mismatch between degree of economic and political European integration may harm efforts to sustain the welfare state (see Chapters 1, 2 and 11). It is too early to say – and probably always will be (!) – what kind of political entity the EU will become. But a stronger 'Political Europe' may be conducive for relatively advanced national welfare states to survive, and a more cooperative political Europe may – in a long-term perspective – play a more active independent role in guaranteeing the survival of some form of a 'Social Europe'.

The state is likely to play a relatively less dominant role in the future social Europe given large, economically well-off middle classes which may demand exit options, choice and differentiated services (see Chapter 1). More space for market and other non-governmental welfare solutions has been opened within and across

European nation-states. Although more dual public–private welfare states are likely to appear, national governments enjoy a number of policy instruments to regulate and control developments in order to affect access to quality services for all and relatively egalitarian income distributions (if so wished). Whether to maintain and develop welfare states, and what kind of welfare states to develop, are questions of institutional structures and interrelationships, of institutional 'conservatism', of 'strong' rights, 'privileges' and entitlements, and of vested interests. But they are also questions of political preferences and choices by governments, organisations, firms and individuals – choices that are influenced by institutions, experience, values, social structures and economic opportunity.

Europeans value state welfare more than people elsewhere, but welfare states develop everywhere. More state welfare elsewhere may alleviate the pressure of globalisation on European welfare states. There are more social security schemes in the world now than ever before in history (*Social Security Programs Throughout the World 1997*), and many more nation-states than only 10 years ago, and more states may be born (or re-born), even in Western Europe. This politicisation of territorial organisation may seem a paradox given the simultaneous market drive for lower national barriers to promote global trade, capital mobility and financial transactions. The more nation-states, the more social security schemes. The welfare state itself is undergoing globalisation.

A number of major 'welfare state reforms' were introduced in East and Southeast Asia during the most recent economic miracle period (1985–96), particularly in Korea, Taiwan, China and Thailand. And in spite of more poverty, unemployment and social misery, there are few signs of 'welfare dumping' after the 'crash of the summer of 1997' (Hort and Kuhnle, forthcoming 2000). In fact, the lag between industrialisation and major state intervention for social protection was greater in Europe than in industrialising and modernising Asia, despite the assumed or contended importance of Confucian values and traditions of family welfare provision. If America is not, a number of Asian countries are looking to Europe for solutions to state welfare policies.

These trends of Asian welfare development are no guarantee for the survival of European welfare states. The observation that state welfare schemes are spreading and moving up on the political agenda in the globalised world may, however, indicate that some of the external pressure for retrenchment and down-scaling of European welfare states may gradually be alleviated. In fact, because of fairly well-developed welfare states, Europe may – if not in the immediate short term – be better prepared to meet the challenges of demographic and socio-structural change in the modern world than other regions of the globe. European countries in which, for example, social policies to support families exist (kindergartens, cash transfers, home help for the elderly, public support for institutional care), may be better prepared for global competition than countries in which welfare provision is solely or primarily a family responsibility.

Many factors influence decisions about investments, production and location of production facilities – not only low wages and maximisation of profit. Skilled labour, efficient public bureaucracy, little corruption, little poverty, limited social inequalities, public safety, social and political stability, democracy and political accountability, are all factors which have a bearing upon decisions about where, how and at what cost to produce goods and services. The advantage of low wages for investments is not always logically more important than the advantage of (more expensive) high-skilled and qualified labour. There is no empirical evidence for the idea that removing social safety nets for people, and making them more insecure, contributes to making firms more competitive or to furthering national economic growth (but firms and governments may make decisions without considering likely effects or evidence of effects). Social protection and economic growth can hardly be looked upon as alternatives, but in some way as complementary. There will always be a demand for social security, health and welfare services, and if not provided by the state, others will have to provide welfare – and also at a price (see Chapter 13).

From the discussion above follows that solid, comprehensive welfare states may present a comparative advantage. European welfare states may, with a number of continuous adjustments of social policies, and with a somewhat different 'welfare mix' in the future, fare well. As chapters to this volume bear out, European welfare states are likely to maintain or advance universal coverage of major welfare rights. The format of the welfare state may look different in coming decades, however, than what it was during the period of the most intense 'happy marriage' (Hagen 1998) between the nation-state and the welfare state in Europe, c. 1950–80.

There is no question or exclamation mark at the end of the title 'Survival of the European Welfare State'. This is to convey the clean and sober message that survival is possible and likely – and desirable – if one listens to the voice of the majority of European voters. Voice counts.

References

Ferrera, M. (1993) *EC Citizens and Social Protection. Main Results from a Eurobarometer Study*, EC Commission, Div. V/E/2, Brussels.

Flora, P. (1993) 'The National Welfare States and European Integration', in L. Moreno (ed.) *Social Exchange and Welfare Development*, Madrid: Consejo Superior de Investigaciones Cientificas.

Hagen, K. (1998) 'Towards a Europeanization of Social Policies? A Scandinavian Perspective', paper presented at MIRE Conference, Gilleleje, Denmark, 4–6 September.

Hort, S. E. O. and Kuhnle, S. (forthcoming, 2000) 'East and South-East Asian Miracles, Social Dumping and Welfare Models', prepared for a special issue of *Journal of European Social Policy*.

Social Security Programs Throughout the World 1997 (1997) Washington DC: Social Security Administration.

Index